The Corruption of Economics

*When everybody is swept away unthinkingly by what
everybody else does and believes in, those who think
are drawn out of hiding because their refusal to join
is conspicuous and thereby becomes a kind of action.*

Hannah Arendt, *The Life of the Mind*

Other books in this Series

A Philosophy for a Fair Society
Michael Hudson, G.J. Miller and Kris Feder
Hdbk ISBN 0 85683 161 1
Ppbk ISBN 978-1-916517-01-1
ebook ISBN 978-0-85683-557-5

Land and Taxation
Nicolaus Tideman (Editor)
Hdbk ISBN 0 85683 162 X
Ppbk ISBN 978-1-916517-02-8
ebook ISBN 978-0-85683-558-2

GEORGIST PARADIGM SERIES
Series Editor: Fred Harrison, MSc

The Corruption of Economics

Mason Gaffney and Fred Harrison

The Georgist Paradigm is a model of political economy that offers comprehensive solutions to the social and ecological problems of our age. At its heart are principles on land rights and public finance which integrate economic efficiency with social justice.

Shepheard-Walwyn (Publishers) Ltd.

in association with

Centre for Incentive Taxation Ltd.

First published in 1994 by
Shepheard-Walwyn (Publishers) Ltd.,
in association with
Centre for Incentive Taxation Ltd.
www.wearerent.com

Second Edition (eBook) 2022 published by
Shepheard-Walwyn (Publishers) Ltd.,
107 Parkway House, Sheen Lane, London SW14 8LS

British Library Cataloguing in Publication Data

A catalogue record of this book
is available from the British Library.

Mason Gaffney and Fred Harrison
Ppbk ISBN 978-1-916517-00-4 (2nd Edition)
eBook ISBN 978-1-8568-3554-4 (2nd Edition)

www.shepheardwalwyn.com

Cover design by Andrew Candy, www.tentacledesign.co.uk

Printed and bound in the United Kingdom by 4edge Limited

Contents

Corrupting the Body Politic

Fred Harrison

Students are taught that, unlike their peers in the natural sciences, social scientists cannot treat people as guinea pigs in laboratory experiments. True, except that laboratory-like conditions may prevail in the real world. Political ideologists manipulate people. In doing so, they transform whole societies. Such cases, of which there were three in the past 30 years, enable scientists to test hypotheses against outcomes. At the same time, these cases enable us to imagine what might have happened if, instead, reform of the social structures had been undertaken on different terms.

What if (as proposed by the authors of the present volume) those three countries had abolished taxes on wages and on the profits of value adding entrepreneurs and funded public services out of an alternative source of revenue? That fiscal model is the organising method for delivering a justice-based society by placing both rights *and* their corresponding responsibilities at the heart of politics. Some scholars contest that vision. They argue that the fiscal policy would corrupt the body politic by inviting "collusion and corruption in government".[1] This issue, it appears, is fruitful both empirically and theoretically. Our case studies are South Africa, Russia and China.

In the 1980s, the leaders of those countries explored ways to transform their societies. They had two choices. One was to gravitate towards one of the variations of capitalism. The only viable alternative was the classical model, which originated in the 18th century with the French Physiocrats. Adam Smith elaborated the economics of their model of governance in *The Wealth of Nations* (1776). American journalist Henry George, in *Progress and Poverty* (1879), restated that model in fulsome terms, on the basis of

---

1   See below, p.242.

which he was able to initiate the first global reform movement in history. The bedrock policy is the treatment of rent as the public's revenue. Nobel Prize economists like Joseph Stiglitz and William Vickrey rigorously reaffirmed the virtues of the policy.

The rent to which they referred was not the commercial rent paid for hiring an apartment or motor vehicle. It is the net income (*economic rent* – hereafter: Rent) that people cooperate to create. In evolutionary terms, that Rent made possible the formation of humanity.[2]

In textbooks, Rent in its privatised form is analysed as a "transfer income". This stream of value is appropriated from people who produce it, in return for nothing. There is no exchange. It is the classic "free lunch". This behaviour is also known as free-riding (on the backs of producers). Does the privatisation of Rent lead to the corruption of economics and – as a consequence – the fabric of society? Or, on the contrary, does the pooling Rent in the public purse – while abolishing the tax burden on wages and profits – induce corrupt behaviour? To determine which of these theses is closer to the truth, we can interrogate the evolution of governance in South Africa, Russia and China since the publication of *The Corruption of Economics* in 1994.

South Africa: Nelson Mandela's post-apartheid constitution

A truth and reconciliation commission was assembled to heal the wounds inflicted by decades of apartheid. The segregation of indigenous people in "tribal lands" had excluded them from mainstream civil and political life. The new constitution deemed everyone equal. Land was to be restored to traditional holders. That was the prospectus.

Most of the towns collected revenue directly from location Rent. The ANC government could have extended this policy in a revenue neutral reform: collecting more Rent from the resource-rich territory while reducing taxes on earned incomes. Instead, the government cancelled Rent-revenue policy in 2004. Some outcomes: social mobility was not enhanced for indigenous people; more of them were relegated to the shantytowns, and a new form of apartheid was practised. Spatial segregation was based on the standard model of post-classical economics as authorised by agencies such as the International Monetary Fund.

---

2   Fred Harrison (2020), *#WeAreRent*, London: Land Research Trust.

Corruption? Symbolic of state of governance was the fate of Jacob Zuma. He rose from freedom fighter to become President in 2009. In 2021 he was imprisoned after being convicted of corruption. During his service at the head of government, rent seekers manipulated the power of governance to enrich themselves out of the nation's Rents. All the while, the fiscal system and its related property rights crushed the post-apartheid aspirations of the people.

Russia: Boris Yeltsin's anti-communist prospectus

He stood on top of a tank in 1991 and proclaimed Russia independent from the Soviet Union. Boris Yeltsin was not driven by ideology, but the Soviet Union was no more. Western governments and think tanks lost no time: they urged him to adopt the naked form of capitalism. One American professor (Jeffrey Sachs) toured the crumbling Soviet empire, prescribing a "shock therapy" transition to the market model.[3] The competing view, promoted vigorously over a 10-year period, urged the Kremlin and Duma (Parliament) to vary the terms of governance employed by the standard capitalist model. Instead of taxing labour and capital, rely on the Rents of land and natural resources, which were already in public ownership. A leading advocate was Dr Dmitry Lvov, who headed the economics department of the Russian Academy of Sciences.

Yeltsin chose to privatise the nation's land and natural resources and adopt the western version of taxation. This facilitated the emergence of a class of oligarchs whose fabulous wealth enabled them to compile portfolios of real estate stretching from the South of France through London to New York. While the rent seekers enjoyed the High Life, the working population suffered a decline in living standards and life expectancy. Corruption became the norm, with politics skewed to favour the coterie of oligarchs who gathered around a Kremlin that shifted from democracy to autocracy.

China: Deng Xiaoping's quest for equality

In discussions with Britain over the return of Hong Kong to China in the 1980s, the Communist Party's Paramount leader asserted the constitutional principle of "one country, two systems". Mainland China would remain socialist "with Chinese characteristics". Hong Kong would retain its own

---

3   See below, p.218; and www.nytimes.com/1993/06/27/magazine/dr-jeffrey-sachs-shock-therapist.html

economic and administrative system of government, independent from the policies pursued in Beijing.

Land and natural resources on the mainland were retained in public ownership. Rent, however, was privatised. Municipal governments sold the leases, an arrangement marred by extensive cases of bribery and corruption involving civil servants and developers. Developers, in scrambling for capital gains, locked vast amounts of capital in unoccupied residential tower blocks (the "ghost towns" phenomenon). Middle-class workers accumulated property portfolios in pursuit of the capital gains from vacant apartments.

Inequality became an intractable problem. House prices were the central political crisis for President Xi Jinping. The scramble for privatised Rents distorted the economy and damaged people's lives. One consequence was a dangerous decline in the fertility rate. House prices helped to drive up the cost of getting married, which caused a decline in weddings.[4]

In 2021, as property developers found they could not fund their debts, President Xi intervened to tighten the Communist Party's grip on real estate; without reforming the fiscal system so that China could grow on sustainable terms.

The nature of corruption

Corruption is more than just bribes paid to politicians and individuals or corporations applying monopoly power to skew economic activity to gain super-profits at other people's expense. This requires a nuanced approach to analysing corrupt behaviour, as when attributing unjust outcomes to the system of public finance.

In China, for example, because of the mistreatment of Muslim Uyghurs, the Communist Party is accused of crimes against humanity.[5] In Hong Kong, pressure from Beijing led the legislature to renege on the "two systems" promise. The National Security Law diminished liberties. Citizens were barred from standing as candidates in elections if they did not support the party line ("patriots"). School textbooks were censored to curate the

---

4   Sun Yu (2021), "China weddings reach 13-year low in blow to drive for more births", *Financial Times*, Dec. 9.

5   https://uyghurtribunal.com/wp-content/uploads/2021/12/Uyghur-Tribunal-Summary-Judgment-9th-Dec-21.pdf

knowledge going into the minds of children. There is no apparent link between these forms of egregious behaviour and the fiscal system.

If we dig deeper, however, we may perceive the way in which these violations of human rights are the consequence of the absence of the Rent-as-public-revenue form of governance.

Rights have corresponding responsibilities. A tax regime that draws revenue from earned incomes is a feature of a social paradigm that ruptures rights from responsibilities. Such a system is an irresponsible system. Government draws revenue on terms that do not acknowledge a proportionate relationship between the payments and the benefits received. This results in an irresponsible form of power, which is not under the control of the people who pay the revenue into the public purse. This kind of politics contrasts with the Rent/revenue paradigm. People who pool Rent into the public purse do so on terms that are proportionate to the benefits they receive. Each citizen acquires a direct stake in the kind of governance that prevails. Under those circumstances, governance becomes accountable. The cumulative effect is a responsible form of politics.

By analysing the fiscal system, we see how the way in which revenue is raised sets the moral parameters for political behaviour. The issue is control over state *power*. Under the Rent/revenue model, everyone has a personal and direct stake in scrutinising and holding politicians accountable. This results in a democratic form of power.

This analysis leads us to ask questions that are awkward for the ideologists who prevail in western democracies. For example, if Russia *had* adopted the fiscal system advocated by Dmitry Lvov, the economy would have prospered from the bottom up. Might that have led the occupants of the Kremlin to steer their country in a different direction, with the outcome akin to authentic democracy? Under those conditions, it would not have become necessary to distract Russian citizens from the systemic suffering they endure today. It would not be necessary for the power brokers to embark on foreign adventures, like digital interference in the elections of the US and Europe and military threats against Ukraine.

The Rent paradigm . . . What if?

The Corruption of Economics lays out the principles on which the three countries could have preserved their cultural identities while adopting a social contract grounded in the principles of justice. The litmus test is the method of funding public services.

If South Africa, Russia and China had adopted the Rent-based fiscal system, the net income would have flowed into the public purse instead of fuelling corruption. Instead, they opted for the tax regime that penalised people who worked for their living and who saved to invest in the capital equipment that their economies needed.

Western democracies are a case study in that form of corruption. Constraints imposed by the fiscal system on people's aspirations are opportunities for the free riders. Policy-makers are aware of that fact. Remedial action, however, is limited. President Joe Biden, for example, has "vowed to crack down on 'criminals, kleptocrats and others' paying cash for houses to launder money as part of a broader anti-corruption drive".[6] His clean-up project is restricted to chasing the profits of drug cartels and tax-dodging corporations, which use real estate to wash "dirty" money. The effective way to cleanse those sources of corrupt finance would be for government to employ the justice-based system of public finance. The most profound damage to society is inflicted through the stresses and distortions rooted in the tax regime. Governments intentionally employ the tax tools that impose "deadweight losses" on their citizens.

Joe Biden, when he arrived in the White House as President, announced that the single biggest challenge the world faced was the contest between the democracies and autocracies. That conflict will not be resolved in favour of authentic freedom for so long as democratic governments purposefully inflict traumas on their electorates. Those stresses surface as poverty and inequality; they deepen the distrust of public authorities; and they drive people into the hands of politicians who favour the arbitrary power of autocracy.

The evidence is in. It is now for people in the court of public opinion to mandate changes to the way they pay for the services they share in common.

London
January 2022

---

6   www.reuters.com/markets/funds/biden-targets-cash-homes-deals-anti-corruption-drive-2021-12-06/

Prologue:
Who's Afraid of Henry George?

Fred Harrison

Henry George had to be stopped. The American journalist who wrote a pamphlet in the early 1870s had, 15 years later, become a threat to the power elites throughout the world. His crime was to inflame the masses with the idea that social justice was a real possibility in this world, not just the hereafter.

Henry George had to be stopped, because he did more than develop his vision into a coherent political philosophy: he also expressed the idea in a language that could be understood by the millions of people who read his book, *Progress and Poverty* (1879).

Henry George had to be stopped, because he turned political: he took his message to London and Dublin, where he gave direction to the discontent among the workers who had been denied a fairer share of the benefits of industrial society. And then, his gravest mistake - he started to fight elections in New York with a manifesto based on the reform of taxation and land policy. This manifesto, if embodied in the law of the land, would have destroyed the privileges of those people who had become accustomed to living off the labour of others.

So he was stopped.

How do you stop what had become a global movement, in which Henry George's book had become the best-selling text on economics ever to be published? The way in which Henry George was neutralised is uncovered by Mason Gaffney in what will now be seen as one of the most heinous episodes in the history of the development of scientific knowledge. *Those who opposed Henry George's vision of The Good Society paid money to buy scholars to bend the truth – to prevent people from insisting on their democratic rights.*

The way in which the scholars accomplished this feat, unwittingly aided by academics to this day, was to corrupt our language. They redefined economic terms, creating a jargon language to confuse public debate. By doing so, they prevented the evolution of rational public policy. That, in turn, meant that the existing flaws in society were preserved; flaws which, to this day, result in the unnecessary deaths of tens of thousands of people, as Dr. George Miller explains in a companion volume in this series.[1]

Henry George had to be stopped, because his was the rational, evolutionary path to The Good Society. The practical significance of this approach can be assessed by the response of the power elites to Karl Marx. Both George and Marx were the major influences on the development of working class consciousness in Britain in the 1880s.[2] Both men wanted to change the world, but each was opposed to the other's approach to change. Henry George would have nothing to do with the red-in-tooth revolutionary ideas promoted by Marx.

George and Marx employed the language of the classical economists, but they were diametrically opposed on a large number of issues. The key test relates to the rights of ownership of capital. The American said that what people created with the toil of their hands and the use of their brains and by saving was their private property; Karl Marx wanted capital to be collectively owned. The American wanted to preserve a one-man-one-vote democracy; Karl Marx wanted a dictatorship of the proletariat. The American wanted reform through social evolution; Karl Marx wanted revolution.

One would have thought that the power brokers of late 19th century Europe and North America would have been more terrified of Marx than Henry George. Not at all, and a revealing insight into the attitude towards these two men was displayed by the way in which their proposals were treated by scholars. As an example, we can refer to the 1909 edition of *Palgrave's Dictionary of Political Economy*. This described Henry George's tax and tenure proposals, and added the verdict:

The danger of these opinions has become more apparent as time goes on.[3]

But what was the pronouncement on the works of red revolutionary Karl Marx? Evidently there was no "danger" here, for readers of the entry in *Palgrave's* were invited to ruminate on Marx's "singularly brilliant" style, an assessment controverted by two others who, in German and Latin, were of the opinion that, stylistically, Marx was cumbersome, imprecise, obscure and unintelligible.

Marx was evidently no threat to the class interests of those who controlled society; he could be left alone to wade through his manuscripts in the British Museum, and even allowed to inspire revolution on the outer reaches of eastern Europe. Henry George was another matter; he had to be stopped, and to this day we live with the consequences of that plot to kill his message.

The story that unfolds in these pages will not be well received by the economics profession, for it explains why academic economists have spent a century taking people down blind alleys with their abstract models and algebraic equations. It will explain why governments have persistently failed in the quest for full employment and the elimination of poverty in the midst of plenty. It will explain why, today, government economists believe that the business cycle is a "natural law" which cannot be eliminated by public policy.

So absolute is the flaw in the foundations of our social system, so uncompromising are the lords over our land, so overwhelming are the crises that confront us, that qualitative reforms cannot now result unless the public first engages in a profound debate. For the dialogue to yield policies beyond the banal, we cannot avoid a radical reappraisal of the institutions and values of civilization itself. The risk for the power elites is that, if that debate occurs, the chains of power that have corrupted the rights of the individual and destroyed the cooperative basis of the community will once again be exposed.

War as social process

Civilization is the history of territorial conflict punctuated by periods of peace. This tells us something terrible in its awesome significance and simplicity: civilization must be built on exceedingly unstable foundations.

It began to go wrong in the Bronze Age, 4000 years ago, when people embarked on a path of cultural diversification that is now impossible to sustain. They developed a set of social institutions and processes that separated, on a systemic basis, the people from the land. Not everyone was thus alienated from his or her territorial roots; but the customarily unthinkable principle – that it was possible to tolerate an inequality of rights of access to land – was accepted. Falteringly, at first; but accepted, slowly transformed into what we have today: a blind acceptance of the correctness of exclusive ownership of the benefits of land. This unnatural prejudice – unnatural, because anti-evolutionary, in the Darwinian sense – was legitimised by convention and law, through Greece, Rome and its later medieval manifestations in Western Europe.

The social origins and cultural evolution of that history of property rights is explained by Michael Hudson in *A Philosophy for a Fair Society*. Here, I want to explore what we do about it, now, as a world in turmoil heads for the 21st century. For there is a general acceptance that change there must now be. The problem, of course, is twofold: first, the nature of the appropriate change; and, second, how that change can be brought about with the least possible social disruption to a fragile social system.

In the past, the impetus for change usually came after a bloody war. This was logical, for conflict over territory was the clearest expression of a fundamental misalignment in the primordial relationship of People+Land, and an expression of the need to redefine that relationship. One way was for society to turn in on itself, by victimising a part of its population: ethnic cleansing. Historically, the Jews were good scapegoats for the tensions rending civil society, for which they were in no way responsible.

The most effective way to distract a people from the intolerable strains that have built up in their society is to focus their attention on the enemy without, which involves a voyage forth on a crusade of territorial conquest. This mobilises the whole population behind a common cause, and does so by promising rewards for everyone (more land for the nation-state); with the prospect of distress restricted to the conflict "over there", on the disputed territory outside the population's boundaries. But as Saddam Hussein was reminded, when he tried to incorporate Kuwait into Iraq's boundaries, precision bombing can inflict terrible damage on the home territory.

The Second World War was a classic example of this process. Europe was in the grip of the aftermath of The Great Depression. It was imbued by an awareness of failure – witness the derelict factories, the palsied trading systems, the unrequited demands for new wealth to raise the living standards of millions of people stricken by poverty – and the need to introduce substantive reforms. But there was no coherent expression of a viable alternative to the boom/slump capitalism that had itself been victimised by seemingly uncontrollable economic forces: by the 1930s, Marx was embodied in the Stalinist reign of terror, and Henry George was the merest flicker of an idea in the minds of a few British parliamentarians. Thus, Hitler served a purpose which, given the traditions of civilization, was valid. He did not step outside the bounds of history, to try and conceptualise a solution to Germany's problems that excluded territorial conquest. Why should he? He was a child of that civilization, an admirer of its greatest imperial achievement – the Roman empire. So it was predictable that someone like Adolf Hitler would step forward, and in this case turn his eyes on the land to the east.

Similarly, and as a reciprocal benefit, the rest of Europe benefitted from Hitler-as-stooge-of-history, by being provided with the necessity – in the postwar period – to create a land "fit for heroes". Would the Welfare State have emerged so completely in Britain, had the nation been denied the opportunity to participate in the catharsis of what turned out to be a world war? Was the ritualised murder of millions of men and women (not 20m dead in the USSR alone, we are now told, but more like 40m) really necessary, to provide the impetus for social change? (I say *ritualised* because programmed killing is a defining ceremony of civilization.)

That is one issue that remains to be readdressed by historians. Of immediate concern is whether it is possible to think another unthinkable thought: the possibility of qualitative changes to society without a war. If it is possible, we can be sure of one thing: the programme of change, if it is to serve its social purpose, has to address the problem of the distribution of the benefits from land, which was Henry George's central thesis a century ago.

Agreement on how to resolve the land question is a precondition for any substantial change, for the most serious social and economic conflicts originate with circumstances that can be traced back to the failures of the system of land tenure and public finance. When all the economic, legal, sociological and historical diagnoses have been performed, what it boils down to is something very simple: a maldistribution of the benefits of land in society. So if we wish to avoid the civilised remedy – a war – we need the assurance that land is part of the settlement. Only in that way can we obviate the necessity for a global war at any time between now and the first decade of the 21st century.

Power and public finance

There is one proposal only for restoring order to the chaos of contemporary society which locates at its heart a solution to the land question. This approach entails a reform of the system of public finance.

In the conditions of industrial society, any package of reforms has to resolve two distinct problems. One: if people are to be free to work and invest their resources in wealth-creating enterprises, they must have a legally protected right of private possession of land. Two: there is not enough land to go round, but the rest of us *must* share in the benefits of land – somehow. Solution: those who occupy land pay rent to the community for the use of land or the natural resources beneath, on or above land.

This is the principal policy of the Georgist paradigm. Henry George (1839–1897) did not, in fact, originate the policy, but he rediscovered it, and his genius was to represent it in terms that could be understood by peasants on the remotest crofts of Scotland and Ireland, and by semi-literate factory workers in Burnley (Lancashire) and Birmingham (Alabama). The policy of sharing the economic benefits of land via the system of public finance predates civilization. Indeed, the fate of that policy is another one of the defining characteristics of civilization: the privatisation of the traditional source of public revenue (the rent of land).

In modern terms, the policy was first articulated by the French Physiocrats. The proposal found its way to the British Isles via Adam Smith and *The Wealth of Nations*. So we could have called the social paradigm implied by this fiscal policy by one of a number of names, but in contemporary terms it happens to be most closely associated with Henry George.

The contributors to this series of books share the view that, at this historical juncture, we would all benefit from the implementation of the key fiscal policies that flow from the Georgist paradigm. Could it happen? Could the world transform itself without the self-indulgence of another world war? If so, why is the policy ignored in the corridors of power? The answer is a simple one: those who have power wish to retain it, and this is most effectively accomplished when those without power are distracted from the source of their sorrows. In other words, confusion about the nature of power itself is the most effective weapon for retaining it where (in what is supposed to be a democracy) it does not belong.

One of the remarkable features of the social sciences in the past century has been the failure to identify the roots of power. By failing correctly to analyse the defects in 19th century capitalism, the philosophical field was left open for a vulgarised Marxism to emerge in opposition to the social system which has at its heart the economics of the market.

This was not entirely the fault of Karl Marx. This we can detect from his horror when he read the programme that was drafted for European socialists, who met in congress in Gotha in 1875. Marx strongly dissociated himself from the wording of the programme. At the heart of the disagreement was the nature of power.

Marx got it right. In his *Critique of the Gotha Programme*,[4] Marx traduced those socialists who claimed that labour was the sole source of wealth. "Labour is *not the source* of all wealth," he wrote. "Nature is just as much the source of use-values (and surely these are what make up material wealth!) as labour."[5]

But what of power? Well, according to Marx – if we are correctly to interpret his words – the capitalist was as much a victim as the worker. Why? His single most important pronouncement was thrown away in a parenthesis:

> In present society the instruments of labour are the monopoly of the landowners (the monopoly of landed property is even the basis of the monopoly of capital) *and* of the capitalists.[6]

The Gotha programme reserved its vitriol for capitalists. But Marx pointed out that the landowners were a class in their own right, and he stressed the significance of that distinction when he noted: "In England, the capitalist generally does not even own the land and soil on which his factory stands".

For the sake of analytical clarity Marx ought to have added that if the workers suffered from the primary power of the land monopolist, then so did the capitalist who also relied on access to land for his activities. He could not have done so, of course, because had he added these words his house of cards - the one built on the theory of exploitative capitalists – would have crumbled in one swift sentence!

Marx was to reiterate the primary significance of the power of land monopoly in Vol.3 of *Capital*. Unfortunately, this was published posthumously; by that time the damage was done by the lopsided analysis in the first two volumes, which were not perceived as a fatal threat to the interests of the power elites and were therefore not subjected to the forensic examination that they deserved. That ought not to have been fatal for the evolution of culture in the 20th century, however, for the radicals of the 1880s were provided with a full analysis of land as the basis of power from the pen of Henry George.

At the time of the Gotha congress, the American was in San Francisco, where he was working towards an understanding of how land monopoly – when placed in the hands of a minority – was the most destructive force in history. If the socialists had built on Marx's laconic observations with an appreciation of Henry George's analysis, they would have been directed along a more fruitful path of social activity. Instead, the flow of historical influence was to be in the reverse direction. People like George Bernard Shaw were inducted into an understanding of economics by Henry George, but they then went on to become Fabian-style socialists.[7]

The general public was not so gullible, and its response set the alarm bells ringing among the conservatives in society. Henry George was recognised as the most serious threat to the *status quo*. It was therefore necessary to neutralise him, but the price of this retaliation was the betrayal of economics as a social science.

At the turn into the 20th century, economists abused their discipline by sieving off the reality of life. They turned political economy into a pseudoscience. They did so by abandoning the real world in favour of metaphysics, a device they concealed by glossing their new terminology with the comforting rigour of abstract models. Their legacy has been a discipline which, far from clarifying the real-world processes, is now used to prescribe policies that are as mystifying as the preachings of Schoolmen of the Middle Ages. That much is now being recognised on both sides of the Atlantic. For example, Prof. Paul Ormerod notes:

Good economists know, from work carried out within their discipline, that the foundations of their subject are virtually non-existent. . . . Conventional economics offers prescriptions for the problems of inflation and unemployment which are at best misleading, and at worst dangerously wrong.[8]

So far, however, no-one has exposed the origins of the problem. For that, we have to turn to the work of a professor of economics at the University of California.

Neo-classical mystification

Mason Gaffney is a life-long student of the economics of America's most famous home-grown social reformer, Henry George. As a teacher of economics, he has long been disconcerted by the surreal streak in his subject – the streak that happens to dominate the lecture theatres of universities throughout the world. He has had to explain how his discipline became detached from the real world during the course of the 20th century.

Prof. Gaffney questions the motives of the neo-classical economists. He charges many of his predecessors with wilfully distorting some of the key concepts of classical economics. In particular, they emasculated their discipline when they conflated "land" into "capital". This was not an exercise designed to elevate economics to a higher level of usefulness to society, so why should they do that? In Gaffney's view, this was a ploy to avoid coming to terms with the inexorable logic of one of the most clearcut findings of their discipline. And what was that? Over the preceding 150 years, economists had rigorously defined the elements of the best, most rational, socially just approach to public finance; and the economists at the turn of the century (or their paymasters) did not like the conclusion.

Prof. Gaffney's accusations are serious. He charges professional economists with confusing their obligations as scientists with their private interests as citizens. In the process, they abused the minds of generations of students. This is how he put it in correspondence to me:

Systematic, universal brainwashing is the crime, tendentious mental conditioning calculated to mislead students, to impoverish their mental ability, to bend their minds to the service of a system that funnels power and wealth to a parasitic minority.

This is a serious charge that invites scrutiny, but of one thing we can be sure: today's politicians, when it comes to formulating fresh policies that address the root-cause of social problems, cannot expect much help from their professional advisers. For they are frankly at a loss to *understand* why, for example, in the 1990s, the world economy slumped into the deepest depression since the 1930s.

The neo-classical economists, by abusing the language of their discipline, exposed the world to the Soviet experiment. It need not have been so. The rational policies that flow from classical economics, especially on the subject of public finance, had they been adopted, would have changed for the better the world of the 20th century.

It was not to be. An understanding of how – and why – economists reworked the language of economics to suit the ideology of "capitalism" is crucial. It is a pre-requisite of any attempt to rescue the much discredited practice of economic thinking.

Economic with the truth

The restoration of economics as a tool for analysing problems is imperative in today's turbulent world, in which local fissures are magnified to global proportions by the interconnectedness of people on the planet. But we will not get far if we rely on the theoretical and institutional conventions that were established by neo-classical economists who, because of their conceptual prism, are unable to comprehend the precise nature of the problems that are now faced by humanity.

This claim can be illustrated by re-examining the intellectual biographies of the leading economists: influential men like John Kenneth Galbraith, the Harvard University professor of economics who is famous for his critique of what he called the affluent society. By discovering how their sincere desire to improve society has been frustrated by their distorted language, we can glimmer the policies that must be adopted.

Embarrassed by the global depression of the 1990s which they failed to predict, economists ought to be reappraising radically their understanding of how the world really works. Galbraith's approach, as an exemplar of the would-be reformer, remains locked in the discredited perceptions of the past century. Today, he is one of the few remaining critics of capitalism who still offers a vision of The Good Society that relies on a confused combination of the analytical tools of neo-classical economics and the ideology of welfare capitalism.

The legacy of economists like Professor Galbraith is a reaffirmation of the poverty of conventional economics. This assessment was confirmed by Professor Galbraith in January 1994 in his lecture at the Cardiff Law School. He said:

> Once all economic and social thought turned on a bilateral economic and
> social structure. There were capital and labour, the capitalist and the worker.
> There were also a landed and a peasant population: the landed often
> serving in government as the surrogate of the capitalist class, the peasants
> scattered and politically irrelevant. Capital and labour; capital versus
> labour: this was the basic dialectic.[9]

Galbraith's association of land, its ownership and use, with the peasant economy, safely relegated the third factor of production to an age that even predated the era of the allegedly exclusive capitalist/worker nexus. Land, its power, and the role of landlords, are subordinated to the capitalist, conceptually smothered by a dualism that conveniently simplified life for economists, but condemned economic thinking to irrelevance (at best) and the socially injurious (in the main).

The idea of a bilateral conflict never was a realistic characterisation of the industrial economy (as Marx had noted). Its restatement by Galbraith illustrates the source of the continuing confusion in economic thinking.

The professor's views have moved on; alas, to yet another bilateral dichotomy. We now have the managerial bureaucracy of the big corporations and "the comfortably situated who have replaced the once-dominant capitalist". Unfortunately, this is likewise of no help in trying to figure out what is wrong with the economy.

Professor Galbraith's economic analysis fizzles into sociological categories, the imprecisions of which distract him from the causes of the poverty to which he addresses himself. The analytical problem is illustrated by Galbraith's attempt to explain the recession that gripped the industrial nations in the 1990s.

> There is no simple reason for this, but two factors stand out. There was the
> extreme speculation of the 1980s, especially in the United States of
> America and Japan, with its depressive aftermath. Banks, builders,

corporations generally, and individuals were led or forced, in consequence of debt or financial disaster, to restrain investment and employment. And in the 1980s, there was a marked redistribution of income to the very rich....[10]

Here was a description that offered the starting point for developing remedial policies. Deeper reflection would have revealed that the primary target of speculation was land in all the market economies – not especially the USA or Japan.[11] Destabilisation was the consequence of speculation; which, surely, was not beyond the wit of mankind to eliminate? Professor Galbraith is pessimistic:

> Perhaps there is something we can do to restrain the speculative mood and to avoid its aftermath. I am inclined to believe, however, that it is a basic tendency of the market system, of its deeper character and motivation.[12]

If speculation is "a basic tendency of the market system"; and if the Left now accepts "the market" as it is at present constituted (said Galbraith: "The basic market system and its managers the good society accepts") then we might have to share this pessimism. In fact, such resignation is not warranted once we realise that the major problem is with that variety of speculation associated with land; and that an effective remedy does exist, one that is consonant with the optimum system of public finance and private welfare.

Unfortunately, generations of students have been misled by pronouncements from the lectern. Today, we are told, pragmatism rules: "This is not the age of social and political doctrine," says Professor Galbraith. "It is the age of practical decision." The world has not been short of practical decisions, these past 100 years, and the scale of poverty and of social distress in its varied forms continue to mount.

So we are left with a gospel of despair; one that calls for the alleviation of suffering rather than the demand for preventive action; which deepens dependency on the State rather than personal liberty. The Left – now aligned with the Right in accepting the inevitability of the business cycle and the misery which this causes – has no strategy for neutralising the forces that destroy private initiative and productive enterprise. We have come to the end of a philosophical epoch.

Economists close their minds – and ours

Economists have a remarkable achievement to their credit. They have banished from public discussion a policy that is grounded on impeccable theory and which evokes a beautiful vision of a healthy society based on justice.

This they could accomplish only if they closed their minds to the Georgist paradigm. That was the challenge set for what we now call the neo-classical economists. Their brief was to stop the debate on the Single Tax. And they are paraded for this purpose to this day, most recently – as Dr. Feder explains in her contribution to this volume – in South Africa. Frank Knight is the guru of an author representing the views of The Free Market Foundation, which exists "to promote economic freedom". President Nelson Mandela may wish to harmonise the interests of black and white citizens in the post-apartheid society, but if the "free marketeers" have anything to do with it, he is certainly not going to be allowed to put the Single Tax to the test! (The Free Market Foundation's chairman is a director of Anglo-American, which operates the diamond cartel and has little interest in providing its customers with the benefits of the free market.)

The influence of the turn-of-century economists could not have been sustained to this day without the compliance of successive generations of academics. How did the latter-day economists convince themselves of the need to close their minds to the Single Tax; and, in the process, close our minds as well? How, during the age of the Welfare State, when scholars were genuinely concerned about the plight of millions of citizens who were excluded from the productive capacity of the capitalist economy, was the neo-classical propaganda fed into society?

The methodology is illustrated by the treatment accorded the Single Tax in the history books. Again, we shall take the words of Prof. Galbraith as exemplar. *A History of Economics: the past as the present* (1987) is widely available as a Penguin paperback, a resource to which students resort when they need to set the diagrammatic strokes of the chalk on the blackboard against the facts of history. Does Prof. Galbraith offer enlightment? Or does he colour people's views with his subjective preferences?

That the views of Henry George may be of interest – if not relevance – to us, is suggested by this acknowledgement:

> In his time and even into the 1920s and 1930s, Henry George was the most
> widely read of American economic writers both at home and in Europe. He
> was, indeed, one of the most widely read of Americans. (1984: 166) ...
> *Progress and Poverty* ... in various editions and reprintings, had a
> circulation in the millions. (p. 53, n.5).

In terms of public appeal, the impact of Henry George was so substantial
as to merit attention by scholars – at the very least, by those who purport
to provide a history of their discipline. Henry George's theories may have
been wrong, and therefore of no practical value to us today. But they could
hardly be ignored in a work of history. And yet, notes Prof. Galbraith:

> His *Progress and Poverty,* despite its continuing social influence
> notwithstanding, receives only passing mention or none at all in the
> standard works on the history of economic thought. (pp. 166–67: emphasis
> added)

Why? A century ago the neo-classical economists, who perverted their
integrity for the benefit of their paymasters, were so successful that their
prejudices have been deeply implanted into the minds of their successors.
They, in turn, have joined the brigades that patrol their discipline, to ensure
that young minds are not contaminated by this allegedly dangerous theory.
That most teachers perform this function unwittingly does not diminish
the damage that they, ultimately, are responsible for inflicting on society.

The first step in the process of mind-control is self-censorship of ideas.
This is achieved by exiling the Single Tax into the nether regions of
theology. Thus, Prof. Galbraith's characterisation of Georgists as "a small
but fervent band of believers". (Page 53, n.5). The language has its
subliminal effect. Students of the economics of Henry George are mere
believers of the gospel! Are the advocates of Adam Smith and Karl Marx
less *fervent* in their commitment?

Every "band of believers" needs a bible. Sure enough, the word pops up
in Prof. Galbraith's reference to *Progress and Poverty.* That book he declares
to be "the bible of a small but articulate group of true believers". (p.166)

But the reputation of the leader of the "band of believers" must also be
neutralised, if the process of discrediting the theory is to be complete. This
is how Prof. Galbraith executes that little exercise. Henry George, he says,

... was also an early but lasting demonstration of the fact that no journalist
can ever be taken quite seriously as an economist. (p.166)

Ironically, few professionals today enjoy less credibility than do
economists!

How can economists continue to disparage a treatise that rates as one of
the most remarkable literary achievements since the Industrial Revolution?
By claiming that there are problems with the theory. They do not generally
feel obliged to substantiate their claims; merely to assert the statements, *ex
cathedra*, and we are supposed to, well, *believe them!*

Prof. Galbraith identifies four problems with Henry George's
formulation, "and they may perhaps account for some of the disdain of the
professional economists". (p.167) First problem:

> Increasing land values were far from being the only fortuitous form of
> enrichment. Many others besides landowners, not excluding passive
> investors in all manner of industrial, transportation, communications and
> banking enterprises, were similarly enriched and had similarly a free ride.
> (Pp.167–68)

This is a curious form of argument that does not lend itself to common
sense (which was the whole point of the neo-classical stratagem). There is
an adage which says that "two wrongs don't make a right". If we accepted
this argument of the economists, slavery would not have been abolished
(as we note below).

Prof. Galbraith triumphantly caps this argument with a question: "Why
single out the owners of land as uniquely culpable?" For the good reason,
as Prof. Gaffney explains in *Land and Taxation*, that the characteristics of
land are unique. The claim that there is no difference between land
ownership and the ownership of capital (as in railroads and steel mills) is
not based on fact; it is part of neo-classical metaphysics.

But there is an element of truth in Prof. Galbraith's observation. Insofar
as transporation and steel mills benefit from the exploitation of the rent of
location and depletable natural resources, they fall within the embrace of
the Single Tax. Second problem:

> Nor should the return from the increased value of the land be confiscated
> after the fact. (p.168)

This argument was used in defence of slavery. Prof. Galbraith revives the argument in these terms:

> ...to come later and by taxation reduce, even confiscate, the property values of those who had bought land as distinct from those who were investors in railroads, steel mills or other appreciated property was surely discriminatory.

The asset that appreciates in railroads, steel mills and other property is land, not the rolling stock, mill or other real property which depreciates, so this objection is meaningless. There is no discrimination.

The private appropriation of the rent of land is the primary discriminatory act. It has to be corrected before economic efficiency and social justice can be achieved. Are we to lock into our system, forever, the discrimination that consigns millions of people to unfair treatment such that, if they are born into the working class, their children are more likely to die at birth, and they are more likely to die before they can enjoy their pensions?

Prof. Galbraith, a humane man, would not endorse such a prospectus. Indeed, his proposals for the discriminatory taxation of people's earned incomes were supposed to correct the flaw in the system. Alas, they did not do so. Third problem:

> There was also solemn discussion and some calculation as to whether Henry George's tax would, indeed, pay all the costs of the modern state. (p.168)

The discussion was rarely solemn, in fact; more often, passionate, both by the advocates and opponents of the proposal. But be that as it may, at the end of the 19th century there was little doubt that the Single Tax afforded a sufficient tax base to finance the needs of the state: which is why the policy had to be scotched! Economists today certainly question the proposition: in their (completely uninformed) view, the rent of land is assumed to be a derisory sum, of anywhere between 2% to 8% of national income. Prof. Galbraith, in alluding to the alleged problem, offers no evidence to suggest that the doubts were justified. The reader is left with the impression that the rent of land and natural resources does not provide a sufficient tax base for the modern state.

But notice a curious feature of this argument against Henry George. Economists who are hired to advise governments on fiscal policy do not exclude from their proposals the need for a tax on wages, or a tax on corporate profits, on the grounds that the revenue from one of these taxes would not be sufficient to pay for all the needs of the state. So why emphatically exclude from debate, in the corridors of power, a tax on the unearned income from land?

Modern economists limit their reflections in a manner that they need to explain. First they fail properly to calculate the revenue that would flow from land in *a tax-free society* (Henry George's prescription). They then assume that revenue from the rent of land would be insufficient to meet the finances of the modern state - finances that had to be rigged to compensate for the shortcomings in an unstable system. And they then proceed to ignore land a Welfare State source of revenue, while turning their attention to labour and capital (thus capitulating to the ideology of their neo-classical predecessors). Fourth problem:

> A final and most considerable difficulty went largely unmentioned: that was the very large number of landowners, rich and less rich, and their certain, strongly motivated and decisive political opposition. (p.168)

In fact, there was a massive debate about the wrecking power of the landowners. And at the time, they were not numerically significant (in democratic terms); they just happened to control the fortunes with which to finance the propaganda campaigns against the Single Tax. As Prof. Galbraith notes:

> Though a compelling idea, [the Single Tax] aroused no enthusiasm from owners of real estate, who were not a negligible political force. (p.53)

Today, the vast majority of landowners are the owners of residential land: the small plots beneath their homes. They would be financially richer if their wages and profits were untaxed in favour of the Single Tax, a fact that is not explained to them by economists.

In Henry George's time, the Single Tax proposal aroused the support of millions of ordinary folk. But they were not the paymasters of the economists. In fact, they were the victims of those paymasters, who hired the economists to close their minds. Today, we pay the price for the corruption to which the science of economics was subjected by the rent-seekers.

Quest for alternatives

To leap across the vortex into which society is now sinking, we need the help of a comprehensive description of how the world really works. The Georgist paradigm constitutes such a framework. It yields some large claims about the transformation of society, starting with self-esteem, moving on to a renewal of interpersonal relationships, then on to the quality of society and a redefinition of our basic relationship with Nature. It exposes the weakness in the foundations of society, and it specifies the conditions for achieving the optimum balance between the private and public sectors, by removing monopoly power from the market and funding the public sector out of public value (the rent of land). Thus is the union between individual liberty and social welfare consummated.

Henry George, in advocating this prospectus, recognised that he would be stirring controversy. But that controversy was not so much because of question marks over his theoretical or moral arguments: theological, philosophical and economic thinkers through the ages have consistently endorsed the principal tenets which he integrated into a programme of action in *Progress and Poverty*. This was recognised by the audiences that received him with rapture in most places where he spoke. His engagements took him from the United States to the debating chamber of the Oxford Union; to the town halls of Ireland and Scotland, and all the way to Australia and New Zealand. No; Henry George became the target of special opposition because his remedy did not seek to disturb society by revolutionary means. But he did seek to undermine – by democratic means, through the system of public finance – the monopoly power exercised by people who were misappropriating the income of society to finance their private lifestyles.

One consequence of that state of affairs, noted George, was the relationship between poverty and scientific and technologial progress. There was no paradox, he explained, once we recognise what happens when the relationship between man and land is broken. And that was where the neo-classical economists stepped in – to sever the conceptual tools which, in Henry George's hands, had exposed the causal mechanisms.

To what extent would the prescriptions embedded in George's paradigm lead to the abolition of poverty? He was confident about committing himself to a large claim. Everybody who was not work-shy, he insisted, would be able to enjoy a decent standard of living.

> What I mean is, that we all might have leisure, comfort and abundance, not
> merely of the necessaries, but even of what are now esteemed the elegancies
> and luxuries of life ... I do mean to say that we might all have enough wealth
> to satisfy reasonable desires; that we might all have so much of the material
> things we now struggle for, that no one would want to rob or swindle his
> neighbor; that no one would worry all day, or lie awake at nights, fearing he
> might be brought to poverty, or thinking how he might acquire wealth.[13]

Today, the men who lie awake at night worrying about being unemployed
or being made redundant have a statistically greater chance of dying than
their neighbours who are secure in their jobs. This is a tyranny that no
"civilised" society ought to tolerate; Henry George's analysis leads to the
inexorable conclusion that the only circumstance under which such deep-
seated terror can be abolished is through the reform of public finance.

Was Henry George over-optimistic? Did he overstate his claims? He did
not shirk the challenge of the sceptic, for he immediately confronts his
vision with the question: "Does this seem an utopian dream?" His provocative
claim that poverty can be abolished confronts scholars with an obligation to
test George's insistence that the correct system of public finance would
liberate us all from the existing restraints that deprive millions of people of
their material needs.

Such an enquiry is now inevitable, because the Welfare State is fast
discovering that it can no longer find the money to supplement the lowest
wages. Could the market economy be reconstituted in such a way that
poverty would be abolished?

And what of the business cycle? In 1993, over 30m people were without
jobs in the rich nations that are members of the Organisation of Economic
Co-operation and Development. Economists have resigned themselves to
the belief that booms and slumps are "natural" – an epidemiological feature
of the industrial economy. Solutions to the cyclical disruption of production
have escaped their algebraic equations. Henry George claimed that business
activity would be smoothed out if we removed the parasite in the body
politic – the private appropriation of the rent of land, the pursuit of which
drives people (through speculation) to feverish distraction. This is a testable
hypothesis that needs to be subjected to empirical research. Alas, it is a
subject that is ignored by economists. Result: pessimism.

Little, it seems, can be done to change substantively the structure of the market economy. Every possible twist and turn has been tried, and policy-makers are now retracing their steps – re-creating, in fact, institutional conditions that bear a striking resemblance to market conditions of the 19th century. In contrast, Henry George's paradigm encourages us to be optimistic, for it deepens our understanding of the meaning of freedom and equality. There is much work still to be done, and precious little time left in which to do it if we are to avoid what one French commentator[14] regards as the onset of a New Dark Age.

The need for a reappraisal of the foundations of capitalism is necessitated by the overwhelming scale of today's economic, political and environmental problems. These are systematically defeating governments throughout the world. Could Henry George's remedy – untaxing people's wages and profits, and relying on the rent of land for public revenue – carry the burden we now collectively face? Reflect on the assessment of Professor Galbraith himself:

> If a tax were imposed equal to the annual use value of real property ex its improvements, so that it would now have no net earnings and hence no capital value of its own – progress would be orderly and its fruits would be equitably shared.[15]

Is that not what we want? Orderly progress, in which the "fruits" would be equitably shared? Within such a framework, would we not be able to correct the accumulated problems of the past? I believe so. Yet it is the dogged determination not to translate this one theoretical insight into a set of practical policies that is at the heart of the crisis of western political philosophy. There is no practical reason for refusing to treat the rent-revenue policy seriously. The administrative apparatus for implementing the policy exists in countries as diverse as Denmark and New Zealand; Jamaica and South Africa.

Curious, then, that economists should by their silence circumscribe the choice of people. They do so, because they presume to know what is politically feasible – acceptable to the electorate. This intervention in the democratic process, using ideology disguised as scientific expertise, forecloses people's options by closing their minds. This, surely, is intellectual totalitarianism that warrants further investigation?

Whether the process of social disintegration is reversed, now, or corrective action is postponed until after some planetary-scale tragedy, depends on democratic pressure from the citizen. There is reason to be hopeful; for most people have less invested in the old ways of thinking about the world than those who have most to lose from change. This series of books on the Georgist paradigm is dedicated to helping people to come out of hiding and challenge the failed wisdoms that afflict our age.

References

1 G.J. Miller, "The Health and Wealth of the Nation", in Michael Hudson, George Miller and Kris Feder, *A Philosophy for a Fair Society*, London: Shepheard Walwyn/CIT, 1994.

2 C.R. Fay, *Life and Labour in the Nineteenth Century*, Cambridge: University Press, 1920, Ch.20.

3 "George, Henry", *Palgrave's Dictionary of Political Economy* (Editor: Henry Higgs), Vol. II, London: Macmillan, 1926, p.873.

4 Page references are to Karl Marx, *The First International and After*, Harmondsworth: Penguin, 1974.

5 *Ibid.*, p.341. Marx's emphasis.

6 *Ibid.*, p. 343. Marx's emphasis.

7 R.V. Andelson (editor), *Critics of Henry George*, Rutherford: Fairleigh Dickinson University Press, 1979.

8 Paul Ormerod, *The Death of Economics*, London: Faber, 1994. *Wall Street Journal* economics editor Alfred L. Malabre (*Lost Prophets*, Boston: Harvard Business School Press), has noted research which suggests that the US economy performs better when the President's Council of Economic Advisers was without a chairman (1994:3).

9 J.K. Galbraith, "The Good Society Considered: The Economic Dimension", Cardiff Law School, University of Wales College of Cardiff, 26 Jan., 1994; pages not numbered.

10 *Ibid.*

11 Land speculation in the second half of the 1980s was a generalised phenomenon in the market economies of the world. For the most recent survey, see Mason Gaffney and Fred Harrison, *Land Speculation and the Business Cycle*, London: Shepheard-Walwyn/CIT, 1995.

12 Galbraith, *op. cit.*

13 Henry George, *Social Problems* (1883), New York: Robert Schalkenbach

Foundation, 1981, pp.70–71.

14 Alain Minc, *Le Nouveau Moyen Age*, 1993.

15 J.K. Galbraith, *The Affluent Society*, Harmondsworth: Penguin, 1987, p.44.

Neo-classical Economics as a Stratagem Against Henry George

Mason Gaffney

1

Neo-classical economics is the idiom of most economic discourse today. It is the paradigm that bends the twigs of young minds. Then it confines the florescence of older ones, like chicken-wire shaping a topiary. It took form about a hundred years ago, when Henry George and his reform proposals were a clear and present political danger and challenge to the landed and intellectual establishments of the world. Few people realize to what degree the founders of neo-classical economics changed the discipline for the express purpose of deflecting George and frustrating future students seeking to follow his arguments. The strategem was semantic: to destroy the very words in which he expressed himself. Simon Patten expounded it succinctly. "Nothing pleases a ... single taxer better than ... to use the well-known economic theories ... [therefore] economic doctrine must be recast" (Patten, 1908: 219; Collier, 1979: 270).[1]

George believed economists were recasting the discipline to refute him. He states so, as though in the third person, in his posthumously published book, *The Science of Political Economy* (George, 1898: 200–209). George's self-importance was immodest, it is true. However, immodesty may be objectivity, as many great talents from Frank Lloyd Wright to Muhammad Ali and Frank Sinatra have displayed. George had good reasons, which we are to demonstrate. George's view may even strike some as paranoid. That was this writer's first impression, many years ago. I have changed my view, however, after learning more about the period, the literature, and later events.

Having taken shape in the 1880–1890s, Neo-Classical Economics (henceforth NCE) remained remarkably static. Major texts by Alfred Marshall, E.R.A. Seligman and Richard T. Ely, written in the 1890s, went through many reprints each over a period of 40 years with few if any changes. "It was for the Chautauqua Literary and Scientific Circle (1884) that I wrote the first edition of my *Outlines*, under the title *Introduction to Political Economy*. In this first edition of the *Outlines* there is to be found the general philosophy and principles that have shaped all future editions, including that of 1937" (Ely, 1938: 81).[2]

Not until 1936 was there another major "revolution," and that was hived off into a separate compartment, macro-economics, and contained there so that it did not disturb basic tenets of NCE. Compartmentalization, we will see in several instances, is the common NCE defense against discordant data and reasoning. After that came another 40 years of Paul Samuelson's "neo-classical synthesis". J.B. Clark's treatment of rent, dating originally from his obvious efforts to refute Henry George (see below), "has been followed by an admiring Paul Samuelson in all of the many editions of his *Economics*" (Dewey, 1987: 430).

Clark's capital theory ". . . gives the appearance of being specially tailored to lead to arguments for use against George" (Collier, 1979: 270). "The probable source from which immediate stimulation came to Clark was the contemporary single tax discussion" (Fetter, 1927: 142). "To date, capital theory in the Clark tradition has provided the basis for virtually all empirical work on wealth and income" (Dewey, 1987: 429; cf. Tobin, 1985). Later writers have added fretworks, curlicues and arabesques beyond counting, and achieved more isolation from history and from the ground under their feet, than in Patten's dreams, but all without disturbing the basic strategy arrived at by 1899, tailored to lead to arguments against Henry George.

To most modern readers, probably George seems too minor a figure to have warranted such an extreme reaction. This impression is a measure of the neo-classicals' success: it is what they sought to make of him. It took a generation, but by 1930 they had succeeded in reducing him in the public mind. In the process of succeeding, however, they emasculated the discipline, impoverished economic thought, muddled the minds of countless students, rationalized free-riding by landowners, took dignity from labor, rationalized chronic unemployment, hobbled us with today's counterproductive tax tangle, marginalized the obvious alternative system of public finance, shattered our sense of community, subverted a rising economic democracy for the benefit of rent-takers, and led us into becoming an increasingly nasty and dangerously divided plutocracy.

The present study sets out to identify the elements of NCE that were planted there to sap and confound George, and show how they continue to warp, debase and vitiate much of the discipline called economics. Once a paradigm is well-ensconced it becomes a power in itself, a set of reflexes to sort the true and false. Any exception spoils the web of interpretation through which art seeks to make human experience intelligible. Only the young, the brave, the energetic, the sincere and the sceptical can break off such fetters. This work is addressed and dedicated to them.

The Imperative to Put Down Henry George

Neo-classical economics makes an ideal of "choice". That sounds good, and liberating, and positive. In practice, however, it has become a new dismal science, a science of choice where most of the choices are bad. "TANSTAAFL" (There Ain't No Such Thing As A Free Lunch) is the slogan and shibboleth. Whatever you want, you must give up something good. As an overtone there is even a hint that what one person gains he must take from another. The theory of gains from trade has it otherwise, but that is a heritage from the older classical economists.

Henry George, in contrast, had a genius for reconciling-by-synthesizing. Reconciling is far better than merely compromising. He had a way of taking two problems and composing them into one solution, as we lay out in detail below. He took two polar philosophies, collectivism and individualism, and synthesized a plan to combine the better features, and discard the worse features, of each. He was a problem-solver who did not suffer incapacitating dilemmas and standoffs.

As policy-makers, neo-classical economists present us with "choices" that are too often hard dilemmas. They are in the tradition of Parson Malthus, who preached to the poor that they must choose between sex or food. That was getting right down to grim basics, and is the origin of the well-earned "the dismal science" epithet. Most modern neo-classicals are more subtle (although the fascist wing of the otherwise admirable ecology movement gets progressively less so). Here are some dismal dilemmas that neo-classicals pose for us today. For efficiency we must sacrifice equity; to attract business we must lower taxes so much as to shut the libraries and starve the schools; to prevent inflation we must keep an army of unfortunates unemployed; to make jobs we must chew up land and pollute the world; to motivate workers we must have unequal wealth; to raise productivity we must fire people; and so on.

The neo-classical approach is the "trade-off". A trade-off is a compromise. That has a ring of reasonableness to it, but it presumes a zero-sum condition. At the level of public policy, such "trade-offs" turn into paralyzing stand-offs in which no one gets nearly what he wants, or what he could get. It overlooks the possibility of a *reconciliation*, or synthesis. In such a resolution, we are not limited by trade-offs between fixed A and B: we get more of both.

Popular responsiveness to problem-solvers

Voters faced with two candidates, each coached by a neo-classical economist, also face a hard choice. They often appear apathetic and take a third choice, staying home. However, history denies that voters are intrinsically apathetic. They have been excited by candidates who try to lead up and away from dismal trade-offs.

In 1980 it was Ronald Reagan. Instead of the dismal Phillips Curve ("choose inflation or unemployment"), he offered the happy Laffer Curve: lower tax rates would lead to higher supplies, higher revenues and lower deficits, he promised. Lowering taxes, said Laffer, would eliminate the "wedge effect".[3] He often cited Henry George in support of his position.[4] Thus he would unleash supply, and collect more taxes while applying lower tax rates. The voters were sick of second-generation Keynesians who had been reduced to preaching austerity, so they were game (if not wise) to buy into Reaganomics as advertised.

Unfortunately, the Laffer Curve turned out to be wildly overoptimistic, and Reaganomics partly fraudulent and hypocritical[5] in application. The voters again tuned out and seemed apathetic. They are not saying, however, that they don't care. They are saying "come back when you have something better, mean what you say, and deliver what you promise".

From 1936–70 it was John Maynard Keynes and his apostles who had a long run with the voters, in spite of virulent critics. Keynes' winning political formula was that consumption and capital formation are not alternatives to be traded off, but complements that reinforce one another. Raise wages, he said, raise private and public consumer spending, and get more capital formation as a happy by-product. "We can have it all," he said. Who would not prefer that to long-faced moralizers preaching that we must suffer for the prodigalities of the past, or for the sake of a remote and uncertain future? Even puritans learned better as children from Longfellow's "Psalm of Life".[6]

When the theory of the propensity to consume, and the multiplier, lost their charm, and some strong trade unions (like Hoffa's Teamsters) showed their nastier side, the American voters tuned in to John F. Kennedy and "business Keynesianism" in which the emphasis turned to fostering new investment. Keynes had been shrewd enough to cast his theories to accommodate either emphasis. Here the formula was to raise the "marginal efficiency of capital" (today we say the marginal rate of return) after taxes by giving preferential tax treatment to new investment, keeping tax rates high on income from old assets like land. It was a species of Georgism, applied via the Federal income tax.[7] The key devices were fast write off for new capital, and the investment tax credit. There was no talk or thought, however, of enriching capitalists by impoverishing workers. The promise was to enrich capitalists and workers together, as higher investment raised aggregate demand for labor and its products through the "multiplier" effect.

In time that happy glow of mutuality turned to ashes. After JFK, with his influential economist Walter Heller, the flame burned low; later leaders stumbled in the dark. They relied too simple-mindedly on demand management through fiscal and monetary policy, carrying them well beyond their power to stimulate supply. Thus they lurched into Stagflation: double-digit inflation and recession conjoined. They blamed the war, then the Arabs. They scolded the public, and they called for sacrifices, as leaders always do when they lack ideas. "You must mature and face the facts of life," they lectured. "There is no way to stop inflation except unemployment. Whichever evil you choose, don't blame us, we told you so".[8] Faced with that, the voters exercised a third choice: they retired the patrons of those new dismal scientists.

Before Keynes there was another great reconciler, Henry George. In 1879, George electrified the world by identifying a cause of the boom/

slump cycle, identifying a cause of inadequate demand for labor, and, best of all, following through with a plausible, practicable remedy. Like Keynes and Laffer after him, he turned people on by saying "Forget the bitter trade-offs; we can have it all".

Henry George came out of a raw, naive new colony, California, as a scrappy marginal journalist. Yet his ideas exploded through the sophisticated metropolitan world as though into a vacuum. His book sales were in the millions. Seven short years after publishing *Progress and Poverty* in remote California he nearly took over as Mayor of New York City, the financial and intellectual capital of the nation. He thumped also-ran Theodore Roosevelt, and lost to the Tammany candidate (Abram S. Hewitt) only by being counted out (Barker, 1955: 480–81; Myers, 1907: 356–58; Miller, 1917: 11). Three more years and he was a major influence in sophisticated Britain. In 1889, incredibly, he became "adviser and field-general in land reform strategy" to the Radical wing of the Liberal Party in Britain, where he was not even a citizen. "It was inevitable that, when [Joseph] Chamberlain bowed out, George should become the Radical philosopher" (Lawrence, 1957: 105–06). It also happened that when Chamberlain bowed out, the Radical wing *became* the Liberal Party. It adopted a land-tax plank after 1891 (the "famous Newcastle Programme"), and came to carry George's (muted) policies forward under the successive Liberal Governments of Campbell-Bannerman, Asquith and Lloyd George.

How could a marginal man come out of nowhere and make such an impact? The economic gurus of the day, even as today, were in a scolding mode, blaming unemployment on faulty character traits and genes and demanding austerity. They were not intellectually armed to refute him or befuddle his listeners. He had studied the classical economists and used their tools to dissect the system. Neo-classical economics arose in part to fill the void, to squeeze out such radical notions, and be sure nothing like the Georgist phenomenon could recur.

Are we imputing too much weight to a minor figure? We are told that Georgism withered away quietly with its founder in 1897.[9] That, however, is warped history. One of the great derelictions of American historians is to have neglected the single-tax movement, 1901–24. It is also a warped view of "The Single Tax" as a discrete, millenial change, a quantum leap away from life as we know it (Gaffney, 1976). Pure Georgism never "took over whole hog," but no single philosophy ever does. Modified Georgism, melded into the Progressive Movement, helped run the USA for 17 years (1902–19) working through *both* major political parties.[10] At the local level, it continued on through the early 1920s. Local property taxation was modified on Georgist lines even as it rose in absolute terms. The first Federal income tax law was drafted by a Georgist (Congressman Warren Worth Bailey of Johnstown, Pennsylvania) with Georgist goals uppermost.[11] Real concessions were made: the politicians heard the voters. Historians of the Populist Party and movement often note that its ideas succeeded even though the Party failed, because its ideas were coopted by major parties. Georgism was a strand of American populism, later wrapped into Progressivism.

Consider, for example, that in 1913 Wm. S. U'Ren, "Father of the Initiative and Referendum," created this system of direct democracy for the express purpose of pushing single-tax initiatives in Oregon. According to U'Ren, another by-product of the single-tax campaigns in Oregon was the 1910 "adoption of the first Presidential Primary Law, which was quickly imitated by so many other States that [Woodrow] Wilson's nomination and election over Taft was made possible" (U'Ren, 1917: 43). To that we may add that another "Father of the Direct Primary," George L. Record of New Jersey, was a mentor of Woodrow Wilson and an earnest Georgist who had raised the tax on railroad lands to the great benefit of public schools in New Jersey, and to the impoverishment of special interest election funds." ... it was the passage of these great election reforms in the Wilson Administration [in New Jersey] that led ... [to] winning the Bryan support and the Democratic nomination for President" (Blauvelt, 1936: 28). That helps explain the gratitude of President Wilson, who included single-taxers in his Cabinet (Newton D. Baker, Louis F. Post, Franklin K. Lane, and William B. Wilson), and worked with single-tax Congressmen like Henry George, Jr., and Warren Worth Bailey (Geiger, 1933: 464; Brownlee, 1985).

Consider that in 1916 a "pure single-tax" initiative, led by Luke North, won 31% of the votes in California (*Large landholdings*, 1919; Miller, 1917: 51; Geiger, 1933: 433; Young, 1916: 232). Even while "losing," such campaigns raised consciousness of the issue to a high degree, such that assessors were focusing more attention on land. Thus, in California, 1917, tax valuers focused on land value so much that they constituted 72% of the assessment roll for property taxation (Troy, 1917b: 398) – a much higher fraction than today. Joseph Fels, an idealistic manufacturer, was throwing millions into such campaigns in several states (Young, 1916; Miller, 1917), having earlier thrown himself and his fortune into the English land tax campaign that brought on the Parliamentary revolution of 1909 (Fels, 1919, 1940).

Consider that there was a single-tax party, the Commonwealth land Party. In 1924 its Presidential candidate was William J. Wallace of New Jersey, with John C. Lincoln, brilliant Cleveland industrialist, for Vice-president (Moley, 1962: 162). In 1919 Georgists began working through the Manufacturers and Merchants Federal Tax League to sponsor a *federal* land tax, the Ralston-Nolan Bill. Drafted by Judge Jackson H. Ralston, it would impose a "1% excise tax on the privilege of holding lands, natural resources and public franchises valued at more than $10,000, after deducting all improvements" (Jorgensen, 1925: 8–9).[12] In 1924 Congressman Oscar E. Keller of Minnesota reintroduced it (H.R. 5733). In spite of Harding, Coolidge, and Hoover, Progressivism still lived in Congress. In 1923, for the first and last time, income tax returns were made public, giving valuable data-ammunition to land taxers. Progressivism also lived in Wisconsin, where Professor John R. Commons in 1921 drafted the Grimstad Bill to focus the property tax on bare land values (Commons, 1922). Commons believed that 95% of "millionaire fortunes" consisted of land and franchise values (1893: 253). Young State Assemblyman (later Professor) Harold Groves was among its supporters.

Consider that in 1934 Upton Sinclair, so-called "socialist," almost became Governor of California on a modified Georgist platform. Two years later, Jackson H. Ralston, by then a Stanford Law Professor, led another California Initiative campaign to focus the property tax on land values. Norman Thomas, perennial Socialist candidate for President of the US, kept a land tax plank in his platform. Daniel Hoan, the "socialist" Mayor of America's model city, Milwaukee, had his tax assessor focus on upvaluing land. Hoan distributed land value maps to the Milwaukee public, to raise their consciousness of the issue.

Historian Eric Goldman (1956) found George to have inspired most of the major reformers of the early 20th Century. "... no other book came anywhere near comparable influence, and I would like to add this word of tribute to a volume which magically catalyzed the best yearnings of our grandfathers and fathers" (Goldman, 1979). Raymond Moley wrote, "... George ... touched almost all of the corrective influences which were the result of the Progressive movement. The restriction of monopoly, more democratic political machinery, municipal reform, the elimination of privilege in railroads, the regulation of public utilities, and the improvement of labor laws and working conditions – all were ... accelerated by George" (1962: 160).

Consider that most American states and Canadian provinces required separate valuations of land, for tax purposes. Professional valuers, responding to the general interest, were routinely valuing land separately from buildings, and developing workable techniques to handle the occasional tricky case (Zangerle, Pollock and Scholz, Purdy, Babcock, Somers, *et al.*)[13] Valuation anticipates taxation.[14] Lawson Purdy, one of those valuers, was Tax Commissioner of the City of New York, a founder of and power in the National Tax Association, a campaigner for George in the 1897 race, and a leader of the Manhattan Single Tax Club. Under this kind of influence, New York City kept its subway fares down to 5 cents, paying for most of the cost from taxes on the benefitted lands (Trott, 1956: 1). It also exempted new residential structures from the property tax for ten years, 1924–34 (Jorgensen, 1925: 159–62).

Consider that Wright Act Irrigation Districts were spreading fast throughout rural California, using Georgist land taxes to finance irrigation works. The Wright Act dated from 1887, and sputtered along fitfully until in 1909 the California Legislature amended the enabling legislation to limit the assessment in all new districts to the land value only. It also let old districts do so by local option (Cal. Stat. 1909: 461). The old districts soon did: Modesto in 1911, Turlock in 1915 (Troy, 1917a; Mason, 1942: 393; Mason, 1957–58; Jorgensen, 1925: 168–69; Henley 1969: 141; Gaffney, 1969; Ralston 1931: 161–63; Geiger, 1933: 439). This was Georgism getting its "second wind," so to speak. Beyond much question, the idea was identified with George. The legislative leader, L.L. Dennett of Modesto, got the idea from his father, an old neighbor of Henry George in San Francisco (Dennett, 1916a,b; Mason, 1957–58: 106–08). In Modesto and Turlock, "The campaign was conducted on pure Single Tax lines" (Troy, 1917a: 54).

In 1917, rural Georgism got a third wind: the California Legislature
made it mandatory for all Districts to exempt improvements (Stat. 1917:
764, codified Stats. 1943, Ch. 368, Div. 10, 11 [California Water Code];
Mason, 1949: 2,6; Gaffney, 1969). They then grew to include over four
million acres by 1927, and to dominate American agriculture in their
specialty crops. They built the highest dam in the world at that time (Don
Pedro, on the Tuolumne River in the Sierra Nevada), financing it 100%
from local land taxes. Albert Henley, a lawyer who crafted the modified
District that serves metropolitan San Jose, evaluated them thus:

> The discovery of the legal formula of these organizations was of infinitely
> greater value to California than the discovery of gold a generation before.
> They are an extraordinarily potent engine for the creation of wealth
> (Henley, 1957: 665, 667; 1969: 140).

They catapulted California into being the top-producing farm state in
the Union, using land that was previously desert or range. They made
California a generator of farm jobs and homes, while other states were
destroying them by *latifundiazation.*

If this is a "minor" phenomenon it is because the neglect of historians
and economists has made it so. One searches in vain through academic
books and journals on farm economics for recognition of this, the most
spectacularly successful story of farm economic development in history.
What references there are consist of precautionary cluckings focused on
attendant errors and failures. "Economic development" theorists neglect it
altogether, as though California's commercial farming had sprung full
blown from a corporate office, with no grass roots basis, and no
development period. It is as though the clerisy were in conspiracy against
the *demos*, under some Trappist oath against disclosing what groups of
small people achieved through community action, and through the
judicious application of the pro-incentive power of taxing land values.

There is a common defeatist notion that "farmers" are implacably
against land taxation. The California experience seems to belie it. It was the
same in other states, also, The Grange and the Farmers' Union were
pushing for focusing the property tax on land during the 'teens (Hampton).
In Minnesota, the Dakotas, and the Prairie Provinces the Non-Partisan
League became a major power in state and local politics, electing a
Governor of North Dakota and swaying many elections. North Dakota

exempted farm capital from the county property tax, taxing land only.[15] The spirit of Prairie Populism straddled the 49th parallel (the international boundary), radicalizing politics in rural Manitoba, Saskatchewan, Alberta, and British Columbia, all of which were focusing their property taxes on land in this period. It would seem that J.B. Clark's allusions to "agrarian socialism" had some basis in fact – he had spent some years in Northfield, Minnesota, in the heart of it. Clark just gave it the wrong name. One could go on: those are just straws in the wind.

George's ideas were carried worldwide by such towering figures as David Lloyd George in England, Leo Tolstoy and Alexandr Kerensky in Russia, Sun Yat-sen in China, hundreds of local and state, and a few powerful national politicians in both Canada and the USA, Billy Hughes in Australia, Rolland O'Regan in New Zealand, Chaim Weizmann in Palestine, Francisco Madero in Mexico, and many others in Denmark, South Africa and around the world. In England, Lloyd George's budget speech of 1909 reads in part as though written by Henry George himself. Some of Winston Churchill's speeches *were* written by Georgist ghosts.

Thus, to the rent-taker, the typical college trustee or regent, George's ideas remained a real and present danger over several decades: the very decades when neo-classical economics was spreading through the academic clerisy.[16] With the development of direct democracy, open primaries, the secret ballot, direct election of US Senators, the Initiative, Referendum, and Recall, and the like, crude vote-buying such as prevailed in the late 19th century would no longer dominate the electorate. Mind-control became the urgent need; NCE was the tool.

George's ideas and the allied Progressive Movement fell, not from failure to deliver, but to the Great Marathon Red Scare that has dominated much of the world from 1919 to 1989. This panic marshalled and energized rent-takers everywhere; by confusion, some of it deliberate, its victims included Georgists.[17] It inhibited them until their message lost its vigour and excitement and became just a minor local tax reform. Its leaders have moved to the trivial center, downplaying George's grand goals for full employment, catering to the practical but small and prosaic advantages of median homeowners at the local level. Now, with the fall of the Berlin Wall, Progressive ideas might very well pick up again where the original Movement was aborted.

2

The Reconciler and Problem-Solver

Let us itemize the several constructive reconciliations in George's reform proposal. This will explain its wide potential appeal and hence its ongoing threat to embedded rent-takers with a stake in unearned wealth. It will explain why they deployed neo-classical economists to work so hard to put this genie back in the bottle.

(1) George reconciled common land rights with private tenure, free markets and modern capitalism. He would compensate those dispossessed and made landless by the spread and strengthening of what is now called "European" land tenure, whose benefits he took as given and obvious. He would also compensate those driven out of business by the triumph of economies of scale, whose power he acknowledged and even overestimated. He proposed doing so through the tax system, by focusing taxes on the economic rent of land. This would compensate the dispossessed in three ways.

• Those who got the upper hand by securing land tenures would support public services, so wages and commerce and capital formation could go untaxed.

• To pay the taxes, landowners would have to use the land by hiring workers (or selling to owner-operators and owner-residents). This would raise demand for labor; labor, through consumption, would raise demand for final products.

• To pay the workers, landowners would have to produce and sell goods, thereby raising supply and precluding inflation. Needed capital would come to their aid by virtue of its being untaxed.

Thus, George would cut the Gordian knot of modern dilemma-bound economics by raising demand, raising supply, raising incentives, improving equity, freeing up the market, supporting government, fostering capital formation, and paying public debts, all in one simple stroke. It is quite a stroke, enough to leave one breathless.

In practice, landowners faced with high land taxes often choose another, even better, course than hiring more workers: they sell the land to the workers, creating an economy and society of small entrepreneurs. This writer has documented a strong relationship between high property tax rates, deconcentration of farmland and intensity of land use (Gaffney, 1992).

(2) George's proposal enables us to lower taxes on labor without raising taxes on capital. Indeed, it lets us lower taxes on both labor and capital at once, and without reducing public revenues.

(3) Georgist tax policy reconciles equity and efficiency. Taxing land is progressive because the ownership of land is so highly concentrated among the most wealthy,[18] and because the tax may not be shifted. It is efficient because it is neutral among rival land-use options: the tax is fixed, regardless of land use. This is one favourable point on which many modern economists actually agree, although they keep struggling against it, as we will see.

George showed that a tax can be progressive and pro-incentive at the same time. Think of it! An army of neo-classicalists preach dourly that we must sacrifice equity and social justice on the altar of "efficiency". They need that thought to stifle the demand for social justice that runs like a thread through the Bible, the Koran and other great religious works. George cut that Gordian knot, and so he had to be put down.

The only shifting of a land tax is negative. By negative shifting I mean that the supply-side effects of taxing the rent of land will raise supplies of goods and services, and raise the demand for labor, thus raising the bargaining power of median people in the marketplace, both as consumers and workers. This effect makes the tax doubly progressive: it undercuts the holdout power and bargaining power of landowners *vis-a-vis* workers, and also *vis-a-vis* new investors in real capital. This effect also makes the land-rent tax doubly efficient.[19]

(4) A state, provincial or local government can finance generous public services without driving away business or population. The formula is simple: tax the rent of land, which cannot migrate, instead of the incomes

of capital and people, which can. By eliminating the destructive "Wedge Effect", the land tax lets us support schools and parks and libraries and water purification and police and fire protection, etc., as generously as you please, without suppressing or distorting useful work, and without taxing investors in real capital.

(5) Georgist tax policy contains urban sprawl, and its heavy associated costs, without overriding market decisions or consumer preferences, simply by making the market work better. Land values are the product of demand for location; they are marked by continuity in space. That shows quite simply that people demand compact settlement and centrality. A well-oiled land market will give it to them.

(6) Georgist tax policy creates jobs without inflation, and without deficits. "Fiscal stimulus," in the shallow modern usage, is a euphemism for running deficits, often with funny money. George's proposed land tax might be called, rather, "true fiscal stimulus". It stimulates demand for labor by promoting employment; it precludes inflation as the labor produces goods to match the new demand. It precludes deficits because it raises revenue. That is its peculiar reconciliatory genius: it stimulates private work and investment in the very process of raising revenue. It is the only tax of any serious revenue potential that does not bear down on and suppress production and exchange. As I have noted, George's fiscal policy takes two problems and composes them into one solution.

(7) George's land tax lets a polity attract people and capital *en masse,* without diluting its resource base. This is by virtue of synergy, the ultimate rationale for Chamber-of-Commerce boosterism. Urban economists like William Alonso have illustrated the power of such synergy by showing that bigger cities have more land value *per head* than smaller ones. (Land value *is* the resource base of a city.) Urbanists like Jane Jacobs and Holly Whyte have written on the intimate details of how this works on the streets. Julian Simon (*The Ultimate Resource*) philosophizes on the power of creative thought generated when people associate freely and closely in large numbers. Henry George made the same points in 1879.[20]

(8) Georgist policies encourage the conservation of ecology and environment while also making jobs, by abating sprawl. It is a matter of focusing human activity on the good lands, thus meeting demands there and relieving the pressure to invade lands that are now wild and marginal for

human needs. Sprawl in the urban environment is the kind most publicized, but there is analogous sprawl in agriculture, forestry, mining, recreation and other land uses and industries.

(9) Georgist policies strengthen public revenues while in the same process promoting economy in government.

Anti-governmentalists often identify any tax policy with public extravagance. Georgist tax policy, on the contrary, saves public funds in many ways. By facilitating the creation of jobs it lowers welfare costs, unemployment compensation, doles, aid to families with dependent children and all that. It lowers jail and police costs, and all the enormous private expenditures, precautions, and deprivations now taken to guard against theft and other crime. Idle hands are not just wasted, they steal and destroy.

Ultimately, Georgist policy saves the cost of civil disturbances and insurrections, and/or the cost of putting them down. In 1992 large parts of Los Angeles were torched, for the second time in a generation, pretty much as foreboded by Henry George in *Progress and Poverty,* Book X.[21] Forestalling such colossal waste and barbarism is much more than merely a "free lunch".

George's program would abort other, less obvious wastes in government. It obviates much of the huge public cost now incurred to reach, develop and safeguard lands that should be left in their natural submarginal condition. Today, people occupy flood plains and they require levees, flood control dams and periodic expenditure on rescue and recovery. Others scatter their homes through highly flammable steep brushlands, which call for expensive fire-fighting equipment and personnel, and raising everyone's fire insurance premiums. Others build on fault lines; still others in the deserts, calling for expensive water imports. Generically, people now scatter their homes and industries over hundreds of square miles in the "exurbs", or urban sprawl areas, imposing huge public costs for linking the scattered pieces with the centre, and with each other.

This wasteful, extravagant territorial overexpansion results from two pressures working together. One force is that of land speculators. They manipulate politics by seeking public funds to upgrade their low-grade lands so that they may peddle them at higher prices. The other force is that of landless people, who seek land for homes and jobs, and public funds for "make-work" projects.

Both these forces wither away when we tax the rent of land and down tax the incomes of labour and capital. This moves good land into full use, meeting the demand for land by using land that is good by Nature, without high development costs. It also creates legitimate jobs, which abates the pressure for "make-work" spending. Above all, it takes the private gain out of raising the value of marginal land at public cost. Such lands, if upvalued by public spending, would then pay for their own development through higher public revenues.

These nine compelling features of George's program should be enough to persuade one that it had the potential to become very popular. Its premise was socializing land rents. Its very strengths were its undoing, however, for they evoke a powerful, intransigent, wealthy counterforce.

3

The Empire Strikes Back

Rent-takers and their wordsmiths could abide the classical economics of Locke, Hume, Smith and Ricardo, who stopped short of challenging the distribution of wealth. Quesnay's slogan of *laissez-faire,* and Smith's good name, were even coopted as bywords for social conservatism, after death muted their tongues to deny it. John Stuart Mill came closer to kicking over the traces: his distaste for unearned wealth shows clearly in his writings, and he proposed to socialize all future unearned increments. The feeling grew stronger with the years, and his last years were focused on land reform.

Still, Mill could be patronized into oblivion as "the saint of socialism": "saint" apparently meaning something like "scrupler". It was Mill who popularized the idea of raising taxes on landowners only after first compensating them, thus buying the right to tax them. It was a selective scruple: neither Mill nor anyone, to my knowledge, ever proposed compensating workers, consumers, or the owners of capital before taxing them. It was something of a red herring, because it assured that net revenues would be about zero. It simply gave debaters something to chew on while precluding meaningful action. Nevertheless, Mill set the stage for George by analyzing the matter clearly, and putting reform on the table. On the continent, H.H. Gossen, Auguste Walras, and later his son Leon Walras took up the idea - Leon with great passion and *elan.*[21] It was then only left for George, who corresponded with and respected Mill, to convert theory into action.

J.E. Cairnes, who took the lead against English support of US slavery, also was a member of Mill's and Wallace's land Tenure Reform Association. He proposed imposing maximum rent controls in Ireland. F.Y. Edgeworth, scion and heir of Irish landlords, snapped menacingly, faulting Cairnes' mathematical technique; it is not known if that succeeded in intimidating Cairnes, but it is likely that others of lesser standing took the hint.

Still, classical political economy was a remarkable phenomenon. Its major writers in England were able to portray the dominant class of rent-takers as idlers and superfluous drones. One surmises they got by with this because the idlers were proud of it. In their value-system, labor was not respected; conspicuous leisure was. Saving was regarded contemptuously as stinginess: conspicuous consumption was the mark of a gentleman and aristocrat.

In the later 19th century, however, especially in America, values were changing. The franchise was broadening. Pure rent-taking could not be defended in its own terms; it was reeling under attacks from the new functionalists. This is when George could go the rest of the way, showing how to use classical economics to rationalize land distribution through tax reform. Fred Foldvary well-calls him a "geo-classical"[23] political economist. Worse, George was a popular public figure with high-flying ambitions, a large constituency, a bias for action, and a sense of urgency.

The menace George posed to rent-takers is clear from how he viewed them. To George, the landowner *per se* is nonfunctional (unproductive), a layabout drone, a drain on the hive, a transferee, a welfare case. Worse than that, he or she often makes the land itself lay about, too: then he or she is *dys*functional or counterproductive, a double-dipper. Worse yet, landowners become triple-dippers when they use their discretionary income and wealth to dominate politics and drain away yet more treasure through subsidies, public works and services, protections from competition, cheap credit, and so on. Often they are not just passive drones, but active predators.

As to the academic clerisy, George first suspected, and then impugned their motives. They were myrmidons of the rent-takers, using smoke and mirrors to addle, baffle, boggle, and dazzle the laity. He provoked, supplying motive for venomous reaction from those whom the shoe fits.

The inevitable counterattack came to be called "neo-classical economics" (NCE), as though it were simply a natural development and improvement of tried-and-true classical economics. Rent-taking had to be made to appear useful in functional economic terms. The classical underpinnings of George had to be undone in a fairly subtle way, to seem simply evolutionary. There had to be some legitimacy of apostolic succession, while also nodding to the cult of progress. "Neo-classical" was an inspired stroke of public relations, suggesting modernity coupled with continuity of tradition. It is not, however, an accurate description. It was a radical paradigm shift. The task was to vandalize the stage Mill had set for George, torch the old furnishings, and reset the stage permanently in ways to discomfit George and frustrate future Georgists.

Personal Involvement of George with Early Neo-classicals

Several major figures in the neo-classical revolution had personal contact with George. Among these were J.B. Clark, Philip Wicksteed, Alfred Marshall, E.R.A. Seligman, and Francis A. Walker. Wicksteed was friendly; the others decidedly not so. There is no doubt George was much on their minds and in their hearts, not with the warmth of friendship but the fire of enmity.

JOHN B. CLARK

No single figure personifies the change from classical political economy to neo-classical economics, but J.B. Clark exemplifies it. His aim was to undercut Henry George's attack on landed property by erasing the classical distinction of land and capital. His method was to endow capital with a Platonic essence, a deathless soul transcending and surviving its material carcass. Some characterize Clark's concept as "jelly capital", some as "plastic," some as "putty," but those concrete images rather trivialize the abstract, even spiritual element, and the power of mystical traditions he could marshal to support it. There was an element of reincarnation, evoking Hinduism, transcendentalism, and Rosicrucianism. Clark even uses "transmutation," evoking alchemy. Capital was an immaterial essence, a spiritual thing, that flowed from object to object.

There is nothing inherently mystical about noting that capital turns over: every storekeeper and banker experiences that routinely. A remarkable quality of Clark's capital, however, is that it can ooze ("transmigrate," in Clark-ese) into land, becoming land itself. That is the only apparent reason for the mysticism, smoke and mirrors.

Clark's capital being deathless it is just like land, and theorists after Clark have made land just another kind of machine. The economic world was thenceforth divided into just two elements, labor and capital. "... that destroys the equality of capital to accumulated savings, and dismisses all Ricardian and Malthusian problems in one fell swoop" (Tobin, 1985). He might have added, it dismisses all Georgist, conservationist, spatial, temporal and environmental questions. It put blinkers on economic theorists which they wear to this day.

J.B. Clark's bibliography includes at least 24 works directed against George, over a span of 28 years, 1886–1914. These are in the bibliography to the present work. They begin with *The Philosophy of Wealth,* 1886. In this work Clark refutes "financial heresies and strange teachings concerning the rights of property ..." (1886: 1–2). The only such strange teaching specified waits to p.126, where a "Mr. Henry George" is accused of "ignoring the productive action of capital". That is a strange complaint to raise against one who recommended untaxing capital, but there it is.

Clark points out that wealth is created "from the mere appropriation of limited natural gifts ..." and that repelling intruders "is almost the only form of labor which exists in the most primitive social state" (p. 10). The atmosphere as a whole, showers or breezes, "minister transiently to whomsoever they will, and, in the long run, with impartiality". Therefore they are not wealth. Those who appropriate them create wealth by so doing. The essential attribute of wealth is "appropriability," to create which "the rights of property must be recognized and enforced,. ... Whoever makes, interprets, or enforces law produces wealth". He gives to commodities "the essential wealth-constituting attribute of appropriability". He goes on in that vein: those who seize land and exclude others thereby produce its value; George, who would untax capital, is guilty of ignoring its productive action.

Next came *Capital and its Earnings,* 1888. Frank A. Fetter, a disciple of Clark, commented as follows in the course of an encomium to Clark:

> The probable source from which immediate stimulation came to Clark was the contemporary single tax discussion. ... Events were just at that time crowding each other fast in the single tax propaganda. *Progress and Poverty* ... had a larger sale than any other book ever written by an American. ... No other economic subject at the time was comparable in importance in the public eye with the doctrine of *Progress and Poverty. Capital and its Earnings* "... wears the mien of pure theory .... but ... one can hardly fail to see on almost every page the reflections of the contemporary

single-tax discussion. In the brief preface is expressed the hope that 'it may be found that these principles settle questions of agrarian socialism.' Repeatedly the discussion turns to 'the capital that vests itself in land,' ... (Fetter, 1927: 142–43)

Clark's argument rose from an "original polemical impulse...". (*ibid.*: 144).

Remember, those are not the words of a critic, but a militant disciple of Clark. Fetter was more Clarkian than Clark, criticizing him only for his occasional backing and filling. He was certainly more forthright and importunate. The very candor and extremism of Fetter's exposition, giving a quick take on Clark, makes his chapter a good display of Clark's essential polemical motivation.

Fetter might have written the same about Clark's major work, *The Distribution of Wealth* (1899), which is mostly a compilation of earlier writings. "One can hardly fail to see on almost every page" Clark's focus on undercutting George. Clark's attacks continue to 1914, "Dangers of Increased Land Tax," whose title tells not only where Clark stood, but that the land tax was a live issue in American politics in 1914 (cf. Alvin Johnson, below). Such attacks, direct and indirect, constituted most of Clark's career up to 1914.

In 1890, J.B. Clark confronted George personally in a debate at Saratoga (c.1890). Clark's title was "The Moral Basis of Property in Land". Here he draws on the concept that capital is an abstract essence that "transmigrates" from capital objects into land, a concept he first advanced in 1888. In 1888 a reaction was sweeping the country after the Haymarket Riots of 1886. In this atmosphere, it was timely to strike at the radical who had been trendy and lionized since 1880 (Henry, 1994).

Another personal confrontation was with George's chief lieutenant, the lawyer, journalist and future Assistant Secretary of Labor, Louis F. Post.[24] This was in a debate at Cooper Union (Clark, 1903).

In 1891, in his review of Marshall's new *Principles of Economics*, Clark virtually ignores Marshall for 26 pages while attacking the concept that land rent is a surplus, and/or that other incomes are not surpluses. The preoccupation with George is transparent.

Clark moved to Columbia University in 1895. It has been suggested that he was recruited thither partly in response to his running dispute with Henry

George, a nemesis of Columbia President Nicholas Murray Butler. Actually, Butler was then still waiting in the wings, a strong Dean destined (pre-selected?) to become President in 1902, but this only strengthens the point.[25] How so? Because the real President of Columbia in 1895 was preparing to run for Mayor of New York - against Henry George himself. This was the wealthy patrician Seth Low (Barker, 1955: 616–18).

President Seth Low personally recruited Clark, working out a Byzantine scheme to have him paid by Barnard College while teaching at Columbia (Rozwadowski, 1988: 199). To secure Clark, Low had to outbid another powerful anti-Georgist, Daniel Coit Gilman of the Johns Hopkins University, recently founded with B&O R.R. money (Barber, 1988: 223). Clark was a hot property: the new Rockefeller Baptist (aka The University of Chicago) and The Southern Pacific R.R. (aka Stanford University) had also bid on him. An academic myrmidon on tap would be most useful in all such settings; J.P. Morgan's (Low's) need was the most urgent and/or the best-funded.

George was also in a running dispute with E.R.A. Seligman, Chairman of Columbia's Department of Economics over many, many years under both Presidents Low and Butler. Seligman was an ally of Clark's at the Saratoga debate. Butler, in turn, was the funnel through which the wealth of Wall Street, personified by the dominating banker J.P. Morgan, patronized Columbia, making it the wealthiest American university for its times.[26] Money poured into the Department of Economics. Under Seligman, his Department swelled from two members to "forty or fifty" (Hollander, 1927: 353).[27]

This was a period of secularization of US colleges. Businessmen were replacing clergymen on boards. The new broom swept out some old problems, no doubt. At the same time, it posed new threats to academic freedom, threats of which Butler was the very embodiment. Clerics, after all, owe some allegiance to Moses, the Prophets and the Gospels, which are suffused with strident demands for social justice. They were displaced by others more exclusively attuned to the Gospel of Wealth. Academic tenure was a distant dream: top administrators hired and dismissed with few checks and balances. They only needed to dismiss a radical occasionally: others got the message. *Dartmouth College v Woodward* had established that[28] Boards of trustees were self-perpetuating and unaccountable: "checks and balances" never applied to them (except in the banking sense). They were interchangeable with directorships of major corporations, many of them great landowners and/or franchise-holders.[29] Pressures on academics were extreme: it was placate or perish (Sinclair, 1923).[30]

Some of these pressures were specifically anti-Georgist. For example, Professor Allen Eaton was fired from the University of Oregon for successfully pushing a series of characteristically Georgist measures: municipal ownership of the Eugene waterworks;[31] taxation of waterpower sites; direct election of US Senators; keeping valuable State-owned timberlands from being given to Southern Pacific (Sinclair, 1923: 171–74). These advocacies put him directly in league with W.S. U' Ren, leader of the Oregon single-tax campaigns, and Joseph Fels, his supporter. Elisha Andrews was forced from Brown University for favoring populists George and Bryan (Barber, 1988a: 93–94).

Scott Nearing was fired in 1915 from the University of Pennsylvania (Sass, 1988: 238–39). Pennsylvania Trustee Joseph Rosengarten explained that "men holding teaching positions in the Wharton School introduce their doctrines wholly at variance with those of its founder and ... talk wildly and in a manner entirely inconsistent with Mr. Wharton's well-known views and in defiance of the conservative opinions of men of affairs" (Sass, 1988: 239). Mr. Wharton's views are not stated, but might be inferred from the Wharton estate's holding of 100,000 acres in New Jersey, lying between Philadelphia and Atlantic City. This land supported towns and industries in the 18th century, but under the Whartons went out of use (Ackerman and Harris, 1946: 154).

What were Nearing's "variant" ideas? Modern socialists claim Nearing as their own, but it is relevant here that in 1915 he published in *The Public,* a Georgist organ (Nearing, 1915). Uncowed by the Wharton Trustees, in 1917 he was speaking for the Joseph Fels Lecture Bureau, a Georgist organization based in Philadelphia, along with prominent Progressive Georgists Warren Worth Bailey, John Dewey (yes, *the* John Dewey), Frederic C. Howe, and George L. Record (J.D. Miller, 1917: 462). He published an analysis of the "occupations" of the trustees of most US colleges and universities (Nearing, 1917), fodder for Sinclair and Veblen, whose books on the same subject followed soon after. His best-known "variant idea" was opposing child labor (Sass, 1988: 239; Sinclair, 1923:

100–110). This was exactly the cause advanced by George's lieutenant and biographer Louis F. Post, founder and long-time Editor of *The Public,* in which Nearing published. As Assistant Secretary of Labor under Wilson, Post (with Julia Lathrop) founded The Children's Bureau in the US Department of Labor.[32] The community of interest with Nearing is evident.

The safe route for academics was to work for a patron and grovel. Clark's record is fairly clear. He began as a favorite of Julius Seelye, President of Amherst (Dewey, 1987: 429; Henry, 1994, Chap. 1). Later, Seelye moved to Smith College, and in 1882 hired Clark there. Life under Seelye could be perilous for the truly scholarly. In 1884, Seelye peremptorily fired one of John B. Clark's colleagues, the homonymic geologist John Clarke, for "heterodoxy" (Schuchert, 1925: 54). Clarke was competent enough: he went on to publish several books and 450 professional papers in his field. He became Director of the New York State Geological Survey, and organizer of the State Museum in Albany. His "Memorial" in the *Geological Society Bulletin* runs to 25 pages. His fault at Seelye's Smith had been giving geological evidence of evolution.[33] J.B. Clark was not one to commit such a social gaffe of loose-cannon scholarship.

Before 1886, J.B. Clark had engaged in some "socialist posturing," briefly made fashionable by the depression of the 1870s, and the labor revolution of the early 1880s.

> With the formation of the Knights of Labor, then viewed as a dangerous, revolutionary organization, and the Haymarket affair of 1886, such a flirtation was no longer 'respectable' ... academics were subject to close scrutiny, a recantation of previously held views was demanded, and firings occurred in the case of recalcitrants. Clark, as a most respectable economist, quickly and vociferously abandoned all of his seemingly socialist posturing, separated himself from those who were suspect (Ely, for example),[34] and framed his new position which demonstrated his loyalty to prevailing authority (Henry, 1992: 32, citing Furner, 1975, and Ross, 1977–78: 52–79).

George was a very present danger at this time to the rent-takers of New York City, where he now resided, published, lectured, and organized politically. He had been nearly elected Mayor in 1886, and probably really was but got counted out by the Tammany machine (Barker, 1955: 480–81). This had been a major event: future US President Theodore Roosevelt "also ran". Indeed, it was a national event. New York City was "a point of vantage worth contending for, since the moral effect of such a victory of the working class would be incalculable, ... Such rebellious movements are highly contagious .... in New York, the labor movement had plunged boldly into political action ...". (Myers, 1907: 356).

It was even an *inter*national event, in George's vision. With Michael Davitt, he saw rebellious Ireland as a staging ground for a truly radical program he might then reexport to America through the militant Irish-Americans of New York City, George's major ethnic voting bloc (George, Jr., 1900: 347). Considering that these Irish-Americans had recently staged the Fenian invasion of Ontario, their militancy and their ties with the Ould Sod, while not overwhelming, were substantial enough to alarm conservatives. George was preparing to run again in the 1897 campaign, which finally took his life. It seems entirely believable that men like Low and Butler in a city like New York would patronize a man like Clark at a University like Columbia of 1895 to subvert a man like George.

By this time (1895) Clark was promoting his 1890 theme (of spiritual, transmigratory capital) in debate with the Austrian capital theorist, Böhm-Bawerk (Clark, 1895; Böhm-Bawerk, 1895). Clark's concept of capital "... gives the appearance of being specially tailored to lead to arguments for use against George" (Collier, 1979: 270).

Some modern radicals, schooled mainly in Marx, interpret Clark as being motivated to undercut Marx and communism (Henry 1982, 1983, 1992).[35] This view runs into the difficulty that Clark's concept of capital is much like Marx's, and was obviously tailored to refute George, as Collier says. Clark's theory is that land and capital are the same, because "pure capital" is abstract value, and value moves from capital to capital, and also from capital to land, by "transmigration" and "transmutation". When capital "transmigrates" to land it "vests itself" in land, which is a "receptacle for value". Thus land "is made to contain" the capital of those who buy it (Clark, 1890). Remember, Clark introduced these ideas in a debate with Henry George, head-to-head, at Saratoga.

Clark's concept of capital tracks Marx's rather well. Here is Marx: "The value of commodities ... in the circulation ... of capital, suddenly presents itself as an independent substance ... in which money and commodities are mere forms which it assumes and casts off in turn (1867, rpt. 1906: 172).

"Land as capital is no more eternal than any other capital" (1847: 138). Clark's concept of capital, on which he insisted so dogmatically, was not aimed against Marx; it is almost as though he borrowed from Marx. It was aimed against Henry George, just as Marx aimed his salvos against Pierre Proudhon. Proudhon, like George, offended Marx by distinguishing land from capital.

Another difficulty for the anti-Marx hypothesis is that Clark does not address nor name Marx. Rather, he addresses George, his works, his ideas, and his proposals. Clark does not address communism, but "socialism". Clark regularly used "socialism" as a mischievous surrogate for Georgism. In various passages he lumps Georgist ideas with "socialism," and "agrarian socialism". Marx, on the other hand, is not in the index to *The Distribution of Wealth*, nor have I seen him named in any of Clark's works.

In Clark's world, "Marxism" was rather a remote, inchoate menace, an exotic import easily put down as alien, atheistic and un-American. Georgism was different: it was quintessential native radicalism. It found support with labor: Samuel Gompers and Terence Powderly both backed it. It also had immediate political potential with small farmers, with small urban businessmen, with renters, and with small homeowners. Its leader was neither atheistic nor fundamentalistic, but in step with the popular social gospel movement of the times. He was a WASP married to an Irish Catholic, popular with Irish ethnics and liberal Jews. Single-tax had been part of Populism, and was to become part of Progressivism, rising to a crescendo between 1913–24, during Clark's later career. It was easily implementable by a simple turn of the tax screw, using institutions already in place, and carrying forward tendencies already moving in practice. For Clark and his contemporaries it was the clear and present danger. Even in England, "When Karl Marx died in 1883, there must have been dozens of Englishmen who had argued about Henry George for every one who had even heard of" Marx. (Douglas, 1976: 48).

If Clark had focused on confuting Marx, he would have naturally allied with the Austrian School, whose members had that paramount objective. Instead, he attacked the Austrians and their capital theory (1895a, 1907), opening a vendetta that Frank Knight, Clark's follower, later carried to outlandish lengths, as we will see. Anti-Georgism could not tolerate anti-Marxism. Knight in turn imposed it on the whole Chicago School of neo-classical economics, which he dominated from its inception.[36] George Stigler, echoing Knight, objects to the Austrian-School concept of a "period of production" because it presumes a difference between capital, which has one, and land, which does not (Stigler, 1941: 278). Stigler's only objection to the dogmatic, intransigent Clark is that Clark made too many concessions (*ibid*.: 217).

Another consanguine element of Clark and Marx is Hegelianism. Clark's early work contains astonishingly Orwellian passages deifying the state. For example, "The State and no other may say into what form pure capital may go. It has said that it may go into land. For ends of its own it has so decided; and the ends are good" (Clark, 1890c: 27). Such abject sentiments would not shock Clark's contemporary economists: most of them, like himself, had taken their graduate training in Bismarck's Germany. R.T. Ely's prospectus for the "Platform" of the new American Economic Association began with this: "We regard the state as an educational and ethical agency whose positive aid is an indispensable condition of human progress". Even that was "toned down," according to Ely, from what Simon Patten and Edmund James wanted, which was to be an American carbon of the *Verein fur Sozialpolitik* (Ely, 1938: 132–49). Such sentiments served, however, to isolate the whole economics profession from the median American.

The Austrians' goal was to show that capital and its owners are productive; Clark's goal was to show that land and its owners are productive. To this end he, and his followers to this day, were and are willing to accept substantial taxation of capital, and call it benign (Seligman, 1916; Stockfisch, 1957; Harberger, 1968). This concept informed the architects of the Tax Reform Act of 1986, under which American businesses and workers now moil, travail, ail, and fail. "… to date, capital theory in the Clark tradition has provided the basis for virtually all empirical work on wealth and income" (Dewey, 1987: 429). Let's recap that. A concept "specially tailored to lead to arguments for use against George" (Collier, 1979: 270) is still "the basis for virtually all empirical work on wealth and income" (Dewey, 1987: 429). Could that help explain why land and rent are minimized in this empirical work (Kurnow)?

The survival and coexistence of Marxist economics and neo-classical economics among modern academicians, and the submersion of Georgist

thinking, may be in part a logical outcome of this semantic consistency of
Marx and Clark. It makes for easier mutual vituperation at a visceral level.
In this odd sense, the warring camps "need" each other. The dominant neo-
classical schools can debate comfortably with Marxists who share their
naive dualistic or two-factor view of the world. Issues can be reduced to
prejudices, with routine appeals to known biases. Neither party needs to
budge or think; each enjoys belaboring the other. Basic definitions are not
questioned. Each group makes an easy foil for the Pavlovian posturing of
the other.

Coping with Georgism, on the other hand, calls for actual cerebration,
reexamining basic concepts. After all, how is a Chicago economist to
explain why he, a dogmatic, extreme spokesman for private property as a
social panacea, favors socializing part of capital through taxation? How
can he damn the "radical, confiscatory" Georgist who would relieve capital
from taxation? A Marxist might damn the Georgist for that, as Marx
himself did: he called George the last ditch defense of capitalism. But the
Chicago School? Where previous radicals like Marx would wield the
meataxe blindly against all property, George would strike surgically to tap
the rent of predatory and dysfunctional property. He, George, would spare
and nurture functional property. He would distinguish the drones and
predators from the creators and conservers of capital. This is a hard one to
deal with, especially for the drones and predators.

In 1899 Clark delivered his other main stroke against George, his
doctrine of factor symmetry. By now George's sharp tongue was silenced
by death, but Clark prefaces his *Distribution of Wealth* with this. "It was the
claim advanced by Mr. Henry George.." that led him to generalize the
theory of marginal productivity (p.viii). It was not intended as a
compliment. Chapters VII and VIII of the book are aimed at "Mr." George,
by name. When he is not attacking George directly, he is getting at him
through Ricardo.

In fact, no one who has read George can study Clark's *magnum opus*
without recognizing it as a tract leveled against the unwashed "Mr." George
almost from beginning to end. Throughout, the obvious idea is to merge
land with capital, by whatever device. On p.2, the rent of land is merged
with interest "for reasons that will appear later". This begins a kind of
"proof by infinite retreat". The promised reasons are later put off again to

Chapter XXII, which puts them off to Chapter XXIV, where they finally disappear in the fine print of one of the longest footnotes in history: 395–98. Along the way he repeats his idea that capital is immortal, reprinting earlier works as chapters. At one point he says rent is interest because it equals the interest rate times the price of land. Elsewhere he says unearned increments are really part of the wages of workers who are also landowners. Device after device is used; deferral after deferral of promises to treat central matters "later". Meantime, however, rent is interest and land is capital throughout the book.

Clark had telegraphed his anti-Georgist intent in the 1891 review of Marshall: 142–43, in this convoluted passage:

> If the special product of land be treated as the only true rent, and if land be thereby separated from other productive instruments, then the principle becomes a barrier against the attainment of a general law of distribution. Identify land with other instruments, as embodying one general fund of invested wealth, and you may apply the Ricardian principle to the income from all of it. The return from invested wealth, or the interest of capital in the abstract sense of the term, is, as we have said, a differential gain as truly as is the special return from labor applied to good land.... the principle of differential gain will be seen governing the entire *static* income of society ... interest is the rent of a pure fund of invested capital, so wages are the rent of a ... fund of labor force; and both are as amenable to the Ricardian law as is the income derived from a fertile farm.

Whatever we may think of the outcome, Clark thought he was refuting Henry George.

Clark's enduring influence, and its ideological content, may be inferred from Paul Homan's paean (1928):

> When ... he published *The Distribution of Wealth*, the logical beauty and precision of the system of theory there displayed was like an illumination from Heaven to many of those whose goal for economic science was the reduction of economic life to terms of law and order.

The evidence suggests that this light was inspired by an urgent need to blind students to the message of Henry George.

As to capital formation, depreciation, and obsolescence, Clark simply assumed them away by postulating a static state. He alleged that was the correct way to analyze basic economic principles; dynamics was too complex, and muddied the waters. One might study dynamics *after* mastering the basic principles of statics, a mastery somehow never quite achieved in time to get on to dynamics. Ever since, micro-economic theory has been largely lacking a time-dimension: a curious lack for a discipline using calculus and aping the methods of physics. Clark purged time, and relations of sequence, from micro-economic theory.

George was the first economist to address head-on the problem of "recurring paroxysms of industrial depression," as he called them. He made this an integral part of his theory. Even Karl Marx, who nominally recognized the problem earlier, and appeared to make much of it, addressed it mainly with a jumble of press clippings on the suffering of the unemployed (Marx, 1867, Chap. XXV, Sect. 5, Articles d-f). George adumbrated a cost-push analysis of depression, in which cyclical overpricing of land was the prime cause. Veblen's later cost-push model of the upper turning point looks suspiciously like George's, but with the term "goodwill" substituted for price of land. Wesley Mitchell, Veblen's disciple, pioneered further work in business cycles, but in a militantly Baconian way that let his work be compartmentalized, separated totally from mainstream NCE as framed by Clark.

Clark's static state assumed the problem away; NCEists chose to live in a dreamworld free of depressions. Thus, by 1929, NCE stood defenseless against the overwhelming catastrophe that broke. Even Harry Gunnison Brown could only refer to it as a "period of slack business". Brown was in many ways a George supporter, but he tried to reach NCEists in their own paradigm, and became so habituated to it that he had no way to cope with chronic unemployment.

Even when Keynes developed macro-economics to try, at least, to deal with relations of sequence, macro was carefully segregated from micro. To this day, micro, the "core" of economics, remains static and Clarkian. The failure of economists to integrate micro and macro is an ongoing scandal of professional dereliction or incompetence. Compartmentalization has been the profession's response to many of its problems, as we will see further.

During the Great Depression there was some reaction against the NCEists whose self-imposed blinkers had made them lead us into it. With the nation's attention focused on World War II, however, NCEists recaptured the academies, if they had ever lost them. The reform spirit was safely deflected overseas. Radical land and tax reforms were accomplished in Japan, to the everlasting credit of academic economists like Shoup and Vickrey who worked there under Mac Arthur. Reforms were pushed (but much too gently) in the Philippines. The Soviets were allowed – who then could stop them? – to crush the Junkers. Economist-reformers crowded into U.N. agencies. It was safe fun, working from privileged sanctuaries, telling little third-world nations how to reform themselves.

Meantime, the home front was a separate compartment. The US invested $7 billion in the "G.I. Bill" education programs, 1945–52. It was a great transforming event; it opened doors of college training to a generation. Veterans fresh from risking life and losing years and body parts to military service now gave more years to being pumped up with human capital. The pump, however, was firmly in NCE control. The returning veterans received from their grateful nation "human capital" like this:

> From every point of view ... land may be regarded as a capital good and the rent of land as similar in every respect to the gross earnings of a produced factor (Scitovsky, 1952: 227–28).

It was everywhere: it hit one from every angle. It was an integral tenet of NCE; you learned to make it part of your reasoning process, or failed your exams. Thus, as far as economic policy went, the great public investment was worse than wasted. The early spadework of Clark and his like came to guide the flow of billions of dollars, and the minds of millions of people.

Clark did not stop at subsuming land in capital. He also makes a great point that wages are rent, too. The policy implication is that wages would make a good tax base. Seligman carried this forward into the income tax, leading to the present tax system which raises much more from payrolls than property.

EDWIN R.A. SELIGMAN

Another debater confronting George at Saratoga in 1890 was E.R.A. Seligman, scion of a wealthy banking family,[37] and Clark's future colleague at Columbia. Seligman drew on his powers of rhetoric to assail George with dagger drawn. "... you come to us with a tale that is old as the hills, ... long exploded, ... unjust, ... one-sided, ... illogical, ... inequitable, ... panacea, ... lop-sided, ..." As Chair of Economics at Columbia, an admirer of Clark, a loyal yeoman of Presidents Low and Butler, and a lifelong antagonist of George, it is reasonable to surmise that Seligman helped Low and Butler identify Clark as their man.

Seligman was a dogged critic of George, to whom George was almost an obsession, like Jean Valjean to Inspector Javert. His *World Book Encyclopedia* biographer notes his lifelong strife against George and Georgists. His *Palgrave* biographer, A.W. Coats, characterizes him as "a severe critic of Henry George". He is also one who "created the field of public finance in America" – in case there is any doubt how the twig was bent, and by whom. It is not that all academic economists scorned George. The founders of the National Tax Association included Lawson Purdy, and other Georgist names. Rather, those who did favor or tolerate his ideas were gradually isolated, ridiculed, silenced, or, if necessary, proscribed and ostracized.

Clark was the theorist, who set things up; Seligman was "the mailman" who delivered the message at the point of impact. Seligman was a frequent witness before the New York City Council, repeatedly working to stifle proposals from the Manhattan Single Tax Club (Marling, 1916), a large and active organization. He was influential in shaping the new Federal income tax, although, as to that, he was trumped in Congress by Congressmen Warren Worth Bailey, Henry George, Jr., and other "single-taxers" who shaped the original income tax legislation of 1916 along their lines (Brownlee, 1985). Seligman's attitudes, however, dominated the economics profession, and slowly prevailed over the popular position, first in the ivied halls where young minds are molded, and then in the legislatures where these molded minds act on the ideas that shaped them.

In his major work, *Essays in Taxation* (1895 plus many reprintings), Seligman devotes Chapter 111, 31 pages, to savaging "The Single Tax". The manner is openly critical; there is not even a gloss of objectivity or impartiality. He gleefully quotes from Voltaire's "*L'Homme aux quarante écus,*" a sarcastic attack on Quesnay, who had proposed taxing just farmland (George's tax was aimed mostly at city land, but never mind, any device was relevant and respectable when used to put down Henry George). Voltaire proceeds from the strange position that the poor people own all the land, an oxymoronic premise that Seligman implicitly endorses without the burden of responsibility. Seligman himself describes the work as "caustic . . . mordant sarcasm" – and continues to cite it approvingly through ten or more editions of *Essays in Taxation.*

The spirit of invective is not the spirit of science nor philosophy. The spirit of Seligman's reference group seems to have been that any stick will do to beat Henry George, for whom decorum may be suspended, and for whom no upright scholar would demand fair treatment or equal time. Again and again we see the arts of drawing-room violence practiced against George: the artful sneer, the sarcasm, the giggle, the condescension, the feigned incredulity, the manufactured data. Seligman is not alone in his attitude: no one could pull this off alone, he would appear outrageous. There must have been an orchestrated campaign of academic terrorism. Its echoes reverberate down to the present. Note, for example, the admission by Prof. Paul Ormerod, who has taught economics at several British universities:

> The challenge of constructing an alternative, scientific approach to the analysis of economic behaviour is one to which increasing attention is being paid. The obstacles facing academic economists are formidable, for tenure and professional advancement still depend to a large extent on a willingness to comply with and to work within the tenets of orthodox theory. It is a source of encouragement that more and more economists are willing to look at alternatives, despite the risks they take in doing so. (Ormerod, 1994: xx)

Recall, once again, Karl Marx. Seligman was anything but provincial. He was a historian of European thought on tax policy. Yet, neither "Marx" nor "communism" are in his index. The modern bias is to marginalize George and to characterize all conservatism as a reaction to Marx. That appears to be bad history. Seligman's guns, like Clark's, were trained on Henry George, clear through the 1920s. Clark dominated neo-classical theory; Seligman dominated its applications to tax policy.

Seligman, otherwise known as a sober scholar, let his hostile rhetoric lead him into multiple contradictions and inconsistencies. These are detectable with only a modest effort, and have been detailed elsewhere (Andelson and Gaffney, 1979). However, otherwise they have passed unchallenged within the profession: an indication that the "academic reward system" was luring or driving "objective" scholars in other directions. The most blatant misrepresentations of George, the most superficial arguments, may be and are advanced without rebuke.

Seligman had the practical sense to use Clark's strongest weapon against George. This was *not* the demonstration that land is productive (has a marginal product). The fact that land is productive does not say the owner is responsible, nor gainsay that land income is a taxable surplus. After all, Quesnay and his group had championed land taxes in the belief that land was not just productive, but the *only* productive factor. Wicksteed, who worked the kinks out of marginal productivity five years before Clark published, continued to favor special taxation of land (Barker, 1955: 382; Steedman, 1987: 915). Actually, the fact that land has a marginal product turns out to be a useful tool of the Georgist case: it shows that the return to land may be separately imputed, and measured for tax purposes.

So, rather, Seligman uses Clark's mystical capital theory. This is the essential, distinctive Clark. Seligman writes that if *land* is taxed, this drives capital out of land, into housing, misallocating capital in favor of housing (*Essays in Taxation*: 92).[38] That presumes land is convertible into capital, and *vice versa,* just as Clark said when debating George at Saratoga in 1890. Thus, the essential for neutrality in taxation is uniformity, including uniformity between land and capital. Seligman goes on to apply this to income taxation as well as property taxation. (Others have applied it to excise taxation.) Like Clark, he believes that wages are another form of rent, and just as fully taxable as property income.

Seligman's doctrine of uniformity has grown mighty through the years. It is the theoretical basis for the watershed tax reform act of 1986 under which the American economy briefly boomed before crashing dismally. Neo-classicals were in command, led by Charles McLure.[39] *Uniformity* was the touchstone. The 1986 reformers did away with devices like the investment tax credit, which favors new investing. They did this to help lower tax rates that apply to the income from old assets like land. The reaction to Henry George, reached a century through time to mold our tax system in the name of the "level playing field".

Seligman is much more applied than Clark, but his theoretical assumptions are in harmony. Seligman was perhaps the most influential American tax economist of all time. His ideas form the basis of much of modern tax theory, the cutting edge of neo-classicism in policy. Like Clark, he faults George for thinking capital supply is elastic.

> It may be asked ... where all this additional capital which is to be invested in houses is coming from. There is no fund floating about in the air which can be brought to earth simply by the imposition of the single tax [i.e. by untaxing capital – M.G.J; ... (Seligman 1895, rpt. 1921: 92)[40]].

Seligman makes the above views even more explicit in "Tax Exemption through Tax Capitalization" (1916). As with Clark, the supply is fixed, by assumption. This is purely static analysis at a point in time. Significantly Arnold Harberger (1968), the more recent Chicago tax theorist, is also known for rejecting the view that housing taxes are shifted off capital, and by the same line of reasoning.

PHILIP HENRY WICKSTEED

Philip Wicksteed is another who knew George personally, but on much friendler terms (Barker, 1955: *passim*). Wicksteed, upon first reading *Progress and Poverty*, wrote George ecstatically, it "has given me light I vainly sought for myself. You have opened "a new heaven and a new earth," he wrote George, and thanked him for a "freshly kindled enthusiasm" (Barker: 381). He sat with Michael Davitt on the platform during one of George's major addresses in England (Barker, 1955: 397).

George Bernard Shaw, another George fan, also engaged Wicksteed to instruct him in the basic Ricardian economics he needed to extricate Fabianism from Marxist theoreticians. Shaw found these too mystical and cryptic. Wicksteed's and Shaw's common interest in George helped to bring them together, and deeply affected the Fabian Society, which continued to support George after Hyndman and his Social Democrats turned against him. After being tutored by Wicksteed, Shaw attacked the Marxist Hyndman caustically, as Wicksteed never would, but GBS himself could (Shaw, 1889). Concerning rent, he wrote "... profit to the proprietors of the more favourable raw material (is) economic rent, the main source of 'surplus value.' Without a thorough grip of this factor it is impossible to defend Socialism ..." Marx's failure to see this point makes *Das Kapital* "useless" (1889: 196–98).

Defending George, Shaw wrote in the London *Star* "... by his popularisation of the Ricardian law of rent, which is the economic keystone of Socialism, and concerning which the published portion of Marx's work leaves his followers wholly in the dark, Mr. George is doing incalculable service in promoting a scientific comprehension of the social problem in England" (June 7, 1889, cit. Lawrence, 1957: 86). Shaw claimed credit for first putting land taxation in the platform of the Liberal Party in 1892 (Fabian Society, 1950: 208, cit. Lawrence, 1957: 171). The voice was the voice of Shaw, but the hand was the hand of Wicksteed.

George was system-minded and sought to unify the laws of production and distribution in a coordinated harmonious system. His theoretical framework foreshadows the marginal productivity theory of wages, which he integrates with Ricardo's rent law. The idea that the wage rate equals the marginal product of labor is simply George's law of wages formalized and rounded out.[41] The title of Wicksteed's masterpiece, *An Essay on the Coordination of the Laws of Distribution* (1894), is paraphrased closely from *Progress and Poverty*, Book III, Chapter VII, "The Correlation and Coordination of These Laws (of Distribution)," (George, 1879: 218). Wicksteed was formalizing, in more elegant form, an insight from his friend George.

In the process, Wicksteed wrote that land and labor are coordinate and symmetrical, and none yields a surplus any more than any other. He was expressing a mathematical insight, not an anti-Ricardian dogma. He was saying that distribution exhausts the total product when every factor, including land, is paid its marginal product. He showed that the same laws of distribution may be established regardless of whether land or labor is arbitrarily treated as the variable. It is a valuable insight, and fully compatible with recognizing land rent to be a taxable surplus (Gaffney, 1962: 149–54; Alonso, 1964: 46–49).

It has been used by some, like Clark, to claim that land rent is not a taxable surplus, but that was not Wicksteed's purport at all. "... (the logic) ... so far from weakening the position of those who regard rent as a surplus, by showing that the use of land is paid for in accordance with the marginal utility of the service rendered by it, shows what is indeed Mr. Wicksteed's object to prove, that the two views are essentially contained, each in the other" (Flux, 1894: 312). He even credits part of his insight to Graham Wallas (1894: 40,n. 1) Wallas, a Fabian socialist, was surely not intent on justifying private collection of land rent in the manner of J.B. Clark. On the contrary, Wicksteed's life history demonstrates that one can see this element of factor symmetry – one can even discover it, as he did – and see land-rent as a taxable surplus.

Wicksteed remained sympathetic to George and his cause. "He remained always loyal to *Progress and Poverty's* central idea, land nationalization, to be achieved gradually by way of taxation ... remained a conviction to the end, with Philip Wicksteed" (Barker, 1955: 382). The lasting Georgist element in Wicksteed is discussed in Wicksteed (1933) 1, vi-vii; II, 686–90, and in Herford (1931: 213–14).

ALFRED MARSHALL

Alfred Marshall is another who debated George heatedly. This was in a meeting at Oxford in 1883. Feelings ran high and sharp words were spoken. Marshall was egged on by Oxford students, including scions of titled landlords. Dignified, scholarly, academic Oxford, of all places, was one of only two venues on George's speaking tours of Britain where there was "organized disorder" evident (Lawrence, 1957: 36). We may surmise Marshall disapproved of the organized disorder, but felt pressed to uphold himself on his home turf against the unpedigreed, upstart foreigner. The mature Marshall wisely never published these immature polemics, so they hardly bent the course of economic thought.[42] He never reacted so drastically as Clark and Seligman. Marshall is called a neo-classic, but great economists seldom fit tight molds, and it would be hard to identify him with the ideas of Clark and Seligman, as limned above.

Marshall's reaction to George is rather one of caution, compromise, ambivalence, and gradualism. It was the lack of these qualities in George, the importunate activist (plus a touch of xenophobia and caste-feeling in Marshall?) that exercised Marshall at the Oxford debate. Marshall's imprint on neo-classicism is his two-handedness, that notorious quality of economists that later disturbed President Harry S. Truman. In one of the 1883 lectures, Marshall grants the merit of nationalizing land after 100 years. At the time it must have seemed safely temporizing; it is a sobering thought that that centennial is now eleven years behind us.

George Stigler (1969) seeks to invoke Marshall against George, but that is to misrepresent him. Marshall actually supported Lloyd George's land-tax budget of 1909, accompanied though it was with Henry Georgist oratory, political upheaval, and social ferment (Hutchison, 1969). It is possible that Marshall had weathervane tendencies. This tradition, too, is powerful in the profession. In the end, however, George could hardly ask for a more useful, constructive critic than Marshall. Marshall was cautious to a fault, and surrounded by rent-takers with whom he had to live, but in spite of all, quite sincere and honest.

Marshall actually accepted much of George's case, although probably preferring to trace its provenance to others. His opposition was not simply captious, but thoughtful and constructive. He even improved on the case with his concept of "the public value of land" (1891, rpt. 1947). Marshall's public value is what George means by "community-created value," the joint result of nature, location, public works and services, settlement, and community synergy or "urban linkages". Marshall saw that urban values were outgrowing rural values, and provides an appropriate concept.

He also spotted (along with Cannan, 1907) the flaw and upper limit on raising *local* land rates (in Britain, local property taxes are "rates") to high levels, noting that this would distort locational decisions by over-attracting people to jurisdictions with higher rate bases – a kind of "tragedy-of-the-commons" effect, working through the rating system and locally financed public services. He leaned toward a benefits-received limit on rates, describing rates in excess of benefits-received (narrowly construed) as "onerous". The viewpoint is that of the upper-middle class or retired landowner in a suburb.

This was not an unplanned problem, to be sure. The Tory political leader Sir Austen Chamberlain (Neville's half-brother), thinking ahead, saw this as how to keep down public charges on land.

> It is certain that if we do nothing the Radical Party will sooner or later establish their national tax, and once established in that form any Radical Chancellor ... will find it an easy task to give a turn of the screw. ... On the other hand if this source of revenue ... is once given to municipalities, the Treasury will never be able to put its finger in the pie again, ... (cit. Douglas, 1976: 150).

That was by no means the limit of Marshall's horizon, however. If we shift to national land taxes, the "overused commons" problem disappears.

George has been faulted for not specifying in *Progress and Poverty* what level of government should collect land taxes, but his later career made clear that he wanted national governments to rely heavily on land taxes, for approximately the same reasons that Sir Austen Chamberlain wanted to keep them local. George opposed tariffs in large part to force national governments to turn from them to land taxes. His followers in both Britain and the United States pushed for national land taxes after Marshall wrote and, as noted above, Marshall supported the Lloyd George land tax budget in his own country in 1909. Marshall's successor, A.C. Pigou, wrote favorably (if hypercautiously) of land taxation (1949). The core of overt anti-Georgism is not to be found in British economists, but American.

FRANCIS A. WALKER

General Francis A. Walker, first President of the American Economic Association, President of M.I.T., and Director of the US Census was another who confronted George personally. He engaged George in a furious, cutting debate in the semi-popular press over the concentration of farmland (1883a). In a word, Walker thought in terms of simple means and George in terms of Lorenz Curves[43] (a term not then yet invented). Walker, waving his credentials, led with his chin in an arrogant, condescending, offhand manner, and was demolished. If he had any sense of the situation, he must have been dreadfully embarrassed.

Walker's first reaction was to go into denial. He wrote of George's proposals, "I will not insult my readers by discussing a project so steeped in infamy" (1883b, rpt. 1888). Walker soon discussed it anyway (1883c), and with some slow return toward objectivity. In spite of his initial arrogant approach to George, he was perhaps too large-minded to nurse a grudge for years, or let it reshape his entire way of thinking. He was a person of leadership qualities, soon to be demonstrated when he pulled together dissident factions to launch the American Economic Association (see discussion under Richard T. Ely, below). For others, however, silence has become a pillar of the neo-classical tradition. It has proven effective, but how sturdy a structure can be supported, and for how long, by silence and denial?

Walker was generally forthright, but clumsy and heavy-handed. He lacked the kind of sneaky subtlety Clark used to undercut George by recasting economics. He remained a Ricardian in methodology. He flirted with the notion of Leroy-Beaulieu that rent was declining in importance, but then seemed to dismiss it (1883b: 147, 191). Later in the same year, however, he came back with the interesting point that public works that raise the value of specific lands have the reverse effect in the aggregate (1883c). This is the doctrine now identified with the name of Robert M. Haig (1926). Haig was the Seligman *protégé* who had earned his spurs at Columbia by minimizing the benefits of the then-popular movement to exempt buildings from property taxes (Haig 1915a, b, and c). This idea from Walker has been much used by others then and later, to trivialize Henry George (Seligman, W.I. King, 1921, 1924; Ely, 1922; Schultz, 1953). Ely was to italicize it as (what he calls) a "formal definition": "... *in a progressive society, ... with increasing wealth and stationary population, land values will decline* (Ely, 1927: 131).

Walker also criticized George for alleging that the progress of technology was always labor-saving and land-using. George had overstated this case in a rhetorical flourish (1879: 253), even though Mill, his classical mentor and foil, had written that technology might also be land-saving (1872, Article 4). Granting that Walker wisely corrected an overstatement in George, however, Walker went to the other extreme and remained there. To him, capital formation is the salvation of labor.

Since then NCEists have presumed that capital is always complementary to labor, and a substitute for land. They present it as such a perfect substitute for land that they may eliminate land as a separate term. They thus remove from their purview such events as the disemployment of labor by sheep-capital during the enclosure movements in England, the mechanization and chemicalization of American farming, automation of assembly lines, ATM bank cashiers, barcode checking-out, etc. If there are only two factors of production, as in the NCE dreamworld, then capital must always complement labor. In the real world of three factors, capital may preempt land from labor, as in the cases noted.

J.B. Clark entered in on Walker's side, writing on "The Law of Wages and Interest" (1890d). As a rule Clark assumed the supply of capital is fixed, but he departed in this case. Clark concluded that a rise in the supply of capital acts to lower interest rates, and thus to lower all property incomes, thus transferring all the gains from capital formation to labor.

This leads to "the workman's paradise that we have sought ... more attractive than an ideal vision, since progress toward it is assured by natural law" (1890d: 64–65). The problem with this forecast is that lower interest rates act to raise land rents, whenever land use entails heavy use of capital. Lower interest rates do not eliminate property income, but transfer it from capitalists to landowners. The relationship of rent and interest is clearly inverse, a matter totally lost in NCE by virtue of its identifying land with capital.

Lower interest rates do not just raise land rents in general, but specifically in those land uses that are most capital-intensive, some of which are labor-saving. This important aspect of distribution theory may have been overstressed by Henry George, but NCEists have surely overreacted. They have simply wiped it out of NCE without a trace.

The net result has been a polar contrast between Georgism and NCE. George stressed that land complements labor, and labor may find more jobs by taxing land into use. NCE stresses that capital complements labor, and land taxation may prejudice capital formation. Saving may be fostered by limiting taxes to consumption.

In the hands of modern NCEists, theory teaches that any withholding of good land from use can be no problem. It is easily offset by developing new lands. In the hands of Keynesians and "NCE-synthesists," land monopoly becomes a positive benefit: it creates new investment outlets for capital to develop new frontiers. Alvin Hansen saw public works as the new frontier, replacing the old. Imperialists saw new military and naval frontiers. In all these variations there is a constant: economic land can be created by creating capital, with no limits imposed by nature. In this view, the world is an infinite reservoir of raw land, needing only the touch of mankind and capital to make it into economic land. It took the modern environmental movement finally to blow the whistle on this nonsense (Gaffney, 1993c, and 1994).

4

The Mind Benders

We have given some flavor of the ideas of Clark, Seligman, Marshall, Wicksteed, and Walker. Here we itemize some other economists who attacked George, or who sought to undermine his ideas more subtly. We summarize their points, and put them in the context of their matrices.

CHARLES SPAHR
Charles Spahr (1891) in a short article anticipated many of the points later elaborated by and identified with others. His main points are these.

1) The supply of capital is inelastic. "There is no vast fund of wealth in the air which can be brought to earth by the touch of Mr. George's magic wand" (p.632). This was a phrase borrowed without credit and repeated for forty years in successive editions by Seligman. It follows that taxes on capital are borne by the owner of capital, which Spahr believed. Consistently, the University of Chicago's tax specialist, Arnold Harberger, took that position (Harberger, 1968).

2) "Land is the only form of wealth in America whose possession is widely and well distributed". The allegation is unsupported (and unsupportable). He does not refer to the then-celebrated debate between Walker and George on the subject.

3) The value of land is the value of capital incorporated in it (1891: 627). Public capital has been paid for by past taxes on landowners, who have thus been put upon. That line of thought presupposes each landowner had an entitlement to both the land plus public works to serve it, paid by someone else. That seems extreme for the times, and was perhaps beyond what Spahr

intended. It is, however, in keeping with what NCEists are claiming for landowners today, when they are presumed to have entitlements to receive services far costlier than they pay for.

Consistently with that, Spahr warns that the single tax would turn investment "out of its natural channel" (1891: 632). By "natural channel" in this context he must mean public works. Considering that he lived in a century of insanely emulative bursts of overexuberant public works building, that suggests a blind spot (Cornick, 1938; Hoyt, 1933; Goodrich, 1960).

4) Marginal communities have no land value, hence no land value tax base. This is consistent with his belief that taxes on capital are borne by the owner of capital, a position also taken by Seligman of the Chicago School now. The correct position is, I believe, that all local taxes in a small open economy are shifted so that they must come out of land values. Happily, this "physiocratic" view is now shared by David F. Bradford and others (Bogart, *et al.*, 1992: 11).

5) Land values per head are higher in rich than poor jurisdictions. That is certainly true, but would seem not to argue *per se* against taxing land values. Rather, it argues against limiting such taxes to the local level. Inconsistently, Spahr favored an emphasis on state and local taxation. George had his sights on the national level. He wrote *Protection or Free Trade?* in 1886 only incidentally to promote free trade in the conventional sense. His main idea was to cut off federal excise revenues, forcing Congress to turn to land revenues instead. Alfred Marshall, discussed above, made a similar point, but did more consistently favor using land taxes nationally.

6) "Taxation should be in proportion to wealth" (1891: 633). Spahr is not against taxing property, as one might surmise. He actually supports the property tax vigorously, as well as death duties and land-gains taxes. It is just that he wants to tax all property, which he feels belongs partly to the state. Exempting capital from tax "would impoverish society, by depriving it of the part-ownership which it now holds in every form of wealth, .." (1891: 625). He does not score George for being socialistic, but for being "the most extreme of individualists".

In a later book (1896: 157), he shows that the taxable property of families ranked by income rises much faster than their incomes. That much is certainly true, although forgotten today by those who call the property tax regressive. However, George proposed taxing land, not income. This writer has shown that the taxable *land* of families ranked by income (or by property, either one) rises much faster than their wealth (Gaffney 1970, 1971, 1992, 1993).

In spite of some nativist and racist slurs, Spahr is a strong redistributionist. Low incomes are insufficient for healthful and decent living, while high incomes and properties are "morally perilous to their possessors" (1896: 159). "... the ability to pay taxes increases faster than the private fortune" (1896: 160). George would surely have agreed. It was probably this populistic leveling tendency (he also supported free silver) that caused Spahr to fade into namelessness among the other NCEists whom he otherwise anticipated, and who should have credited him.

ALVIN S. JOHNSON

To understand Johnson, it helps first to understand his matrix, Cornell University. Cornell was named for and in part funded by Ezra Cornell, the creator of the new Western Union monopoly (Gates, 1943: 97), and its appendage, the AP news monopoly. These organizations had victimized a San Francisco journalist, Henry George. He, in turn, had attacked them bitterly. Cornell's attitude toward George may be surmised from the fact that George in 1869 campaigned to have Western Union socialized (Barker, 1955: 118–19 *et passim*). Ezra Cornell was its major owner.

Cornell (both Ezra and his University) also speculated in western lands on a massive scale (Gates). The major obstacle to their financial success was that local governments taxed their lands, something they fought hard for decades. Ezra Cornell "located more than half a million acres of rich lumber (sic) lands in the Northwest with New York Agricultural College scrip" (Hacker, 1947: 394, citing Gates, 1943). To the robber baron, a state University with land scrip was an integral part of the basic business of seizing public domain, the chicane on which George had been first to blow the whistle (George, 1871).

Cornell University was molded by its wealthy first President Andrew Dickson White (q.v., below). Young Richard T. Ely, being scouted by White in Germany, "was interested in his psychology and the way he worked cleverly with Ezra Cornell and with Mr. Sage,[44] a benefactor, and one of the trustees of Cornell University" (Ely, 1938: 57). Western Union - AP was not only the source of Cornell's fortune, it was an instrument of thought control, used for planting stories and bending news, including news about itself (Myers, 1907: 493). We would underestimate Mr. Cornell to imagine he did not understand his University could be used the same way. If he did not, President Andrew Dickson White certainly did.

The power of controlling higher education is greater than merely slanting news stories. The "silver cord" draws us back to love and support *alma mater*. She becomes a thing of worship and purity, a secular Virgin Mary that rises above human failings. She symbolizes our best ideals and aspirations. She is the scene of newly opening vistas, society at a higher level, sparkling friendships, tender sentiments, exciting memories, lifelong loyalties formed "High Above Cayuga's Waters" or "'Neath the Elms" or at "Alt Heidelberg," singing "Thy Sons Shall Ne'er Forget," "A Song by the Fire," "Stand, Navy Down the Field," "Going Back to Old Nassau," "*Gaudeamus Igitur*," "To the Blue and Gold," "Fair Harvard," "Lord Jeffery Amherst," and, in the donative years, croaking out "Golden Days, full of innocence and full of truth". Woe to the messenger bringing news that the Virgin of our Golden Memories was procured to condition our minds for the gain of another. Yet, that is what we must do to understand who created NCE, and why. Truth is also a positive value. It is not always pleasant nor pretty; it is just what shall make you free.

The Morrill Act of 1862 gave land scrip to the states in proportion to their populations, so New York State got the most. Most states sold their scrip for quick cash, but not New York (Gates, 1943: 245). State land offices were quite corrupt, even for that tainted era, so New York handled its scrip in a very clubby way. New York sold Ezra Cornell (E.C.) its scrip at somewhat less than market price. E.C. agreed to use it to enter lands to benefit a Morrill Act College (Agricultural and Mechanical).[45] In general, he seemed to merge and identify his interests with the college. By 1867 he had more agricultural college scrip than any other individual: 500,000 acres (Gates, 1943: 31). The figure later rose to a million acres.

E.C. was, among his other interests, an Ithaca real estate promoter, investing in railways to boost the town. Very likely he had a sincere interest in promoting education, as he professed, but good works and self-interest need not be at odds: he also understood the effect on Ithaca land prices of snaring the new Morrill Act funds. So did rivals around the state, but E.C. had an edge: he was loaded with money from the Western Union monopoly he had created. He gave $500,000 to start the college, and thus secure the Morrill scrip for Ithaca, under his control.

New York State Senator Andrew Dickson White had wanted Syracuse to be the place. He and E.C. both regarded the Morrill scrip inadequate for more than one campus. E.C. won White to the Ithaca site by his large donation of cash (Gates, 1943: 52,55). White then became President of Cornell University. Would we be too cynical to suspect that was part of the deal? E.C. had not forged the Western Union monopoly without mastering David Harum's credo, "If you can't lick 'em, j'ine 'em".

In 1867 E.C. was preparing to sell some scrip, but paused to join with other states to "manipulate the market" to raise the price first (Gates, 1943: 58). Monopoly was in his reflexes. He retained most of the scrip, however, and slowly bought up western lands. He specialized in pine lands in northwestern Wisconsin. His purpose was to create – again – a monopoly (Gates, 1943: 95,97). This was not to be a monopoly of production – there were no mills, no timber culture, no roads built, no river drives – but just a regional monopoly of virgin timber and timberland held for sale at advanced prices. E.C. was a pure speculator and land monopolist, without exception or apology – the very antithesis of Henry George. Gates rates him as a weak business administrator because some of his funds leaked away to grafting agents, but he seems to have understood synergy: everything he did supported everything else, land speculation and monopoly and higher education went hand in hand.

A speculator's ultimate goal is to sell, but some prefer quick gains, even though small, while others favor big gains, even though slow. E.C. was the second kind. His fortune had come from hanging onto telegraph stock for the long pull (Gates, 1943:97), and he applied the same model speculating in Wisconsin land.

This way of investing University funds brought E.C. into intense, prolonged conflict with new towns and counties in Wisconsin. It was not just an adversary but a hostile, emotional relationship, with a high level of dishonesty and self-righteousness on both sides. Georgism was not invented by Henry George, it was endemic throughout the middle border, as Gates' many books have brought out. Local taxes "threatened to swallow up the enterprise" (Gates, 1943: 106). These local property taxes were pure land taxes because land is all E.C. owned in Wisconsin. Gates devotes a full chapter: 137–76, to "Tax Warfare" between E.C. and Wisconsin. Apparently Cornell won out: "in proportion to the price for which its lands were held the taxes were exceedingly light" (Gates, 1943: 175).

If E.C. won out, it was because back in Ithaca it was an obsession:

> When high taxes were threatened … Cornell's (sic) university's officials acted promptly to protect its rights. Cornell's interests were identical with those of other large holders of pine land, and frequently they all worked together … the greatest concern of the Cornell officials was the burden of taxation on the property … (Gates, 1943: 137–38).

That is the atmosphere that prevailed in the Cornell administration in an era when administrators hired and promoted and fired with no checks and balances whatever. It is most unlikely that President Andrew Dickson White or his immediate successors would have tolerated any professor of economics who defended the Wisconsin towns and counties; it is most likely they would have hired someone to defend their position as absentee land speculators. Such a person was Alvin S. Johnson of Columbia, a student of and personal secretary to J.B. Clark.

Alvin S. Johnson (1902) expounded the new definition of rent that NCEists were substituting for the original. As part of this shift, the unit of analysis used in economic theory was shifted to "the firm," or at largest "the industry". The society and the economy as a whole got lost. Formerly, rent was simply the return to land. NCEists redefined it as the surplus over opportunity cost of any resource at any time, thus removing any difference of land from labor or capital. It would have been courteous had they chosen a new word, since they were talking about something different, but courtesy was not the idea. The idea was to remove from land the dangerous stigma of yielding unearned values, targetable as taxable surpluses. (We dispose of this issue below, under Pareto.)

Further to the end, in 1914 Johnson published "The Case Against the Single Tax" in *The Atlantic Monthly*. The influential, topical *Atlantic* would not have been devoting its scarce space to such an arcane topic unless it were alive and impendent at the time. This sea was rising, and Alvin Johnson put his finger in the dike. His theorizing was highly supportive of his political position. That is not uncommon, *per se,* nor necessarily unproductive. At least his ideas, like those of Adam Smith, Ricardo, and Keynes, were relevant to a real issue, unlike most of what is published today. Rather, we should not remain innocent of why NCE is what it is, and what it has done to us.

Was it *really* a live topic? Belittling, even sneering allusions have become standard, suggesting otherwise. In fact, single-tax initiatives were run and running in several western states. A few cities (Bellingham, Pueblo, and Houston, for example) moved to levy property taxes exclusively on land. In California, a "pure single-tax" initiative won 31% of the votes in 1916 (*Large Landholdings in Southern California,* 1919). The Manhattan Single Tax League was knocking on the door (Marling, 1916), and was to get part-way in the door in 1921 (see below under Ely). Cleveland elected two single-tax mayors, over a string of terms, roughly synchronized with the Liberal Party string of Governments in Edwardian England. The first, Tom Johnson, was Henry George's chief political lieutenant and financial angel. The second, Newton D. Baker, was to become a power and Secretary of War in Woodrow Wilson's Cabinet. Toledo, Ohio, had two single-tax Mayors, Samuel "Golden Rule" Jones, and Brand Whitlock. Pennsylvania's Legislature opened the door for Pittsburgh's enduring "graded tax plan," initiated in 1913 (Jorgensen, 1925: 162). Four western provinces of Canada were won over almost completely, helping, among other things, to make Vancouver and Victoria two of the most beautiful cities in the world. Sydney, Brisbane, Wellington, Johannesburg, and other cities were exempting capital completely from the property tax, raising all their local revenues from land alone (Madsen, 1936). The American Academy of Political and Social Science (AAAPSS) devoted 78 pages to it (1915); the National Tax Association devoted 64 (1915); *Great Debates in American History* (1913) devoted 51. Robert Murray Haig delivered his three reports on it in 1915; the Committee on Taxation of the City of New York delivered its final report (Marling, 1916). California's Georgist irrigation districts were revolutionizing state and national agiculture. Yes, it was a hot wire.[46]

Johnson's major theme is that the single tax is "a device for the spoliation of the middle class" (1914: 30), because they own most of the urban land, and all the farmland. Like Willford King later, Johnson's image of America is an idyllic small town, unnamed, where everyone owns the same amount of land.

Johnson's image of egalitarian landowners is projected without benefit of data, and without referring to the earlier well-known exchange between George and Walker. It overlooked the fact that his own employer, Cornell University, had for years sat on over half a million acres of western lands, completely idle. The level of scholarship demanded by NCE editors of those who derided George is seen in the following.

> The Single Tax philosophy originated with a city man, ... a sound agriculture is based on ... the farmer, his ... love of the countryside, the jollity of the country picnic and dance, the fresh cheeked maidens who eagerly accept the role of sweethearts of country boys and develop into contented farmers' wives. (Johnson, 1927: 224).

This publication was sponsored by the American Economic Association. The publication committee consisted of E.R.A. Seligman, R.T. Ely, J. Hollander, B.M. Anderson, Jr., and J.M. Clark (son of J.B. Clark). It was reprinted in 1967: apparently the leaders of The American Economic Association still considered it exemplary scholarship.

Johnson is the link between Clark and Frank Knight. Johnson was a student of, and personal secretary to J.B. Clark. He was soon to be the mentor of Frank Knight at Cornell. One finds "much of Knight's mature thought" in his 1916 Cornell thesis (Stigler, 1987), with extensive credit given to J.B. Clark (Dewey, 1987). The title of Knight's popular 1953 article, "The Fallacies in the Single Tax," is interchangeable with Johnson's 1914 title. Even the "fresh-cheeked maidens" of Johnson show up in Knight, who, in turn, molded the Chicago Department in his image. The chain is unbroken from Seelye to Clark to Johnson to Knight to Stigler, Friedman, Harberger, and now thousands of Chicago-oriented economists. They dominate much of current doctrine and policy, metastasizing through government posts, high banking, academia, editorial boards, granting agencies, and the burgeoning think tanks subsidized by rent-takers to mold opinion for the deepest and most generic of their "deep lobbying".

FRANK A. FETTER

Another Cornell economist, contemporary with Alvin Johnson, was Frank A. Fetter. He graduated from Cornell, took advanced work in

Bismarckian Germany, then taught at Cornell, 1901–11, before moving to a
new career at Princeton. He was very much the insider: President of the
American Economic Association in 1913, consultant to New York State on
taxation, Chair at Princeton, frequent author in establishment journals.
Seligman chose him to write key articles on Rent, and on Capital for his
Encyclopedia of the Social Sciences. He was picked to eulogize Ely and
Clark, and to write key reviews of dozens of new books. He received all
this peer-recognition without adding really anything to economic thought
except an extreme, urgent, repetitive insistence that Clark was right and
George was wrong, and Marshall was wrong to compromise as he did
between the old (Ricardo) and the new (demand-determined value). Fetter
insisted that all the "old lumber" of Ricardian thought be "broken up for
kindling". In 1901a he declared it had happened; in 1901b he predicted it
was going to happen; in 1927 he lamented that it hadn't yet completely
happened; but always he insisted it should happen.

From 1900–14 he wrote on capital, interest, and rent. Murray Rothbard
and The Institute for Humane Studies have brought these together in one
volume, whose paging is used for citations here.

Everything Fetter wrote points towards one objective: to undercut the
Georgist case. His basic style is overgeneralized and abstracted to opacity,
in a failed and painful attempt to be philosophical. A clearer and shorter-
than-normal Fetter sentence reads, "As the truly scientific stage is reached,
the concern of the thinker is with the qualities and aspects of things, rather
than with the concrete objects themselves" (1917: 357). However, he
combines this with a sense of urgency that forces him to lapse occasionally
into clarity. From these lapses, and his admiration for J.B. Clark, we can
pick up his drift. "... rent is the usufruct attributable to any material agent"
(1904: 207). He contributes little that is original, but his interpretations of
certain NCE innovations are insightful.

In 1900 Fetter faults Clark for failing to keep repeating that his "capital"
includes land. "In his earlier utterances, such things are in plain words
included. In the later articles ... a reader new to the author's doctrine
would find no specific statement to this effect ..." (1900: 40). Dogma must
be pure, and repeated every Sunday to satisfy Fetter. The fault of Clark's
thought "was rather that it changed the old view too little than too much"
(1907: 109). It seems likely that Fetter was differentiating his product by

posturing as more Roman than the Pope. He really had no substantial difference with Clark.

Fetter likes the marginal utility (demand-side) explanation of value because it puts all values (land and capital) on the same footing (1901b: 77). No longer may we say that capital is stored-up labor, and so differs from land. We may not even say capital includes stored-up inputs from land and capitalized interest (as Wicksell did). That is because now "we have recognized utility, regardless of the origin of the good, as the measure of value.... When the utility theory displaced the cost-of-production theory of value, this change of the capital concept (to include land, rather than be limited to stored-up labor, etc.) became a logical necessity" (190lb: 77–78).

This gives us some useful insight into the use to which rent-takers and their spokespersons put the new demand-side value theory. It helps us see why they insisted on it so fervidly, and tried to stampede others into "making kindling of the old lumber," and resented Marshall's efforts to synthesize the old with the new. In truth, there was nothing new about the idea of diminishing marginal utility: Adam Smith had expounded it clearly, in his remarks explaining why the price of diamonds exceeds the price of water. What was novel in the 1890s was the use of demand-side value theory to distract attention from the fact that land has value without ever having had to be produced by man.

Fetter applauds Clark for establishing that "Land in all its forms is a part of concrete capital; all concrete goods yield rents; and all pure capital yields interest" (1927: 137). Clark conceived of interest as rent "expressed as a percentage of the value of abstract capital. Thus interest ... did not consist of ... incomes other than those composing rents, but simply was rent, expressed as a price in relation to the price of the instruments that embody the fund" (*ibid*). In other words, ground rent becomes interest, the earning of saved capital, by virtue of being expressed as a fraction of the price of land - never mind that the price of land is originally derived by capitalizing the rent! In 1904: 207, he had said the same. "A more or less durable agent represents a series of rents" (1904: 208).

This was swallowed holus-bolus into NCE, where it remains. Thus originated the purely circular element in NCE capital theory that proved so pathetically vulnerable and indefensible in the recent "Cambridge Controversy," even though the critics in this case were weakly based too -

another story in itself. The point here is that NCE had rendered itself helpless against the otherwise weak Sraffian onslaught by a crude sophistry. The sophistry originated as part of an effort to undercut Henry George.

Fetter rejects any notion of social capital as opposed to individual capital. Like Frank Knight (a Cornell Ph.D.) he fully embraces the fallacy of composition that social capital is simply the sum of individual claims on resources. Economics, to Fetter, is properly the study of private "business" (i.e. property). Economic theory should stop being "remote from actual business usage.... How long must it continue ...? Ambiguity must be banished from economic terminology.... Capital is essentially an individual acquisitive, financial, investment ownership concept.[47] It is not coextensive with wealth as physical objects, but rather with legal rights as claims to uses and incomes. It is or should be a concept relating unequivocably (sic) to private property ... Social capital is but a mischievous name ... When will (the admission of these truths) be made frankly and clearly? When will the dead hand of Ricardianism be lifted from our economic texts?" (1927: 155–56). O, tempora; O, mores! How long, O Lord?

Land in an unimproved state is almost unknown, land must be continually repaired, just like capital (1904: 202, 206). Separating land from capital "must transcend human power ..." (p.203). The line is vague because "... money and artificial agents measured as 'capital' can be and are so often invested in land." Any distinction is "out of harmony with business usage" (p.203). "This fog is lifted when the sources of rent and of interest cease to be considered as physically distinct and objectively differing kinds of goods, and are seen to be simply the same body of income yielders, differently viewed, calculated and expressed for theoretical and practical purposes" (p.206).

There are "varying grades" of capital goods, just like land. Once you measure land by value, rather than acres, there are no different grades of land. The supposed difference of land and capital is merely the result of the convention that land is measured by acres (pp. 196, 207). Fetter's own words at the points cited are so long, pedantic and impenetrable that I will not risk losing the reader by citing or refuting them. They are there for those who want to read them. The point here is that central tenets of NCE were planted therein for the express purpose of refuting Henry George. Fetter's reasoning may be obscure and forced, but his anti-Georgist purpose is always transparent, and his professional acceptance is painfully obvious to all who have been afflicted by having to work with NCE.

5

Rail-roading the Single Taxers

Richard T. Ely[48] took the lead in founding the American Economic Association in 1885. He was a young liberal (in the German sense) with an "elementary, clear, and easy" (and often equivocating) writing style, and an overt Christian social activism. He was highly productive of books and articles over a long, versatile career, whether solo, with collaborators, or as editor. Among his co-authors, and authors edited, were Seth Low, John R. Commons, Frederic C. Howe, Charles B. Spahr, E.W. Bemis, John A. Hobson, C.J. Bullock, Jesse Macy, F.H. Newell, E.B. Fernow, Jane Addams, Elwood Mead, E.A. Ross, H.C. Taylor, T.S. Adams, Max O. Lorenz, Allyn A. Young, W.I. King, R.H. Hess, T.N. Carver, Paul Popenoe, Selig Perlman, Ernest M. Fisher, F.M. Babcock, L.C. Gray, B.H. Hibbard, Nathan W. MacChesney, H.D. Simpson, H.B. Dorau, Paul Raver, Martin Glaeser, Bertrand Russell, Max Otto, Coleman Woodbury, and A. S. Hinman (Ely, 1938, bibliography). It seems he knew everyone and did everything: theory, agriculture, forestry, water, government regulation, conservation, labor, urban studies, taxation, sociology, popular writing, Chautauqua, preaching, business administration, and public policy. He could preach liberal or conservative, as needed, and befriend all sides. (He may have been the model for great Ivan Skavinsky Skavar, who "could sing like Caruso, both tenor and bass, and play on the Spanish guitar".) He must have been a whirlwind, and a great organizer. He was a successful land speculator (until 1929). Besides founding the American Economic Association, he founded the academic discipline of land economics. He was truly a phenomenon, into everything and at the center of much. He also did well selling textbooks. His *Outlines of Economics* was the bread-and-

butter text from 1893 to about 1930. Academicians know what pressures
that brings to bear on a writer.

Ely was brought up short by an attack on his job at Wisconsin in 1894,
for allegedly preaching socialism and fomenting strikes. His colleagues
rallied round and saved him. The University of Wisconsin still preens itself
on its sterling defense of academic freedom. The University itself has
indeed sheltered more than its share of outstanding independent thinkers
like John R. Commons and Harold Groves; but the ebullient Christian
Socialist in Ely was broken forever, save for some residual sanctimonies.
"... young Ely was 'tried' at the University for academic 'heresy.' After the
trial, he carefully denied any connection between his social philosophy and
that of Socialism" (Jaffe, 1979: 108). A useful means to that end was to
disparage Henry George, whom he had earlier labelled a "revolutionary"
socialist.

There was a longer-standing reason for Ely's hostility to Henry George,
in the person of Daniel Coit Gilman. In Ely's youth, even more than today,
the way to promotion and pay was through a patron. Ely's patron was
Gilman, expert exploiter of the Morrill Act (first for The Sheffield School at
Yale, then at Berkeley), first President of the University of California, then
first President of Johns Hopkins University, then first President of the
Carnegie Institution. Gilman was a major founding and funding father of
American higher education, and therefore necessarily something of a
schemer, networker, and truckler to wealth – skills young Ely learned well.
Gilman's network was tight, elitist, and mutually supportive, united by class
consciousness; it was somewhat cabalistic, united by common Bismarckian
graduate education, which was the height of academic fashion in that era,
for those who could afford it. Gilman was the antithesis of George in many
respects, which had led them into a major battle, as we will see.

Under Gilman, Hopkins became the first American university to
specialize in graduate training. From 1876–92 it was virtually alone in
turning out American Ph.Ds in economics (Barber, 1988b: 11), who in turn
took over much of the future profession. Gilman's first hire at Hopkins in
economics was Richard T. Ely, on the say-so of his close friend, Andrew
Dickson White.

Gilman networked closely with fellow Yalie Andrew Dickson White,
President of Cornell. Ely never went to Yale, but his career was pushed by

as thick a club of old Elis as ever pirated beneath the Skull and Bones: White of Cornell, Gilman of Hopkins, Harper of Chicago (Ely, 1938: 83), Barnard of Columbia, and Dwight of Yale.[49] White had discovered and patronized the young Ely in Germany, when White was on leave from Cornell as American Ambassador to Berlin, and Ely a student at Heidelberg under Bismarckian Karl Knies.

Gilman was on top of the Hopkins phenomenon. This was to give him enormous leverage over American education. No less than *eleven* Presidents of the American Economic Association were Hopkins Ph.Ds from Gilman's reign (Barber, 1988: 224). Three other Presidents and founders had taught at Hopkins under Gilman: these were J.B. Clark, R.T. Ely, and Francis A. Walker. Carl C. Plehn, who dominated public finance in California, was an Ely product (Ely, 1938: 115), one who maligned Henry George as naturally as he breathed. Woodrow Wilson was one of Ely's students (Ely, 1938: 108–19. Fortunately for the country, Wilson was later reeducated in New Jersey by George L. Record [Kerney 1931]). Gilman had a long reach.

Enter the Henry George factor. Gilman had arrived at Hopkins because he had earlier been hounded from Berkeley in 1874–75 by a crusading populist journalist, Henry George. George, running the San Francisco *Daily Evening Post*, smelled corruption in Gilman's administration (Barker, 1955: 219–21; Cookingham, 1988: 269–70). He also smelled elitism and improper diversion of Morrill Act ("agricultural and mechanical") funds to "classics and polite learning".

George spoke for the Grange, and some populist Republicans who joined with the Grange to form the Peoples' Independent ("Dolly Varden") Party. Together they made the Berkeley citadel too hot for Gilman, who resented it. It is true, the Establishment immediately gave him a new citadel at Hopkins, just founded by a baron of the B&O Railroad, and loaded with B&O Railroad shares. Still, it must have come as a nasty jolt when the frontier battler for vulgar farmers and mechanics followed Gilman back to his new realm and appeared on the sophisticated Eastern scene as, of all things, a major intellect. This is something Gilman, the networker and administrator, never was nor could be.

Worse, George embarrassed Gilman's friend Francis A. Walker in intellectual combat on Walker's own ground (the US Census). Gilman's feeling toward George would naturally be aped by the upwardly mobile *protégé*, R.T. Ely. Ely's autobiography (1938), 50 years after Ely had left Hopkins, is dedicated to the memory of Gilman, "under whom I had the good fortune to begin my career, and to whom I owe an inestimable debt of gratitude".

Gilman controlled Ely, in part, by playing him off against a rival, Simon Newcomb. To win points with President Gilman, Ely in 1885 followed Gilman's behest to found a professional association: The American Economic Association (Coats, 1988: 354). To do so he enlisted the help of Francis A. Walker (Barber, 1988: 216–17; Coats, 1988: 352, 360–62). (J.B. Clark, E.R.A. Seligman, and Andrew D. White were also founders (Ely, 1938: 179).) Thus, the two most influential men in Ely's early career were both embittered personal adversaries of Henry George: men whom George had met head-on, bested, embarrassed and damaged. A third one, Andrew Dickson White, we have met at Cornell (see Alvin S. Johnson).

To them we should add Abram S. Hewitt. Hewitt was the New York patrician who in 1886 allied with Tammany and the Catholic hierarchy to block Henry George's bid to be Mayor of New York City (Barker, 1955: 453–81). Hewitt was an early financial angel to Ely's new Association. "Need I say that the gentleman holds a warm place in my heart?" (Ely, 1938: 138–39). The pathway to Ely's heart was definitely through his purse. The same might be said of many others, it is true; but how different would the A.E.A. look and act today if purses like Hewitt's had been open to George instead of Ely?

Hewitt's character may be estimated by the methods he used to steal the election of 1886: "... corruption and fraud.... all of the ignoble and subterranean devices of criminal politics ... Tammany repeaters ... fraudulent votes ... tampering with the election returns and misrepresenting them ..." (Myers, 1907: 357–58. Myers was an expert on Tammany, as author of *The History of Tammany Hall*). As to Hewitt's trade, he was an "ironmaster". As to his social philosophy, "The problem presented to systems of religion and schemes of government" is to make men who are equal in liberty content with inequality in property (Goldman, 1956: 71).

Recall the case of Seth Low, who brought J.B. Clark to Columbia. It is noteworthy that both Hewitt and Low, George's major political blockers, were wealthy patrons of NCE. Among the lot, and with J.B. Clark, and the wealthy Andrew Dickson White (Ely, 1938: 57) and the wealthy E.R.A.

Seligman, they founded the most influential, controlling professional association of economists. Walker was President, and Ely Secretary, for the first seven years, time to bend the twig firmly in their direction.

An undemocratic "Council" controlled the early Association, "to prevent our organization from being captured by some economic sect or group of reformers" (Ely, 1938: 162). The main group answering that coded description in 1886 was the single-tax "economic sect or group of reformers," then at a cyclical peak of vitality and widespread support. Non-reformers, apparently, were acceptable. "Businessmen" were entirely welcome; "historians" were numerous (*ibid*: 179).

Yet another factor may have been professional jealousy. Ely was highly competitive, shown by his strife with Newcomb at Hopkins. This side of Ely also surfaced in his intemperate outburst at successful rival author Thorstein Veblen – the outburst that forced Grace Jaffe to leave his employ (Jaffe, 1979: 113). Before the catharsis of 1894, Ely was considered something of a liberal (in the German meaning). In 1886 he published *The Labor Movement in America*, hoping to take some leadership of this movement, and steal a march on Newcomb at Hopkins (Barber, 1988: 219). It made little impact outside the profession. Ely dominated economic teaching in the Chautauqua circuit (he was a native of that County), and prided himself on large sales of his texts. In the same decade, sales of George's books were in the millions: *Progress and Poverty, Social Problems, The Irish Land Question*, and *Protection or Free Trade?* were all best-sellers, and the talk of the labor movement, which supported George warmly. Ely dropped the names of Samuel Gompers and Terence Powderly, but these were among George's organizers and supporters in the 1886 election.

George was a successful lecturer and orator. His spellbinding skill, combined with genuine warmth and exciting message, brought crowds to life: he worked them with relish. Ely rated himself poorly as a public speaker, referring often to his wooden platform performances and chilly receptions (1938, *passim*). He was not modest about other achievements, so his word on this seems credible. George, the ex-journalist, also sensed the pulse of the reading public better. In 1886, with the Haymarket riots and bombing, the public was about to turn against organized labor. George never did that, but 1886 was the year when George published *Protection or Free Trade?*, picking up the incoming buzzword just as the old was losing favor, and Ely was getting around to using it. If Ely was to beat George, it would have to be in Ely's privileged sanctuary, the academy, safely sheltered behind walls green-ivied with funds from rent-takers.

Last, Ely was methodologically a Bismarckian, like J.B. Clark, totally converted by the man he called his "master," Karl Knies of Heidelberg. Is it fair to assume that Knies was "Bismarckian"? Much is said in praise of German university life in this era, but Ely notes, "Public authorities minutely prescribed requirements for these (professional entry) examinations. In this way they controlled the university courses" (Ely, 1938: 53–54). "... they developed their economics out of German life, and the German professors were part of this life.... the universities were largely institutions designed to train men for the civil service ..." (*op. cit.*: 187).

Bismarck was a Prussian before he was a German, and a Junker before he was a Prussian. He was author of the *Kulturkampf*, a form of thought control. He controlled every aspect of German life, with the most efficient civil service and secret police in the world. It is inconceivable he would have tolerated teachings inimical to his Junker class interest. Unvexed by such problems, or even by Adolf Hitler, Ely reaffirmed in 1938 an earlier recommendation "for the state by proper legislation to raise the standard of requirements and so assist the colleges and universities in giving us an able and properly educated set of professional men *as in Germany*" (Ely, 1938: 54). He published this in the year of Munich. When it came to totalitarians, Ely was a slow learner. He shared this problem with another famous battler against land taxation, Neville Chamberlain (Douglas, 1976: 206 ff; Geiger, 1933: 419).

George was in the English classic tradition, which Ely was trying to root out of the profession. Ely was engaged in a delicate balancing act: promoting Bismarckian socialism, safely protective of rent-taking (bolstered by protectionism), while deflecting attacks from those who might confuse this with distributive socialism (Coats, 1988: 357, 364). What better way than to attack George? George favored distributive socialism (via land taxation) without Bismarckian paternalism, and without subsidizing and manipulating public works to enrich land speculators like Ely. Ely wrote a chapter on "Henry George and the Beginnings of *Revolutionary* Socialism in the United States" (Ely, 1885, cit. Young, 1916: 94; emphasis mine). The tactic was to distinguish Ely's Bismarckian socialism, safely controlled by the establishment, from George's distributive proposal which he tars as "revolutionary".

Later, Kaiser Wilhelm II was to make Ely's balancing act even trickier: the Kaiser's arrogance, unpopularity, sword-brandishing, and finally World War I, took the cachet off Ely's German training that had given him his original edge in academe. After 1900, American students stopped training in Germany, while Georgist native radicalism burgeoned. Putting it all together, there were many motives for Ely to preach and intrigue against George: enough and to spare.

By 1920, Ely was 66. He was staring at mandatory retirement, and not ready for it. His vital signs were strong: when admonished by a friend for "chasing girls" at his age, he answered, "Do you want me to commit suicide?" (Jaffe, 1979: 109). He was to live 23 more years, and presently to sire two more children with a young northwestern athlete, Margaret Hale Hahn (Ely, 1938: 250). He began a new career, founding The Institute for Research in Land and Public Utility Economics. It was more than a new career, he founded a new field, "land economics". This much is admirable and *simpatico*: he refused to vegetate and die on schedule. He was a pioneer against age discrimination, at least for himself. Few men found new fields at any age, let alone after mandatory retirement. His achievement was brilliant and outstanding. However, the tale of Faust and Marguerite comes to mind. He had to raise private funding; there was the Devil to pay. Ely apparently chose the "pay-as-you-go plan".

The Mitchell Palmer Raids of 1919–20 signalled a watershed in American history, a replay of 1886 (Post, 1923). The 1920 turn was from Progressivism to reaction, suppression of labor, class warfare, the Ku Klux Klan, J. Edgar Hoover, lower real wages, reneging on promised veterans' benefits, soaring capital gains in land and stocks, and growing inequality. This time, Ely called the turn, right on the mark. In the new era of Babbittry Ascendant, Ely's anti-Georgism reached its peak. He used it to raise funds for his Institute.

His fund-raising appeals may be inferred from the following, from a 1923 address to the American Railway Development Association (cit. Jorgensen, 1925: 18):

> Our Institute ... has a board of trustees which must convey confidence in the
> character of the work. ... Why should not the railways conduct their own

researches? However honest and sincere may be the researches of railway companies, they are ... discounted as coming from interested parties.... our results should command confidence.

One topic that I have mentioned is taxation of land and Public Utilities.... it was an official of one of our railways, Mr. W.W. Baldwin, Vice-President of the CB&Q Railroad Company, who suggested the importance of this special topic and induced the Burlington Railroad to make subscription to our funds. He said that the land and the railways are in much the same situation, and he felt that this was a topic that could well engage our attention. Both are tangible, easily reached and are in no position to escape taxation by flight ... The taxes paid by the railways run into hundreds of millions per year, and their interest in our taxation work must be very great.... we have received endorsement and subscriptions from ... the Great Northern; the Northern Pacific; the Baltimore and Ohio; the Atlantic Coast Line; the Nickel Plate Road; the Chicago and Northwestern; Chicago, Burlington, and Quincy; the Illinois Central; the Minneapolis, St. Paul and Sault Ste. Marie; and the Chicago, St. Paul, Minneapolis and Omaha.

Ipse dixit. One might add that land and the railways are not just "in much the same situation," they are much the same, full stop. Ever since the legendary land-grants of the 19th century, railway companies had been the largest landowners: rural, urban, sylvan, and mineral. Ten per cent of the land in the City of Chicago was in railyards, much of it adjacent to The Loop (the Chicago CBD) itself. Rights of way and terminal and docking sites were, as they remain, the rails' major asset.

"Public Utilities" as part of the Ely Institute's name was a euphemism for the unpopular, highly suspect railway corporations (Ely, 1938: 238, lines 1–4). This was the age of Hiram Johnson and Robert La Follette. Railways in turn were surrogates for land companies. George, an old battler against Leland Stanford, had been the first to document the extent of, and assail these land grants (1871). His followers were proposing, in the Ralston-Nolan Bill of 1920 (H.R. 12,397), to include them in the land tax base. In the Georgist literature, "franchises" are consistently included with "land" in the proposed tax base. Urban mass transit firms were particularly targeted at that time.

Later, Ely the autobiographer volunteers that he was getting funding from various rail and utility magnates: "President Willard of the Baltimore and Ohio Railroad, and Owen D. Young, ... and others like them, including

George B. Cortelyou . .". He assures us, though, that "money which comes to us must be free from any restrictions . .". He praises one Albert Shaw, "who stands shoulder to shoulder with me," whose commitment is to "stating facts, even if they should happen to be facts which seem to be favorable to big business" (1938: 264).

The young Ely had seen merit in public ownership of utilities (Ely, 1938: 160). Ely the fundraiser for the Institute turned about. For this "one-eighty" he took bitter words, and in his *apologia* justifies himself. He illustrates the weakness of regulation in this interesting, perhaps autobiographical way. "Perhaps I am a college professor and the street-car magnate whose rapacity I am called upon to help hold in check has endowed the chair which I occupy. Is it strange that many of us who are called upon to control others of us should simply refuse to do it?" (1938: 253). His harshest critic could hardly have written anything nastier than that, but in his dotage that apparently persuaded him, at least.

He turned against public ownership because "The great mass of the people are interested in games – baseball, movies, radio, and football" (1938: 260). As to this, Upton Sinclair made a good point. "The student comes to college full of eagerness and hope, and he finds it dull. He has no idea why . . . men should be fired if they prove to be anything but dull. All he sees is the dullness, and he hates it, and 'cuts' it as much as he can, and goes off to practice football or get drunk" (Sinclair, 1923: 61). The whole thing is rather circular. The magnate stifles the professor, the professor bores the students, the students get drunk and get blamed for the whole mess.

Hibbard (1921) also reminded the "utilities" that they would be taxed under the Ralston-Nolan Bill. According to Ely, his major contributors were utilities, railways, building and loan associations, land companies, lumbermen, farmers, bankers, lawyers, insurance men, . . . and libraries" (Ely, *Institute News*, October, 1924). We may surmise that the libraries' contributions were not the backbone of the operation.

Ely had not previously published anything on land or resources; there hardly was such a "field" (Ely, 1927: 119). However, he had an old book on local taxation (1888),[50] a big name, and wealthy, motivated clients in the wings. He had an acceptable track record of belittling Henry George (Ely 1885, 1886, 1915). He incorporated his Institute but arranged to use space at the otherwise state-funded and controlled University of Wisconsin at Madison (Jorgensen, 1925: 13). The Institute was not part of U.W. (Ely, 1938: 247), but used its name.

Ely's Institute marked a new salient in the anti-Georgist campaigns. Ely did not rely, like Clark, on removing "land" from the lexicon of economese: "land" was in his new name. That did not stop him from denying that land has unique qualities, but his strategy was rather to preempt the work of those more applied economists – farm economists, real estate sellers, valuers, lenders, urban economists, resource economists, transportation and public utility economists - who had not learned better than to use four-letter words like "land". He guided them away from ideas that might lead to taxing it, and used their money to guide others away.

Ever since, the economics profession has been poised on the balance of wonderful ambivalence. Official Clarkian theory says there is no such thing as land, but just in case there is, it is to be studied under the guidance of Ely, founder of the AEA, in a separate, watertight compartment. Ely isn't so sure there is such a thing as land either, but whatever it is, it must be treated as private property, and taxed only nominally if at all.

The Institute motto, "Under All the Land," is the same as that of The National Association of Real Estate Boards (NAREB). The clientele of the Institute were "courts, legislators, administrative officials, *public utility executives, real estate* dealers and *owners, …*" (1938: 238; my emphasis). "*Banks, insurance companies, and lending institutions*" that had foreclosed became a major concern (*op. cit.*: 243, my emphasis). Their evictees (like John Steinbeck's Joad family), would-be buyers, renters, the job-needy, employees, students, voters, concerned citizens, the average intelligent adult, and the general public are not mentioned. The announced goal of the new Institute was to investigate "all the problems connected with land and taxation" (Jorgensen, 1925: iv; Ely, 1938: 240). Ely appealed for funds "for researches urgently demanded in the public interest, including the taxation of land" ("Organization and Purpose of the Institute for Research in land Economics and Public Utilities," p.8).

He defined his field this way. "Property and value mark out the field of land economics and separate it from those sciences which treat of land with reference to its productive powers …" (1927: 121). "The scope of land economics is as large as that of property rights in land and natural resources. One of the first marks of civilization is the definite allotment of specific rights in the gifts of nature" (1938: 235). Elsewhere in this series on the Georgist Paradigm (*Land & Taxation*) I have itemized ten attributes that distinguish land from capital and labor, and nineteen major economic consequences thereof. Ely's work on land, however, focuses only on land as property, and land as having private value. One might suspect he is rationalizing both of those, and leaving out everything else. He is faithfully replicated today by the private property fundamentalists of our times, Coasians, *et hoc genus omne*, whose panacea is to make every natural resource private property, then punt. They market their creed as "the new resource economics". Perhaps they have some claim to novelty, they are more extreme than Ely, who did favor residual social controls over land use, and at least had some history of social consciousness. However, even Ely didn't invent this. In 19th century England it was called "free trade in land" (George, 1879: 321–22; Douglas, 1976: 18; Lawrence, 1957: 97,105).

Ely's Institute's first output (Hibbard, 1921) was an overtly political attack on the Ralston-Nolan Bill (H.R. 12,397). Drafted by Jackson H. Ralston,[51] Ralston-Nolan would impose a "1% excise tax on the privilege of holding lands, natural resources *and public franchises* valued at more than $10,000, after deducting all improvements" (Jorgensen, 1925: 8–9, 73).[52] The National Association of Real Estate Boards (NAREB), a major contributor to Ely's Institute (Jorgensen, 1925: 6, n.7), published and distributed Hibbard's hit-piece nationwide, using the name of Ely's Institute for academic cover. Emil Jorgensen flayed Ely for presenting this as a product of an "Institute for Research," before any research was done. Ely lamely defended himself, belatedly, that "We have never advocated panaceas" (1938: 239, 241). The relevance of that is only clear if one understands that "panacea" is code language for single-tax. E.M. Fisher, a member of Ely's staff, soon joined NAREB as Assistant Executive Secretary, to take charge of its "educational" work (*Institute News*, June, 1923).

Later the Institute was to follow up by attacking the Bill's successor, the Keller Bill of 1924 (H.R. 5733). In this case the attack was by Ely himself, read into the *Congressional Record* (pp. 3092–93) by Congressman Ogden Mills of New York. Mills, a multi-millionaire, dominated the key Committee on Ways and Means, and was to succeed Andrew Mellon as Hoover's Secretary of the Treasury. Mills, with Ely's help, was to kill Keller in committee (Jorgensen, 1925: 78–81).

Meantime, back in Madison, Ely was charting the path for his Institute by writing *Outlines of Land Economics* (Ely, 1922). This was to let donors know what to expect, and guide the Institute's long-run research agenda – apparently the Hibbard hit-piece was urgent and could not wait upon research. The agenda was ambitious, to consist of some 50 books to guide the trade, and public policy. A staff was assembled, including several names later to become known in applied real estate education. These included George Wehrwein, Herbert D. Simpson, Mary L. Shine (later Amend), Albert G. Hinman, and Herbert Dorau (Jorgensen, 1925: 2,15,189). Ely also mentions Coleman Woodbury, Helen Monchow, Paul Raver, Morton Bodfish, Adrian Theobald, and Herman Walther. The last three were mortgage lenders (Ely, 1938: 246–47).

Normally the promoter of a new topic seeks to stress its distinctiveness. Ely's *Outlines* (and later works) conspicuously do the opposite. According to Ely, land value "is governed by the same laws that govern the values of other requisites of production" (1922, II: 78). "The more recent theory of land income holds that land yields an income substantially of the same character as other forms of income" (1927: 127). "Considered as property yielding income, land and capital are on exactly the same footing. A single-taxer [none are named] is much disturbed because the owner of a certain piece of land receives $30,000 a year in ground rents ... The same man [still unnamed] seems quite unworried by the fact that trust companies are turning over incomes just as great ... to clients ... some of whom are moral delinquents and intellectual incompetents" (1922, II: 21). Land is indistinguishable from capital, and so "we should not tax separately the value of the land ..." (1922, III: 115).

"... there is no surplus in land income.... nobody works harder for what he gets ... than the landowner; and he usually gives a big return to society for what he receives" (1922, II: 39, 53). Rising land prices are a payment for "continuous toil" (1922, II: 36; Ely and Morehouse, 1924: 194, 195), so land is really a labor product. The reader may detect a tendentious quality. What looks like unearned increment to land is really just "rent of conjecture," not peculiar to land (1922, II: 34, 55). Presently we learn that land taxes are shiftable (1922, III: 94), while "It is a great mistake to suppose" that sales and excise taxes are shifted to consumers (1924: 24).

More and more, one wonders why there should be a special Institute to study land, which is so much like everything else.

The promoter of a new topic normally tries to show its importance. Ely conspicuously does the opposite. Minimizing his topic, Ely wrote "... the last hundred years (1822–1922) ... shows the rent of land remaining fairly stationary" (1922, II: 74). "The single tax will not yield enough revenue to meet those (governmental) expenses" (Ely and Morehouse, 1924: 323–24). In the future, he forecasts, land rent will fall further, owing to increasing wealth and technological progress (1922, II: 13; Ely and Morehouse, 1924: 262). Some rents will even become negative, dragging down the value of improvements (1922, II: 73). There is some doubt if he believed this last point himself, because in 1924 he joined the "City Housing Corporation," buying 1100 lots in Long Island City, New York (*Institute News*, May, 1924). He was a Director of Fairway Farms Corporation, speculating in Montana and North Dakota farmlands, "to experiment with the agricultural ladder" (a nice touch) (*ibid*, October, 1924). Still, we have his forecast in print.

Another reason to promote research is to solve perceived problems. Again, Ely minimizes the task. According to him, there are no problems to be solved, except to put down unnamed single-tax agitators who would create problems by taxing land. The market already puts land to the best use, by Ely. "This idea that good land is held out of use in large areas is a fiction" (1922, III: 98). The owner of land awaiting use provides gardens, lawns, and open space while he pays taxes to hold down taxes on the buildings of others (1922, III: 103, 105, 106). "Very uncertain and often inadequate are the gains that finally come to him" (1922, III: 106). Land speculators "purchase and sell land in order to help men acquire landownership". As to competition, it is perfect among landowners. Only non-land assets can be monopolized (1922, II: 52,53,73). Almost like a modern Rochester economist, Ely seems to be saying that land markets are 100% efficient; allocation is handled by the market. One wonders, why found an Institute to study land problems when there are no problems?

As for distribution, that is also as it should be. "Land is the poor man's investment" (1922, III: 98). "The great millionaires prefer other forms of investment[53] ... other things pay better than land" (Hibbard, 1921). Educational and philanthropic institutions rest on landownership (1922, II:

142). "Tenancy is also a good thing when it represents a rung in the agricultural ladder ..." (1922, III: 53). "A properly controlled system of tenancy has a place ... as a stepping stone to ownership" (Ely and Morehouse, 1924: 199). "The evils of tenancy have been grossly exaggerated" (1922, III: 61). The virtues of tenancy are noted at length (1922, III: 51–61). "English agriculture proves that we can have good agriculture with a system of tenant farming" (1922, III: 61). The English Duke of Bedford is a good example, moved by *noblesse oblige* to provide a free bathhouse to the inhabitants of three villages on his estate of 51,643 acres, and to give them jobs building a pond for him (1922, II: 61). Tenancy is caused by "incompetency"; tenants should be made more efficient through social welfare work (1922, III: 59). A desirable percentage of tenancy is about 30% (1922, III: 59).

Ely was well-connected, outstandingly so. His influence reached into the US Department of Agriculture, through Henry C. Taylor, head of the Bureau of Agricultural Economics, who was on his Board, and whom he hired at Northwestern when Taylor was dismissed in 1925. Under Taylor, five B.A.E. employees wrote "Farm Ownership and Tenancy" for the 1923 *Yearbook of Agriculture* (Gray, 1923). They write there that the high price of land has been given "exaggerated importance" as a cause of tenancy, and anyway, "it would be unfortunate to make the road to farm ownership so easy that farm ownership could be achieved by those who are unready". The authors include Lewis C. Gray, who surely knew better. The B.A.E. under Taylor also influenced Census Monograph No. IV, *Farm Tenancy in the United States*, by E.A. Goldenweiser and Leon Truesdell. The B.A.E. input came through O.E. Baker and W.J. Spillman, acknowledged by a note at the end of the introduction. Like the B.A.E. writers, Goldenweiser and Truesdell deal with tenancy as just a "rung on the agricultural ladder," an Ely invention. This is frustrating to the researcher on tenancy, for this classic monograph is a mine of useful information, with stimulating ideas. Something blocked the writers from developing those ideas and data in the direction they seem to lead.

None of the above positions seem to justify research to solve problems. The status quo is seen as satisfactory, except for one thing: overtaxation of land. There is the point of consistency. All the other premises help make a case for sheltering land from taxation. This does seem to be Ely's main point, although he is ever the sidewinder, never seeming to head where he is going. The exasperated Emil Jorgensen, after an exhaustive study of Ely's works, judged him harshly: his methods are the use of "unwarranted assumptions, of wrong inferences, of false suggestions, of insinuation, of half-truths and of outright misrepresentation" (Jorgensen, 1925: 118). That is unkind, but seems to be on the mark in this case. It is consonant with what also irritated his right-wing critic who brought the 1894 case at Madison. Oliver Wells was wrong to persecute Ely, but he had studied his man. He complained that Ely's books are "studiously indefinite and ambiguous ... They abound in sanctimonious and pious cant ..." (Ely, 1938: 220). Just so. Constant equivocating and sidling and backtracking are his ways. Few but those already attuned to the single-tax case would notice how he keeps returning to the major theme of undercutting the case for a tax on land value.

We have seen above in passing some of Ely's penchant for abusing "the single taxer" in the course of making other points. He is now and then a little more direct, although never completely so. "Because a colonization company[54] must operate with a large area of land, a high land tax may hamper or ruin such a company" (1922, III: 29). "Few public utilities will escape taxation under the Ralston-Nolan Bill" (Hibbard). "Many are disturbed because property in land yields income. Is there anything ... which should lead to a special policy of taxation? Unless we are prepared to go over to Socialism ... we must expect to find men receiving an income from property, ... The solution of our land problems is not at all to be sought in confiscation of land values" (1922, III: 102, 103, 105). "The effect of the single tax would ultimately be a system of State tenancy" (Ely and Morehouse, 1924: 324). He favors public land *purchase* (presumably followed by tenancy), but not *taxation*. If we do raise land taxes, we must first indemnify the owners, because they have owned "from time immemorial" (1938: 272). Sales of land to pay back taxes "pained me because of the tremendous economic loss involved ... tragic stories of poor settlers who lost their all, ..." (1938: 234). Land taxes should be capped at 1.5% (1922, III: 115). Without doubt he would be pleased with the 1% cap imposed since 1978 in California, a cap that in only 16 years has helped convert California from the most buoyant to the most depressed American State.

Finally growing bolder, in 1927 he writes forthrightly:

> In recent years the tendency has been for the government to take in taxes
> an ever larger proportion of the income from land. Due to inequities in the
> general property tax system in the United States, this tax burden has borne
> more heavily on land than on other forms of property (1927: 134).

In 1921 New York City, spurred by the Manhattan Single Tax Club,
exempted new dwellings of moderate size from the property tax for ten
years. Ely demurs to this on distributive grounds – because it might
"increase the final burden upon the land" (1922, III: 115). By 1924 he is
sure that it has done so, so that "the inducement to acquire land for
residential utilization has been lessened" (Ely and Morehouse, 1924: 286).
The last statement seems to be spectacularly contrary to fact. Lawson
Purdy and Edward Polak, both officials of New York City and writers in
scholarly journals, reported that building permit requests rose by a factor
of about 5, 1921–23 (cit. Jorgensen, 1925: 159–62).

To avoid taxing land, Ely would tax consumption and labor. Having to
pay taxes simply makes labor work harder (1922, III: 69). (Compare this
with the statement just above, that taxes on land lessen the inducement to
use it for building.) There is a "margin of income for the payment of taxes
by the great mass of people. One has only to watch expenditures for the
'movies' ... to be convinced ..." (1922, II: 119). "On every hand can be seen
an enormous surplus of income over needs of subsistence" (III: 93). There
is no concern that such taxation might be "confiscatory". In the Ely lexicon
only land taxes are confiscatory. "It is really an insult to the workingman to
treat him as a tax exempt person" (1922, III: 90). "We are unable, without
ruin, to meet our growing needs by direct taxation, ... Taxes on
consumption and various indirect forms of taxation must be employed ..."
(1922, III: 93).

Ely did not invent such ideas, but he gave them academic endorsement.
In a few years they were preached from the top by the economic ruler of
America, Andrew Mellon, Treasury Secretary under three Presidents from
1921–31, and by his successor Ogden Mills, Ely's ally in Congress. Both
Mellon and Mills were major owners of the natural resources that Ely
would relieve from taxation. They lost control of Washington in 1933, but
Ely's ideas moved ahead rapidly in the states. The policies championed in

Outlines of Land Economics, 1922, began taking over state governments in the 1930s, and have counter-revolutionized state and local government finance in the last 60 years. They bear major guilt for the decay of our once-vibrant cities and the depopulation of our farming areas.

By 1925 Wisconsin apparently lost its enthusiasm for Ely. La Follette's Wisconsin, of all the States, had least rejected Progressivism. The Regents resolved to accept no more donations from any incorporated educational endowment (Jorgensen, 1925: 154). Ely may have seen this coming: he was already packing for a move to Northwestern. He added to his Board Frank Lowden, former Governor of Illinois and Republican Presidential timber,[55] and Nathan MacChesney, General Counsel for NAREB, and a trustee of Northwestern University. He boasted of his luxurious offices overlooking Lake Michigan, comparable to those he also boasted of in Madison (Ely, 1938: 245,247–48). He and his staff received premium salaries (*ibid:* 248). Ely moved in the highest circles, and to that end went first class. It was an image-making strategy he had learned from watching Disraeli at Berlin in 1878 (Ely, 1938: 55). When he launched his new *Journal of Land and Public Utility Economics* in 1924, it was most attractively presented. He wisely saw that it contained enough objective work to appear to be, and in many respects actually to be, a genuine scholarly journal: this, too, was part of his cultivated image.

"... Ely gradually became more conservative. ... in the 1920s his Institute ... was referred to disparagingly in a report on professional ethics by a Committee of the AAUP, in 1930" (Coats, 1987a: 129). His son-in-law, Ed Morehouse, was its Director, but nepotism was the least of its sins, as we have seen.

Grace M. (Mrs. William) Jaffe became Ely's chief research assistant at Northwestern University in 1929. After they fell out, her memoirs give some insight into Ely's hostility toward Henry George. Doing research for his autobiography, she "discovered some of the less creditable aspects of his academic life, particularly his abject submission when accused of Socialism" (Jaffe, 1979: 113). After that he grew increasingly conservative, and focused more on making money: reprinting and selling texts, consulting for utilities, and speculating in land. "Ely had succeeded in making a small fortune in the Wisconsin real estate business, buying land cheap, and selling it dear. This *modus operandi* brought him into acute conflict with Henry

George's Single Taxers (Jaffe, 1979: 107–08)".

The bitterness of the relationship is apparent in the title of Jorgensen's monograph on Ely, *False Education* (1925). On Ely's side, bitterness is apparent from the material cited above from *Outlines of Land Economics*, etc., and from several disparaging allusions to George, single-taxers, and various pejorative codewords (economic sect, panacea) routinely used for single-tax and single-taxers in Ely's autobiography (1938: 92, 162, 239, 241, 272). Jorgensen's style is heavy, but he did his homework. His charges are carefully researched and backed. They anticipated the later disparagement of Ely by the AAUP Committee on Professional Ethics.

By 1929 Ely was running out of steam, at least professionally (he was yet to sire two more children, when nearly eighty years old). Ely "had retired into a more or less permanent snooze, and was quite content to have the younger generation write his textbook (*Outlines of Economics*) for him.... I was obliged, in order to protect the old man's reputation, to write the pages on 'Rent' and 'The Single Tax' for him.... Every once in a while he would try to write part of his 'own' book. Ely left his MS on my desk. I read it carefully, but with horror. It was a libelous attack on the leader of the Single Tax movement.... signed 'Richard T. Ely.' ... I sat down and wrote the section dealing with the economic theory of rent in general and with Henry George in particular.... that section remained unrevised in later editions.... Whether Ely ever read what his 'ghost writer' had written, I shall never know" (Jaffe, 1979: 109).

This is the man who, in 1929, "was known as the Dean of American Economics" (Jaffe, 1979: 107); who founded The American Economic Association, the academic discipline of land economics, and the Journal that now carries the same name, as an antidote to Georgist teachings about land. "Many of his students went on to distinguished careers in academic or public life" (Coats 1987b). In 1927 he was introduced to President Calvin Coolidge with these prophetic words: "Mr. President, here is Professor Ely, dean of American economists. If anything is wrong with the country it must be his fault" (Ely, 1938: 276). Something was, and it must have been.

The modern American Economic Association holds him to its bosom: from 1963, it honors his memory every year with its invited Richard T. Ely Lecture, a tribute to his enduring influence over the ideas and ideals of the profession. In case any doubt remains over the role models of the Association, it bestows a second and third annual tribute. One is a medal awarded in honor of John Bates Clark, who devoted his career to cleansing the lexicon of words needed to make the case for a tax on land values. The other medal is in honor of Francis A. Walker, he who "would not insult his readers by discussing a project so steeped in infamy" as Single-tax.

The doctrine of "ripening costs"

Aside from his institution-building, what ideas did Ely add to NCE? He endorsed and widely popularized the points advanced by seminal NCE revisionists like Clark, Pareto, Seligman, Edgeworth, and Spahr. Ely saw land value as being mostly man-made. A catalogue of his anti-Georgist teachings is in Jorgensen (1925); we have surveyed them above.

In addition, Ely advanced his own seminal rationalization of land speculation, the doctrine of "ripening costs". Francis Edgeworth (1906: 73) had toyed with the idea in his understated manner, but it was Ely who drove it home to the median midwestern Babbitt. By holding land idle during its rise of value, "I perform social service" (1920: 127). The service is to preempt land from premature underimprovement while it ripens to a higher use. Holding costs and unrealized latent rents are "ripening costs". "*The costs falling upon the holder of land during a period of ripening use are socially necessary and are properly chargeable to the increment in land value resulting from the change in use. . . .* in public utility economics . . . losses sustained during the period of developing a going business are capitalized into the rate base" (1927: 130, and p.130 n.l. Emphasis in original.).

"Ripening costs" marked a shift, but not a rift, in NCE. J.B. Clark (1899: 85–87), Alvin Johnson (1914: 35), H.J. Davenport (1917), and later B.H. Hibbard (1930) credited land speculation with hastening the conquest of the frontier, which they, in the frontier tradition, premised to be an unmixed blessing. The "lure of unearned increment" actually stimulated building (today we call it "rent-seeking"). I find no record that Ely or the others tried to reconcile their polar positions. They were content to unite (notably excepting Davenport) in their damnation of George and the single tax. Clark, Johnson, and Hibbard damned it for slowing down settlement; Ely for speeding it up. No matter: the idea was to damn it, and that they did jointly, unvexed by inconsistencies.

Ely had got ahold of an important and timely truth. Sprawl of all kinds had gone too far; the "cowboy economy" needed reining in. This gave some plausibility, and sense of social responsibility, to what he said. However, he used this truth lopsidedly as a stick to beat down land taxes everwhere. "... it is proposed by some to tax land to the point of confiscation, in order to bring it into use. Yet we find that some kinds of land are being brought into use too rapidly, ... contrary to the principles of conservation" (1927: 121). That is, he blamed land taxes in marginal areas for stimulating development; he never proposed the obvious counterpart, to raise land taxes on better lands to speed and fill out their development, to satisfy demand so that it might stop pushing outwards. He also, without recognizing it, contradicted his ally Seligman, who was still repeating his claim that reliance on land taxes would destroy marginal communities because they would have no tax base. Ely, meantime, with his usual equivocation, was busy speculating in Montana lands for himself and his Institute.

During the Great Depression Ely's doctrine of ripening costs was ridiculed even by George Wehrwein, revising Ely's text, who pointed to empty land that was put into "cold storage, and loading the community with the frozen assets that result" (Ely and Wehrwein, 1940: 149). This was almost Henry George talk! Worse, it was taken from a study by two of Ely's own *protégés*, H.D. Simpson and E.R. Burton (1931: 44). The Great Depression really traumatized people, leading to agonizing reappraisals that lasted for a generation. Today, however, those events and misgivings are forgotten.

Even by his own lights, Ely's "social service" proved negative: his empty land rotted before it ripened, and he lost all in the crash. He was reduced to living on relatives and former students, until rescued by Nicholas Murray Butler, long-time patron of J.B. Clark and E.R.A. Seligman (Coats, 1987b; Ely, 1938: 285). Seligman helped with his autobiography (Ely, 1938: viii).

However, with renewed rising land prices and galloping urban sprawl, the doctrine revived. It found its political outlet in 1957 when Governor Spiro Agnew of Maryland signed the first state law authorizing preferential assessment of farmland around growing cities, a movement that spread like lightning nationwide. In the profession, now consisting mostly of NCE rent-rationalizers, it has again become an article of faith. To them, markets are "efficient" so long as buyers make competitive returns. Whatever actually happens to the land must then be right, by definition. Even if they don't make competitive returns, they thought they were going to when they bought it (again by definition), and that is what really matters. It dovetails nicely with the "perfect markets" and "rational expectations" worldviews that would rationalize markets so perfectly that there is no unearned wealth except by chance.

In my view, the matter was nicely, if unintentionally, disposed of by Friedrich and Vera Smith Lutz (1951: 109–12). They wrote on optimal replacement timing under conditions of progressive obsolescence. All they did was ask how to maximize present value in perpetuity. They found that the expectation of higher future uses leads to speedier, not slower replacement of old by new uses. Their simple, basic mathematics has been entirely ignored by modern economists intent on replicating Ely's feat of rationalizing land speculation. Kris Feder's contributions in the present series of CIT books supplies a bibliography of current writings on the subject. (See also Gaffney, 1973: 141–42).

Another Ely innovation was to sneak in the price of land purchase as a social cost. "... get away from the old dogmatic treatment of the rent of land ... We have also taken over from public utility economics the idea of historical cost. When this method is pursued, it is difficult to find any peculiar or special surplus.... inquiries ... indicate rather a relatively low income on the investment in land; ... need more research" bla-bla-bla. "... land economics ... as a result of observation, statistical inquiry and research, is reaching conclusions in regard to the income of land similar to those formulated years ago by Professor John Bates Clark.... Clark's works ... (use) deductive reasoning of a high order" (Ely, 1927, pp. 127–28). No mere *Methodenstreit* would stand between fellow anti-Georgists.

From this fountain has sprung the whole stream of modern rationalization of markets whereby arbitrage leaves no potential gains unrealized, and this guarantees optimal allocation of land.

Yet another Ely innovation is to make high land prices stimulate saving and capital formation. This may follow directly from Clark's capital theory, but Clark carefully avoided capital formation. He almost always assumed a fixed capital supply, to avoid any difference of capital from land. He focused narrowly on allocation of a fixed quantity of scarce capital among competing ends. Ely, however, sidled into implying that high land prices are a cause of saving:

> Ownership of land signifies saved wealth .... These savings in the form of landed property have been called upon to make heavy contributions.... this puts a premium on spending and a penalty on saving ... encouraging consumption and discouraging productive savings. Consequently, there is considerable scientific support for the view that some of the heavy direct taxes upon land should be transferred to indirect taxes upon certain forms of consumption, i.e., that a broadening of the base of taxation is necessary to avoid confiscation of land values (1927: 135).

After 65 years of such education, Ely has won in academies and think-tanks and legislatures. We have done what he recommended, and more. land prices have risen beyond his wildest dreams. Richly funded think tanks like the American Council on Capital Formation preach his gospel to every Congressman. Interestingly enough, however, the result has been a crisis of low savings rates, high capital imports, balance of trade deficits, and growing absentee ownership of US assets.

6

The Irish Connection

Francis Y. Edgeworth anticipated Ely on "ripening costs". He wrote that land taxes would "force the market". He has a strangely repugnant way of putting it: "In fine, the interest of monopolists is not always contrary to that of their customers" (1906: 73). It makes one wonder what else he is trying to rationalize.

Edgeworth correctly observes that taxing land would weaken the credit rating of landowners. He leaves out the counterpart, that untaxing buildings would strengthen the credit rating of builders. Still, we are in his debt for at least introducing the topic of credit rationing. Otherwise, NCE proceeds as though credit markets are pluperfect, and the highest bidder for land is necessarily the highest and best user. I have treated this point in a companion volume in this CIT series (Gaffney, 1994) and elsewhere (Gaffney, 1973, 1993b).

Edgeworth also thought that land taxes would bite into building profits. It is hard to imagine they would do so more than the alternative of taxing buildings themselves, so his point is obscure, and seems like simple carping. Demonstrably, if land or any other taxes did bite into building profits, the effect would be to defer building, which his first argument posits as a desired outcome. The impression is that nothing would please him because he has some unstated reservation.

One can guess what that reservation might be. Edgeworth was from a family of the "Protestant Ascendancy" in Ireland, Irish landlords, a long line of them reaching back 300 years. They owned Edgeworthtown, which he would inherit and own as an Irish absentee landlord. He was also teaching at Oxford, another great absentee landlord. He was not unaware of the faults of his class – his Aunt Maria, author of *Castle Rackrent*, must have raised his consciousness. That is a far cry from relishing drastic reforms imposed by the state – not even Tia Maria was ready for that.

Henry George had risen from obscurity by attacking absentee landlords generically, and Irish landlords specifically (Douglas, 1976: 15–59; Barker, 1955: 335–72). His 1881 tract on *The Irish Land Question* (later retitled *The Land Question*) is what had sparked initial interest in the more heavyweight *Progress and Poverty*. He was intimately involved in Irish politics, after traveling as a journalist to Ireland to report for *The Irish World* of New York, serving a New York clientele of Irish *émigrés*. These were people who remembered that the Edgeworths and their kind had evicted them from their ancestral land.[56] His wife was Irish; his fellow California land-reformer and employer, James McClatchy of the Sacramento *Bee*, was Irish.

These Irish did not take kindly to economists who told them the usurpers had really created The Emerald Isle. In the NCE cant, this land had been produced by landlords, who were just "supplying" their native land to the Irish renters, and sparing them from having to bear the financial burdens of ownership. That was a hard story to sell in Ireland, or the slums of New York City, in the 1880s. As newcomers, outsiders, common laborers, and the poorest voting whites of 19th Century America, the Irish were George's natural ethnic constituency.

They also supported the revolutionary Fenian movement, as it was then called. They sent their contributions back to Ireland to help roust landlords like the Edgeworths, an irritating skill the Irish developed to a high art. In Ireland, George the reporter also made news, supporting the radical activist Michael Davitt against the temporizing Charles Stewart Parnell (Barker, 1955: 341–56). In propertied England then that was something like preaching abolition in antelbellum Alabama.

Into this powderkeg, George dropped an incendiary note: "It is hard not to feel some contempt for a people so oppressed (as the Irish) who have only occasionally murdered a landlord". It was the harshest, most provocative, impolitic thing he ever wrote. I do not cite it to praise nor blame, but to establish motive. It was only a rhetorical flourish, journalistic hyperbole probably aimed to stir up the passive Parnell. Nevertheless, there it stood on the printed page, seeming to declare open season on Irish landlords like the

Edgeworths. It would have been only human for F.Y. Edgeworth to notice, resent, and fear. It gave him all the motive one would need to undercut George.

This line of causation is consistent with Edgeworth's otherwise inexplicably fierce attack on the mathematics of J.E. Cairnes. Cairnes' book, *The Slave Power* (1862), had played an important role in swinging English opinion against slaveowners, with whom Irish landlords had much in common, during the American Civil War. Cairnes had written of England itself, "The large additions to the wealth of the country have gone neither to profits nor to wages, ... but to swell ... the rent roll ..." (cit. Miller, 1917: 200). More recently, Cairnes' offense was to have written several articles favoring rent control in Ireland. Cairnes had used his authority as a political economist to assert this was compatible with classical rent theory.

With the best will in the world, it would have been hard for a person with Edgeworth's pedigree not to absorb a trace of class and ethnic bias. That would help explain his title: "Recent *schemes* for rating land values". "Scheme" is not a friendly term; "plan" or "proposal" would sound less prejudicial. Edgeworth's bias took the form of eugenics. There are individual differences in the capacity for pleasure, he wrote. He seems to suggest, in his cryptic, elusive way, that human creatures higher on the evolutionary scale (the Edgeworths?) have a higher capacity for pleasure than those below them (Irish tenants?), so that social welfare is maximized when wealth is unequally distributed, pretty much the way it already is.[57]

Quite apart from Irish affairs, T.W. Hutchison (1953: 118–19) has suggested that Edgeworth kept J.A. Hobson from teaching at London, and Hobson attributed it to class bias. Hobson was not a Georgist, but a radical who did pen what Barker calls a "famous appreciation" of George (Barker, 1955: 414–16, 665; Hobson, 1897). This was published after one attack by Edgeworth (1890), and before another (1904). I have no conclusive proof on which to base a firm opinion of the exclusion of Hobson by Edgeworth. Edgeworth's defenders say that either it did not happen, or it was justified because Hobson made an error in calculus (Newman, 1987: 89). Considering that neither Marshall, J.B. Clark, nor Seligman used calculus at all, that would suggest a selective use of technicalities for screening people. Modern academicians are not unschooled in that device.

Edgeworth was a "toolmaker" and model-builder. He was a painfully obscure, opaque writer, little understood by his contemporaries. In most substantive matters he followed Marshall who, as we have seen, was more fair to George than other NCE founders, but who couldn't understand Edgeworth either. In the current toolmaking, model-building era, however, painful obscurity and opacity are at a premium and Edgeworth enjoys a great new vogue. Here is his view of things:

> Imagine a material Cosmos, a mechanism as composite as possible, and perplexed with all manner of wheels, pistons, parts, connections, and whose mazy complexity might far transcend in its entanglements the webs of thought and wiles of passion; nevertheless, if any given impulses be imparted ... each part of the great whole will move off with a velocity such that the energy of the whole may be the greatest possible (1881: 9).

He was, one might say, like a kid with a new toy. Apparently his toy-building technique was excellent. More apposite for us, the subjects that engaged him, and the attitudes he took, are quite congenial to modern "techie" economists. Much of what seems "new" in the last twenty years of grown-up kids playing with toy models is still basic NCE from the 1880s, expressed in less comprehensible forms.

In *Mathematical Psychics* (1881) Edgeworth introduced what is now universally called "Pareto Optimality". The idea is that you cannot measure quantities of welfare, or make interpersonal comparisons of welfare. You can only be sure that welfare rises in the course of voluntary exchanges when at least one person is, and usually two persons are better off, and no one is worse off.

The policy implications are immediate, drastic, highly conventional, and very safe for those who stand to inherit land and private incomes. To begin, all existing entitlements to property, whatever their origins, should be firmed up and frozen. The process has to start somewhere, and any change in the existing entitlements would only delay progress in the orderly march of exchanges leading toward higher welfare. This idea remains central to Chicago School thinking: the economy should "maximize utility subject to the constraints of market prices and *endowments of wealth*" (Reder, 1987: 415). By 1985, "these views and their extensions have become mainstream economics, ..." (Reder, 1985: 417). "The rise in influence of the Coase

Theorem at Chicago has more or less paralleled a decline in the marked concern with income distribution that existed in ... the work of Henry Simons" (Reder, 1987: 417).

All property should be clearly defined and fully alienable, with no strings attached. A series of exchanges, each of them being what is now called a "win-win" solution, must lead always in the direction of greater general welfare. All Robin Hood schemes, based on folk wisdom and Jeffersonian values, like that cited above from Charles Spahr, are without scientific basis, and can only delay progress.

It speaks volumes for modern economists that they have reshaped their discipline around those values. The operational part, of course, is what you do first: firm up and freeze existing entitlements. The rest is mostly moonshine, a promise made to be broken. In practice, "firming up" means wiping out traditional servitudes to the public, so that every "win-win" solution is really a "win-win-lose" solution, with the general public the loser, uncompensated. NCEists often point out how land values are the product of capital in the form of public works. This is all forgotten, however, when land is sold, and this sale is presumed to firm up forever a permanent public obligation to continue servicing and replacing those works. An example is the recent move to convert private contracts to get federally subsidized water in California into perpetual private property, salable to the highest bidder with subsidies permanently attached. NCEists pushing for this overlook that tapping the Treasury, and grabbing water from the public domain, deprive others (Gaffney, 1992, 1993c, criticizing proposals of Richard Wahl, Zach Willey, Sotirios Angelides, Eugene Bardach, and others).

In 1879, the year George published *Progress and Poverty*, Edgeworth was thinking thoughts like these.

> But equality is not the whole of distributive justice ... in the minds of many good men among the moderns and the wisest of the ancients, there appears a deeper sentiment in favour of aristocratical privilege – the privilege of man above brute, of civilised above savage, of birth, of talent, and of the male sex. The sentiment of right has a ground of utilitarianism in supposed differences of *capacity* (Edgeworth 1879: 77, cited in Newman, 1987).

Peter Newman, who cites the above, doubts that Edgeworth was wholly given to such dark views. They were, however, an important part of his complex nature.

7

Pareto's Power

We turn to Vilfredo Pareto, whom the dark thoughts of Edgeworth evoke. The thoughts suggest that Edgeworth's affinities with Pareto were more than methodological. Pareto's philosophy reads like a tour between Niccolò Machiavelli and Benito Mussolini, with detours through Friedrich Nietzsche. A wealthy heir who married a Russian countess, he has been judged by some as the first fascist, but that label, like most, is too simple. His ideas sound fascistic in internal affairs, on the model of a Latin American dictator; but they lack the populism that gave European fascism mass support, as well as the imperialism that was its downfall. He was anti-militaristic, consistent with his contempt for government in general. "Pugnacious elitist misanthropic libertarian" might be a better fit: it seems to fit many of his modern followers, the NCEists. Here are some of his words: let the reader judge.[58]

> ...no social class can for long hold its property or its power if it does not have the strength and vigor necessary to defend them. In the long run only power determines the social forms; the great error of the 19th century will be to have forgotten this principle (1906: 361).

Society has a dominant class, A, and a subject class, B. Class A divides into A-alpha and A-beta. The alpha part "still has enough strength and energy left to defend its share of authority;" the other part, beta, "is made up of degenerated individuals, with feeble intelligence and will, *humanitarians*, as is said today" (1927: 91).

> The A-alpha try to make people believe that they are working for the common good, ... [but] it [this effort] also decreases the energy of the A-

beta, who take as true what is only a pure fiction and can only be useful as such (1906 p.92).

The error of the humanitarians ... is not in having a religion, ... but in having chosen a religion which is appropriate only to weak beings lacking in all energy and courage, ... (p.364).

One wonders, after that, how Pareto would class those who fancy they have found in "Pareto-optimality" a value-free technique to evaluate issues of public policy? More relevant today, how should *we* view them? Pareto would only appear value-free to those who share his values so thoroughly that they cannot even see that they are value-judgments. It might be fair to say that Pareto disclaims all ethical positions and value-judgments save one: private rent-taking is sacred. In this, of course, he has company; it is a powerful company with most of the world's discretionary income at its disposal to impose its message on impressional young students of economics.

Pareto expressed grudging admiration for the B-alphas, or leaders of the lower classes, so long as they were driven by narrow self-seeking, as he assumed they were. The weak whom "humanitarians" defend are "degenerates". The self-seeking proletarian leaders, or B-alphas, are different. "They are energetic and robust he-men who want to eat when hungry, drink when thirsty, and make love when it suits them ..". "It is self-interest which rules the conduct of the B's, not sentimental twaddle" (p.360).

> ...the struggle to appropriate the goods of others may be favorable to (genetic) selection (p.341).
>
> The numerous cases in which the mob wants *to lynch* malefactors demonstrate clearly that the populace still retains the vigor of the race, vigor which the upper classes have lost (p. 360n).

Pareto does not comment directly on George, but he rejects most of the value premises that might lead one to Georgism, in the following.

> Equality before the law ... is not ... advantageous to society; ... (p.95).

Tories and Whigs "compete for the favor of the common people".... they "fight to see which will prostrate itself more humbly at the feet of the common man" (p.100).

When the suffrage has been given to all men, including madmen and criminals, when it has been extended to women, and, if you like, to children, it will have to stop. One cannot go any lower, unless the suffrage is extended to animals, . .(100).

. . . liberals . . . have paved the way for the demagogical oppression which is now dawning". Taxes on the rich are voted on "by those who do not pay them, . . . shamelessly . . ." (93).

In 1904 in England, "all the parties . . . vie with each other in flattering the workers. The Liberal party, which . . . has given up its principles, moved to socialism . . ." (345).

I will intercede here for historical accuracy. Actually, the English Liberal Party did not move to socialism, it moved towards Georgism (Douglas, 1976; Lawrence, 1957: 37,63,73,105–06,111,126). The "famous Newcastle Programme" of the Party, first adopted in 1891, put both rating (local) and taxing (national) of land values into the Liberal Platform (J.D. Miller, 1917: 102; Douglas, 1976: 114–15; Lawrence, 1957: 171), where it stood for thirty years. That is why people like Pareto's friend Edgeworth (1906) were writing articles against "Recent Schemes for Rating Urban Land Values," and Cannan (1907) was writing against "The Proposed Relief of Buildings from Local Rates". Georgists and Socialists had long since fallen out (Lawrence, 1957: 37,63,73), and it was the Georgists who were accepted into the Liberal Party. Gladstone was not keen on them, but lost out and retired to Hawarden in 1894.

From 1906–14, under successive Prime Ministers Campbell-Bannerman, Asquith, and Lloyd George, the Radical wing of the English Liberal Party came close to implementing Georgist reforms – in the process drawing the teeth from the House of Lords. This did not come out of nowhere, but out of 25 years of organizing and propagandizing, which was no secret. Among other prominent English statesmen supporting land taxation were Winston Churchill, Philip Snowden, Ramsay MacDonald, Josiah Wedgwood, Clement Attlee, and Stafford Cripps – a conspicuous group. George Bernard Shaw, a highly visible Fabian leader, sustained his support for George (Lawrence, 1957: 85–86,171). Presumably Pareto knew something of these facts, and was using "Socialist" as a pejorative for "Georgist," as Clark and Ely did.

It was, rather, Bismarck's Germany that adopted socialism. Bismarck had triumphed by swallowing his enemies whole, and announcing their program as his own. As we have seen, this had an enormous influence on American education in economics.

Returning the floor to Pareto, he says *Tolstoyism* led Russia to lose the war with Japan (358n). Tolstoy was George's apostle to the Russians (Geiger, 1933: 459–61); we may presume Pareto knew this – his wife was a Russian countess.[59] Pareto goes on, "But among the leaders some enriched themselves through customs protection and corruptions, others were besotted by their humanitarian faith" (358n).

"...consumers suffer less harm from (monopolies) perhaps than from shopkeepers and trade unions". We should deplore "the contemporary humanitarian mania to excuse ... all harm caused by workers or by persons of little affluence, ..." (p.338).

Those five quotes leave little doubt that Pareto diametrically opposed most values associated with Georgism, or "The Single Tax".

Next let us look at what economic techniques to associate with Pareto. He makes no bones about how he sees the purpose of techniques.

> Men follow their sentiment and their self-interest, but it pleases them to imagine that they follow reason (p.95).

With that avowal, it would be prudent to be chary, and interpret Pareto's choice of techniques in the light of what we know about *his* sentiment and self-interest. All the techniques to be described have been accepted by NCEists, and folded into the body of NCE.

(1) "Pareto's Law" of distribution tells us that unequal wealth is inevitable, and remains the same between times and places, regardless of human institutions. To Pareto, "leveling" is all sham, it is just the rhetoric of the outs trying to become the ins. The overtones of this kind of fatalism are heard in today's "rational expectations" dogma, which says that all government actions are offset by private investors and other economic agents who anticipate them. However, Pareto's "Law" is demonstrably contrary to fact, e.g. among the 50 American states. Detailed data on this are presented in Gaffney, 1992.

(2) Political economy deals only with how "to compare the sensations of one man in different situations, and to determine which of these he would choose". A second class of theories compares the sensations of one person with another, but these are "most unsatisfactory" (105). This converts

economics from a social science to a study in individual psychology (a bad one, according to psychologists). It dismisses in one stroke all traditional American notions and egalitarian ideals, such as expressed by Charles Spahr, above, who wrote that low incomes are insufficient for healthful and decent living, while high incomes and properties are "morally perilous to their possessors" (Spahr, 1896: 159). "... the ability to pay taxes increases faster than the private fortune" (Spahr, 1896: 160).

Clearly, too, Pareto's view is totally at odds with the case for public education, national defense, social security, universal health care, veterans' benefits, and anything else with any element of social dividend. One could never lead a crew or team, or provision a platoon or a division, or teach a class without comparing the sensation of one person with another. Pareto would seem to have wanted to eliminate both the welfare state and the warfare state, maintaining the military for the prime purpose of putting down domestic insurgencies. The purest applications of his philosophy may be observed today in Guatemala, Honduras, or El Salvador.

(3) Pareto redefines rent as the gain from reallocating a resource – any resource. It is the excess of its current return over its "opportunity cost". He belittles "Ricardian rent" as just a particular case of that (247). This, of course, is calculated to divert attention from land rent as a taxable surplus. This altered definition of rent used often to be called "Paretian rent," or "transfer rent," but modern NCEists have gradually got round to calling it just "rent," as though there were no other meaning.

Logically speaking, that involves the trick of taking a concept appropriate to "partial equilibrium analysis" (theory of exchanges, centered on the firm and the industry) and transplanting it, without advising the reader, to "general equilibrium analysis" (social distribution theory, covering all firms and industries) (Gaffney, 1962: 145–46). It is quite inconsistent for Pareto, who is generally known as a writer on general equilibrium. Frank Knight, as we will see, carried it to the greatest extreme possible.

It has been wrongly imputed to Joan Robinson, who actually saw right through it. Robinson wrote, "From the point of view of society, land ... is provided free, and the whole rent is a surplus and none of it is a social cost" (1933: 107). Another good treatment is by Bronfenbrenner (1971: Ch.14). Ground rent applies to the whole class of land incomes without reference to allocation among different uses. It would obtain even if all land and labor were homogeneous, and produced but one commodity.

Ground rent is distinguished from wages by the curse of Adam, that labor towards suppertime grows irksome, entails sacrifice of comfort, vacations, desired location, self-direction, often personal safety, and at all times represents a sacrifice of pleasant diversions. Wages are also a return on all the costs of rearing and maintaining the worker, and the future costs of retirement. For increasing numbers of people, work also represents a sacrifice of time spent on lucrative or destructive untaxed activities like stealing, rioting, vandalism, looting, mobbing, arson, smuggling, tax evasion, barter, etc. Idle hands are not just wasted, they make mischief. For many, work represents a sacrifice of welfare payments, whether from parents or the state (Gaffney, 1962: 146).

The issue is often couched in terms of whether rent is a "cost" to the individual "firm". That is something of a red herring. Land always has a cost in the sense that use A must preempt land from use B. Land never has a cost of being produced. These are simply two different meanings for one word, "cost"; no one should be bamboozled by that. Joan Robinson was not fooled. To repeat her wisdom (which warrants repeating), "From the point of view of society, land . . . is provided free, and the whole rent is a surplus and none of it is a social cost" (Robinson, 1933: 107).

The operational question is for tax policy, which the diversion about rent as a cost is designed to obscure. This question is, what will happen to the supply of land if you focus the property tax on land value, exempting capital? How will the tax affect the allocation of land? (The effect is at worst neutral, and will probably improve it because of the pressure of the cashflow effect.) How will the relief of capital from taxation affect the supply of capital, and the allocation of land and capital? (It will raise the supply of capital, and improve the allocation of both land and capital.) It is really not so complicated. Long-winded disputes over the meaning of "rent" are beloved by abstract theorists. They just distract us, as intended, from getting to the nub of the central question of public policy.

(4) Pareto introduces the use of indifference curves, crediting the device to F.Y. Edgeworth (1879: 119). The "indifference curve" technique is a way of recasting the discipline in several ways, too long and tedious to recount in full detail. Perhaps foremost, it makes it technically more difficult to explain and perceive simple points, thus excluding more people

from understanding, and facilitating obscure manipulations, insider argot, and unsupportable statements from authority.

The technique helps us shift from "cardinal" to "ordinal" rankings of welfare, avoiding those dangerous interpersonal comparisons (such as that every human body needs about the same daily bread to avoid hunger). It lets us escape from diminishing returns of labor or capital applied to fixed land, and refocus the analysis on the disembodied "firm" as the basic unit. These "firms" pick and choose among "inputs" or "resources," which are treated as perfectly symmetrical, and none of which needs to be called land any more. All can be had in any amount by the firm, and society is just a collection of firms so the society can have any amount of land at any time. Optimal substitution or trade-off is the main emphasis. Technically, the ideas of land rent and taxable surplus can still be expressed by use of the "indifference curve" technique, but only laboriously, obscurely, and indirectly, as intended.

Such is the heritage of the cynical misanthrope, Vilfredo Pareto, who wrote,

> Men follow their sentiment and their self-interest, but it pleases them to imagine that they follow reason (95).

8

The Chicago School Poison

Frank Knight is another pivotal figure. We have seen that he learned his J.B. Clark through Alvin Johnson at Cornell. Then he ruled the Chicago School for many years, bending it to his strong will and commanding personality. "The close personal relations of the Knight coterie, maintained for over half a century, has reinforced the strong common elements in their idea systems ..." (Reder, 1987: 415).

How did Knight come to Chicago? John D. Rockefeller funded Chicago spectacularly in 1892, and started raiding other campuses by raising salaries. Rockefeller picked the first President, William Rainey Harper. Harper picked the first economist, J. Laurence Laughlin, from Andrew Dickson White's Cornell (he liked Laughlin's rigid conservative and anti-populist views). Harper drove out Veblen in 1906, then died, leaving Laughlin in charge of economics until he retired in 1916. He passed the torch to J.M. Clark, the son and collaborator of J.B. Clark.[60] Frank Knight first came to Chicago in 1917 from Laughlin's Cornell. The apostolic succession is fairly clear from Rockefeller to Harper to Laughlin to Clark to Knight.

According to William Barber, the early institutional decisions helped shape the "observable outcome" at Chicago to this day: in plain English, Chicago is still the lengthened shadow of John D. Rockefeller (Barber, 1988d: 242, 248, 263–4, 265). We may assume that the man who hired publicist Ivy Lee to polish his tarnished reputation also picked his own private University President with that in mind. Rockefeller and Harper are long gone, but the problem they exemplify is as perpetual as the maldistribution of wealth and the corruption of politics. "It is not what has been given but what is hoped for that influences most the policy of

The Corruption of Economics

university authorities" (Ross, 1914: 166).

In terms of numbers, and intensity of feeling generated, Knight probably produced more NCEists and NCEism than anyone in history. He made no secret of his firm opposition to Henry George and ideas that might aid or comfort Georgists. His enduring interest and his viewpoint are clear from the title "Fallacies in the Single Tax" (1953).

In treating rent, Knight totally fuses the individual and the social viewpoints. A cost to one firm is a cost to society: there is no aggregation problem, no fallacy of composition, and no remote possibilty that "rent" might have more than the one meaning he assigned to it.

Anyway, to Knight all land value is a human product. The single tax, says Knight, is an invention of city men who never knew the soil (recall Alvin Johnson and his "fresh-cheeked maidens"). Among the human activities and investments that create land, by Knight, is "killing off previous claimants" (1924, rpt. 1952, pp. 167–69). It reads like a caricature of Chicago, but it *is* Chicago, from the fountainhead himself. The American Economic Association has laid on its hands, reprinting it as a "classic".

Consistently, Knight also argues that slave-owners had just title to their slaves, because of society's sanction, and – note this well – because there was open competition for the capture of slaves (1953: 810). Competition is the key, it can justify anything. Presumably this would also justify lesser forms of larceny and embezzlement, so long as thieves compete, but Knight does not address this matter. There is some irony in that Knight's roots lay deep in the "Land of Lincoln". "Summary liberation" of slaves, i.e. Lincoln's Emancipation Proclamation, was unethical according to Knight. Compensation was due the owners – not, apparently, the slaves. He does not tell us what persons in "Society" should bear the necessary taxes to do so. One wonders if the young Knight had ever been allowed to read *Huckleberry Finn*. His paramount value is protecting property in unearned wealth.

"Society" was to blame for slavery, wrote Knight, and society should pay (cf. Ely, 1914: 779, cit. Young, 1916: 305). Could this be the origin of the allegedly "knee-jerk liberal" doctrine that hoodlums who gun down robbery victims are blameless because it is society's fault? Little wonder that Knight later wrote that the competitive system lacks most elements of fairness (1935: 60). Was he not projecting onto the system his own grim fairy-tale of what it should be, and reacting against his own travesty?

Consistently, again, Knight wrote that land yields no unearned surplus so long as competition keeps the returns to individuals at market levels (1924, rpt. 1952: 167–69). A "run of free income" (as Veblen called it), ceases being a surplus to Knight as soon as someone buys it from someone else. Similarly, monopoly profits would become competitive as soon as B bought a share in the monopoly from A. This ideological position was taken also in the same decade by W.I. King (1921), R.T. Ely (1927), and Shannon and Bodfish (an Ely employee) (1929), and has grown universal among NCEists. An "efficient market" is now one in which arbitrage has adjusted purchase prices such that every new buyer makes just a competitive return on what he bought, regardless of what that might be (we have already seen Knight apply this to slaves). The origins of property are of no concern, only the trade in property.

The market is also "efficient" so long as no opportunity for arbitrage goes unexploited. It's a wonderfully circular, self-vouching system of thought: by definition, no such opportunity does go unexploited. Getting back to basics, an efficient land market would seem to be one that got land allocated to its highest and best use. In NCE, this is assumed to be the by-product and result of arbitrage. It is as though betting on a horse-race is what makes a certain horse win. Indeed, William T. Ziemba, Professor of Management Science at the University of British Columbia, has provided us with an appropriate model, a perfect travesty of Knight's idea of an efficient market. "My system is based on the premise that the racetrack, like the stock market, is an *efficient market* – ..". Betting is efficient, says Ziemba, because "The odds created by the betting public generally reflect a horse's actual chances of winning a given race" (Ziemba, 1988). Those ideas overlook that the odds do not affect the outcome (plus, in this case, it does not matter which horse wins anyway). Land prices are in some ways like the horse race. They rise and fall from exogenous causes. Buyers bet on the outcome without affecting it. Knight's thought takes us so far away from basics that a professor of management science can mistake arbitrage for social efficiency.

"Choice" is everything to Knight. "Apart from a necessity of choosing, values have no meaning or existence". "... The cost of any value is simply the value that is given up when it is chosen" (1924, rpt. 1952: 167–69). Knight is clear that this undercuts classical ideas about taxing rent.

Knight did not rest with just defining away land rent. He also saw the need to define away land itself, following J.B. Clark. A strong and easily conveyed argument for untaxing buildings while "uptaxing" land is that it removes a disincentive to replace or remodel decrepit, obsolete buildings and other capital. Capital, unlike land, has a finite life. It depreciates and is reproduced. That is, it turns over. The reciprocal of turnover is a period of time, which the Austrians call a "period of production". This was anathema to Clark, who wanted to erase the difference of land and capital by making capital deathless, like land, and have capital consist of a mystical essence that could "transmigrate" into land and explain its value.

Knight took up Clark's anti-Austrian attack with multiplied vigor. In this context, anti-Austrian means anti-Georgist. Clark attacked Böhm-Bawerk in one or two articles; Knight churned out twelve, by Stigler's count (1987: 57, col. 1), against Hayek, Machlup, Lange, and Kaldor. "Knight denies the existence of any 'primary' factors of production [read land] which contain no capital, and equally he denies the possibility of measuring the period of production ..". Stigler claims "victory" for his old master, using the rather circular survival test that he has used elsewhere to define industrial efficiency. It is doubtful if Stigler would accept a popular vote to choose truth over error. It is no better, and perhaps a good deal worse, to accept the verdict, if that is what it is, of a profession whose role models are the likes of Clark, Edgeworth, Walker, Pareto, Ely, and Knight himself.

In the course of this anti-Austrian attack, Knight goes so far as to commit the "fallacy of the disappearing inventory". According to him, the existence of capital lets us treat inflow and outflow of goods through inventories as simultaneous. Likewise we may treat production and consumption as simultaneous, however long goods are stored up in inventory (Knight, 1946: 387; this traces back to Clark, 1893a). It is something like saying we may treat collegiate matriculation and graduation as simultaneous, so long as there is a stock of students. The result of such thinking is to bypass the whole question of what capital is and does, and, damagingly for George, to erase a primary distinction of capital from land. Knight uses the point for this very purpose.

The lost distinction is that capital turns over; it is continuously being used up and replaced by hiring labor to produce more. The longer it takes capital to work through the pipeline, the more capital is required per worker and per unit of output, and the higher is the ratio of capital to labor. Add to that, the pipeline itself is capital. Likewise, since pipes occupy space, the more land is required. To keep the distinction of land and capital well lost, Clark and Knight were forced to dispute the Austrian capital theory,[61] which each of them did in their oft-cited debates with, respectively, Böhm-Bawerk and Hayek. These celebrated exchanges seem quite tedious and pointless, and even mystical, until one realizes their essential role in the imperative to slam the lid on Henry George and his idea of treating land and capital separately. They were essentially battles of anti-Georgists vs. anti-Marxists.

Auguste Comte, founder of "Positivism," taught that all science deals either with relations of coexistence or relations of sequence. Production economics as taught today deals solely with relations of coexistence, ignoring relations of sequence. The popular Cobb-Douglas function[62] exemplifies the point. "Capital" there simply exists as a quantity at a point in time. Sequence virtually disappeared from standard economics until Keynes revived it in a macroeconomic context. Even Keynesians had to work out a "vertical" or instantaneous multiplier to communicate with people whose system of cognition left them uncomfortable with matters of sequence over time.

Production economics, meanwhile, has evolved into manipulation of symbols purporting to represent quantities of labor and capital conceived as substitutes at a point in time. Micro theorists avoid handling the sequential relationships, that labor produces capital and investment employs labor. They avoid defining capital, and explaining what unit of quantity measures it. The abstract axiomatic reasoning in microeconomic theory that students are forced to take as "The Core" of economics deals exclusively with these stylized relations of co-existence. This reasoning ignores the formation, measurement, meaning, depreciation and replacement of capital. Appreciation of land gets short shrift.

Knight, like Edgeworth and Pareto, had a dark, cynical, misanthropic outlook. "Truth in society is like strychnine in the individual body, medicinal in special conditions and minute doses; otherwise, and in general, a deadly poison. ..." (1947: 325, cit. Stigler, 1987: 59). The spirit is at an opposite pole from that of Henry George. Knight was not born to love anyone so *Menschlich* as George.

9

The Bafflegabbers

Willford I. King believed that land is equally distributed. The Editors of the august *Journal of Political Economy* let him prove this, in an attack on Harry G. Brown, by publishing the following (in which he is sarcastically referring to himself in the third person). "He states that in a certain village with which he is familiar there are about a hundred families of somewhat equal wealth who all own their homes" (King, 1924). Critics of George and his advocate, Harry G. Brown, were not held to very strict standards of scholarship in the Chicago house organ.

The *JPE* did give Harry G. Brown a good deal of space, it is true, but reading the kind of reply they let King publish tells one they were just baiting Brown. King's 1924 article is sarcastic, contemptuous, unedited rhetoric from beginning to end, with no shred of support for its wild-swinging allegations and reactionary value judgments. Brown was a neo-classically trained economist who used neo-classical tools to plead the Georgist case before other NCEists. He projected his own conscientious sincerity onto others. He thought he could reach them through reason, using their own tools and concepts. He was a very capable theorist; he pretty well failed. In one exchange, a critic is said to have written "Brown's mind is as twisted as his leg" (Brown was disabled).[63]

Elitist as Pareto, King is capable of this: "... the man who saves and invests his savings in such property (land) is a citizen worthy of emulation and .. the thriftless man who does not accumulate such 'vested rights' is an object for scorn, derision, or contempt ..." (King, 1924: 608).

King sees the rise of land value as part of the return to capital (1921), hence an incentive payment to stimulate saving and investing in real capital. That is not good investment theory, by today's standards. Today we would call this a "rent-seeking" explanation, and most economists would agree, I believe correctly, that such rent-seeking, where it works out as King posits, diverts investing out of its "natural channels" (as Spahr would have put it). They would also agree that in equilibrium, arbitrage pushes up the purchase price of land at the beginning of the investment cycle such that the land buyer receives only a market return on this price. In the Chicago creed, no opportunity for arbitrage goes unexploited.

The net result is to raise the overall credit requirement for being in business. To a NCEist that means no effect at all, but to small, marginal businessmen and renters of all kinds it is a large effect. It screens out many who otherwise would have enough capital to enter or remain in business – a matter of distressingly little concern to modern economists who, like Stigler, measure success solely by survival (what is it about Chicago that blinds people to circular reasoning?). It forces business owners to be tenants. The writer has developed this point in "Land as a Unique Factor of Production," published elsewhere in this CIT series (1994), in 1973, and in 1993b.

Carl C. Plehn was not a general in the war against George, but a colonel with an important regional command. As such, he is emblematic of many other minor figures, and will be taken as typical. He graduated from Hopkins under Ely, then held the fort at Berkeley from 1896 for about 35 years, as Dean of Commerce and Professor of Public Finance. His *Introduction to Public Finance* ran to five editions, 1896–26. California and some other states "utilized his ideas in the formation of their tax systems" (Cookingham, 1988: 277). Just what those ideas are takes a little inferring. His style is equivocating and divagating: one sentence often seems not to follow from another, but to swap subjects and premises ("bafflegab" and "doubletalk" are popular expressions for it). Here are some of the relevant points in his basic text, 1896 version. I have paraphrased liberally, to "cut to the chase". The impression of chaos and confusion is not injected, but substantially lessened from the original.

Initial street improvements may be charged to the benefited landowners, but all later costs should be charged "to the people" (p.66).

"No nation has ever found it feasible to adopt any single tax as the sole source of its income" (p. 105). George's proposal is a "scheme" with an "ulterior" purpose: "he aims, like the socialists, at a new distribution of property" (p. 106). This is "unjust," "inexpedient" (no reasons are given), and "not feasible". It is unjust because "The value of land, like that of other wealth, depends on the use to which it may be put". This is one of Plehn's many non-sequiturs, without further explanation.

The land tax is not feasible because "in no case would the scheme yield sufficient revenue". "It has been estimated" (no source is given) that the land rent of England is inadequate (p. 108). No data are offered (nor could be, since England lacked a valuation of its land; the constitutional crisis of 1909 was precipitated over a proposal to value land, thus exposing it to taxation). In the United States, according to Plehn, data are *not* available to separate land from building values (p.108). (He seems to have this completely backwards. In fact, in California at that time, land and buildings were valued separately.)

This alleged lack of US data does not deter Plehn, however, from stating with confidence and authority that the land base is too small. Getting into finer detail, George's "scheme" would shift taxes to farming lands. In the "professionalization of economic science," it seems, this paramount rule obtained: any stick will do to beat Henry George. (The revenue potential of land has been estimated in Gaffney, 1970, and is explored further in *Private Property and Public Finance*, a companion CIT volume.)

A high rate of land tax, necessitated by the small base, will "ruin the user of the land, and practically prohibit its cultivation" (p. 109). (No support is given for this, but it certainly is frightening.) Some allege, writes Plehn, that untaxing capital will add to the taxable capacity of land, but that is untrue (no reasons are given) (p. 109). Later he is to contradict this, noting that a property tax on the outstanding balance of mortgage loans is shifted to equity owners in higher interest rates (pp.225,249,252). According to the same logic, a tax on buildings is shifted into lower land prices. Consistency, however, was no problem for Plehn: he was the only authority within 1500 miles.

> Every kind of economic wealth ... frequently ... yield(s) its owner an 'unearned' increment (p. 109).
> A single tax ... will ... defeat its own ends by repressing the existence of the phenomenon which forms the signal for its assessment (p. 109).
> The general property tax is a failure ... it will have to be abandoned.... No words are too strong to express the iniquities of this tax (pp.218–19).

Property should be taxed on its income, not its value (p.219).

> ... modern economic theory does not regard rent as an inevitable surplus,
> ... (p.220)
>
> Unlike the land tax the building tax is regularly assessed each year (p.223).
>
> So few farms ... are rented that they need not be considered (p.254, n.l).

The land tax is partly shifted "when the land is used for agricultural purposes". This leads to a boom/bust cycle in which marginal farmers are often "ruined". In this way, the burden falls on "the farmers," even though the land tax may be shifted. Farmers are overtaxed by the land tax (pp.254–55). Taxes on urban buildings cannot be shifted; they are the same as land (p.255). Likewise, a tax on profits cannot be shifted (p.257).

Plehn's first edition, 1896, says little about income taxation. In his fifth edition (1926: 272, cit. Groves, 1946: 168, n.30) we do find an idea that is curiously missing from other early NCEists, but was just awaiting the 16th Amendment to surface. Plehn refers to unearned increments of land value as "capital gains," a camouflage that has of course become standard. He wants them exempt from income taxation on the grounds that it would be double-counting to consider both the anticipation and the realization of higher rents as income.[64] Harold Groves disposes of this tersely and nicely. Capital gains "arise not as a flow of income from the fountain, but from the sale of the fountain itself. ... If depreciation and obsolescence ... are (negative) income, ... appreciation ... seem(s) entitled to the same status (i.e. as positive income)" (Groves, 1946: 166, 180). Amen.

Interestingly, Plehn's position, seemingly so *simpatico* to rent-takers, took a long time to work its way into NCE, and is not all the way home yet. Professors Haig of Columbia and Simons of Chicago gave their names to the doctrine that increases in a person's wealth are income and should be taxable; they have many followers. How explain this failure of NCEists to press an advantage for rent-takers? Half an answer lies in their recognition of the paramount importance of the doctrine of uniformity. If "capital" gains were not income, that would mean they were unearned and non-functional, hence liable to even higher taxation, or outright confiscation, outside the income tax framework. Another part of the answer is that it is possible, and even standard, to endorse Haig-Simons in principle, but then cop out with the claim that it cannot be administered, winning points with both sides while leaving the money with the rent-takers. Study of NCEists has made us cynical, but the rest of the answer may lie in the actual sincerity of believers in income taxation.

Seligman is Plehn's ultimate authority: Plehn cites him many times, slavishly. The only apparent reason for using his own book instead of Seligman's was to collect the royalties. Nearly all his ideas are borrowed, and garbled in transcription. Plehn illustrates how a writer of practically no ability could hold down and sterilize an important outpost for forty years, contributing practically nothing, so long as he clucked forebodingly against land taxation in the approved NCE manner. Multiply Plehn by 100 or so, multiply that by the average number of students each such professor confused, bored, and twisted, and you have the tragedy of American higher education in economics.

10

The Bitter Harvest

Neo-classical economics has dominated thinking and policy now for half a century or so. The results are better than those achieved in Eastern Europe, but NCEists cannot take credit for our market economy, much as they boast of it. The North Atlantic nations had a well-oiled market economy functioning long before NCE drove out classical and progressive economics. What can NCEists claim as *their* heritage, their contribution to our well-being? "What have they done for us lately?"

They have achieved power, and implemented much of their program. They have dismantled most of the reforms of the Progressive Era, and discredited their rationale. They have successfully stifled the movement to convert the general property tax into a pure land tax. Going further, they have shifted taxes off property, especially land, and onto payrolls and retail sales, beyond Ely's dreams. They have achieved "uniformity" in income taxation, and more, given preferential treatment to land income and unearned increments. They have substantially deregulated utility and railway rates, and seen that regulatory commissions are drawn from the monopolies being regulated. They have privatized, or are privatizing, much of the public domain (including fisheries, the radio spectrum, water, and the right to clean air) without compensation to the public. They have done away with obsolete urban mass transit by substituting average-cost pricing for the old Georgist-Hotelling marginal-cost pricing supplemented by taxes on land value. They have turned the banks loose to lend on speculative land values, and bailed them out when they failed.

They have nullified the Progressive Era electoral reforms by pouring money into politics and "deep lobbying," including higher education, to achieve Abram Hewitt's goal and "make men who are equal in liberty content with inequality in property". In the name of "freedom to choose" they have subsidized land speculators by extending public services in every direction at the expense of median taxpayers who occupy small plots of land. They have starved pre-collegiate education that serves everyone, and subsidized graduate education that serves the few. They have poured ever more of our tax money into prisons, to uphold respect for law and order. Clark and Pareto and Seligman and Fetter and Johnson and Ely, surveying the scene from their heavenly thrones, must glow with pride. Let us, however, look at this Utopia they have created for us.

Worsening condition of labor

1. The share of labor in national income has been falling; the share of property has been rising. (If we include imputed income, unrealized capital gains, interest on the national debt, and pensions, the share goes higher.) In spite of this rise, the rate of saving and capital formation is falling. A rising share of property income is going to aliens.

2. Real wage rates have fallen in the USA since about 1975, for given kinds of work. At the same time, American youth is turned into worse and worse kinds of jobs. Real wages of men with a high school education fell 21%, 1973–91. Those with less than a high school education fell 26%. Wages of young urban black workers fell 50% (sic!) (*Business Week*, 29 June 1992: 91). This has forced women into the labor market. The proportion of women working, or seeking jobs, rose from 38% to 58%. According to David Ellwood, Harvard Professor of Public Policy, this, rather than the welfare system, is what accounts for the rise of single parenting. Women have less incentive to marry, and stay married. Rising welfare may have had some impact from 1960–70. Since 1975, however, real benefits have fallen.

3. Unemployment has risen to chronically high levels. NCEists shrug it off by defining it away. The "natural" or "normal" rate of unemployment keeps rising: 2%, 3%, 6%, 11%, ... there is no natural cap, apparently, on what NCEists will call natural so long as they are in power. Rising employment, once an occasion to celebrate, has become bad news: NCEists automatically tighten money to choke it off. Joblessness is just a personal taste in the NCE cant: "To explain why people allocate time to ... unemployment, we need to know why they prefer it to all other activities"

(Lucas, 1986). Others say the unemployed are just engaged in the vital economic function of "job search".

4. Homelessness has risen to new heights, in spite of decades of subsidies to home-building, favorable tax treatment of owner-occupied residences, and an excessive diversion of national capital into residences. The problem, apparently, is "not production, but distribution," to resurrect an old phrase long discarded by Paretian NCEists. The 1990 Census shows that 10% of all dwelling units in the USA stand empty at any given time – many of these are the second homes of the more affluent. In California, affluent Newport Beach has the highest fraction of its units vacant. As to the homeless, in the NCE world some people just have a "taste" for sleeping over heating grates, under freeways, in cardboard boxes, and in doorways. In the NCE paradigm they are engaged in the vital economic function of "home search," a search they conduct every evening. They are guided in this by "rational expectations". Either that or they are "mentally disturbed": irrationality puts one beneath and outside the NCE system.

5. Hunger is still with us. "Second Harvest," a nationwide network of food banks, reports that children account for half of all people needing help from food pantries or soup kitchens, and 73% of households it serves have incomes under $10,000. As Congress debated terminating The Emergency Food Assistance Program (TEFAP), they got the following advice from Robert Rector of The Heritage Foundation:

> It's not surprising that 10% of the American public is lining up to get free meals. But it doesn't mean they're malnourished. The more welfare assistance you give to people, the more dependence you have. (Dixon, 1994).

It is not reported that he or his Foundation have agitated to lower payroll taxes, which fine people for working, or retail sales taxes, which fine people for supporting their families. Most NCEists support such fines, then join Rector in "blaming the victim".

6. Beggary, once rare, is everywhere, here in the midst of great wealth and capital and new technology and universal education, all the NCE panaceas which are supposed to make jobs. You might call it, "Progress and Poverty," a phrase worth jotting down.

The current NCE answer to these problems is to downsize labor forces in major industries to make them "leaner and meaner". "Efficiency" and "productivity" have become identified with layoffs. In some unknown future this is supposed to create new jobs by making us more "competitive".

Worsening returns to capital

In spite of worsening returns to labor, we also have a worsening condition of capital.

1. The returns on savings are at historically low levels, especially after taxes and inflation.

2. The domestic saving rate is low. This implies a high consumption rate, which Keynes *et al* said would help us, but it does not seem to be working that way – a matter on which neo-Keynesians are silent.

3. Foreign savings rates in Japan and Europe, which bailed the US out in the 1980s, seem to be drying up, too, following the collapse of Japan's "bubble economy," and the onset of recession in Europe.

4. American capital is increasingly decayed and obsolete, as old capital is replaced too slowly. The US has lost much of its steel and auto industries. Many power plants and oil refineries are ancient, with grandfather rights to continue polluting the air people breathe. Much public capital is too old, its replacement made highly expensive by the low density per mile of line. New York City, which in 1902 was able to build and operate a subway charging 5 cents to ride anywhere, now cannot even maintain and operate what it already has, even while charging fares so high they can hardly be collected.

5. The US financial system is a shambles, surviving only by virtue of loading hundreds of billions of dollars of bad debts onto the taxpayers.

The concentration of wealth and income is high and rising

A higher share of the national income is going to property. As a simple test of this, the labor-price of land has risen sharply, for residential or business use. The labor-price of an American farm, for example, has risen from 6 years' industrial wages to 17 years, 1954–87 (Gaffney, 1992a). (In terms of farm wage rates, the labor-price is a good deal higher in both years.)

As to urban residences, The California Association of Realtors publishes a regular "Affordability Index". It shows the fraction of households that could afford to buy the median price house. They assume 20% down, and

30% of income used on monthly payments, with a 30-year mortgage. In November, 1990, the index said that only 32% of households could afford to buy a house at the US median price of $ 130,000. (That means a debt of $104,000, payment of about $11,000/yr., indicating income of about $37,000).

A report by Ernst and Young, and the National Real Estate Index, relates the monthly cost of buying a standard house to take-home pay. It varies from lows of 18% in Omaha and Kansas City to highs of 50% in San Francisco and 49% in Honolulu.

During the 1980s the merger movement reached new heights. It has long since been shown that mergers lead to lower output, more downtime, fewer jobs, and alienation between employer and community. It is obvious to all that "investment" in mergers and acquisitions creates no new wealth nor capital nor jobs.

The number of American farms has fallen from 6 million to 1 million, 1920–90 while the population rose. In 1900 there was one farm per 11 Americans; in 1987 only one per 113. At the same time, the Gini Coefficient (a measure of concentration) among the farms that remain has risen from .57 in 1910 to .76 in 1987 (Gaffney, 1992a). It is possible to adjust the Gini Concentration Coefficient for the loss of farms, by adding the lost 5 million farms to the data universe as farms with zero acres. Doing so, the 1987 Ratio is .92 instead of .76 (Gaffney 1992a).

Income has grown more concentrated, too, but its Gini Ratio is much lower than that for property ownership of any kind. Likewise, its increase is less. That is because so much of income, at least as defined and measured by NCE statisticians, consists of the gross cash flow from labor.

The modern enclosure movement of common property resources proceeds apace. The ocean fisheries, until recently open to all, are being privatized through licensure. While this may be necessary to avoid overuse, it is not necessary to give the newly minted licenses away, as is being done. Former fishermen have become instant millionaires, living in idleness and luxury by renting their licenses to working fisherman, suddenly creating a class structure where before there was equal opportunity. Air polluters, instead of being fined or charged *pro rata* of their effluents, are being given "Offset rights" to sell. The radio spectrum has been and is being given away in valuable chunks. Having once made J. Werner Kluge of Virginia into

America's second richest person, the FCC has now given the McCaw company so much of this public domain that it recently sold out to AT&T for $12.5 billion. Forty-year contracts to receive irrigation water from Federal projects are currently being converted into perpetual ownerships that the original contractors may sell to the highest bidder. These "innocent" purchasers are to receive not just the water, but a right to demand that the taxpayers subsidize their water service (storage, conveyance, quality protection, etc.) forever. The national parks are being turned over to private concessionaires, some of them politically selected, who charge what the traffic will bear while paying no more than token rents to the public that owns the parks. Offshore oil and gas are being auctioned off to private lessees under a system that the major oil firms seem to control and manipulate to their major advantage. The Forest Service is spending $10 on roading for every $1 in forest revenues, in some marginal areas. All these giveaways, the kind of things the Progressives stopped, are back in full fashion to the loud cheering of the "new resource economists," steeped in NCE and Ayn Rand.

Social problems we thought were cured

Americans have experienced a sharp loss of community. There is little place for the sense of public service, or honor or patriotism or duty or loyalty or devotion or dedication or responsibility in NCE: it is cynical of such values. The family is an anachronism, a communistic unit. Private individuals, motivated by individual self-interest, make the system work. Public servants are assumed to be moved by the same self-seeking. Those who think otherwise are fools or hypocrites.

That philosophy has a self-fulfilling quality. It is a short step from that to their viewing themselves as chumps and suckers if they act for the public weal. "Heroic," in NCE lingo, is a term of reproach; "bribery" is rational. Selling out one's country for cash is not inherently bad, in NCE thinking, it is expected. Accordingly, we now have retired Congressmen lobbying for foreign powers, without remorse or rebuke. We even have unretired Congressmen representing foreign powers, does not NCE teach that individuals should serve those who pay them? We have national treasures sold to aliens, we have defense secrets sold to foreign spies, all justified by going for the top dollar. After all, the marginal productivity of the stealth bomber might be higher to Iraq's Air Force than to ours.

"Greed is good," as Gordon Gekko put it, is the central NCE creed. Ayn Rand and Harry Browne are the new Messiahs. Church is still tolerable, but only if it narrows its focus to individual salvation: social concerns (like those of Moses and Jesus) are out. Almost anything public or common is suspect: public schools, public health, public transit, public parks and beaches, public monitoring of weights and measures, public inspection of foods and drugs, common rights of citizenship, public safety, public restrooms, public care of the feebleminded, common waters, common land, common carriers, public utilities, public broadcasting, public courtesy, social behavioral controls, public financing of political campaigns, the public good.... Only the public roads are acceptable, because they may be used and dominated by private vehicles. The individual driver, windows closed except to toss out trash, door locked, air-conditioner running, muffler cut, catalytic converter bypassed, radio receiving advertising, cellular phone in hand, by-passing accidents and road kill to avoid getting involved ... Is this a caricature of NCE, or is this how many Americans spend hours a day in modern sprawl cities, living with settlement patterns framed by NCE values?

The rich used to live in plain view, in the big house on Main Street. They may have flaunted their wealth and abused their power, but they saw and were seen. They took some responsibility for their towns, and exercised some leadership: they and their tenants were in the same boat, their common city. Now, class divisions are reinforced by spatial segregation, as we follow the NCE panacea and "vote with our feet" (wheels, actually). The rich cluster in exclusive suburbs and gated communities, or move off entirely to enclaves at Aspen, La Jolla, or Palm Beach. They never even have to see their tributaries any more, but relate to them through their stockbrokers, agents, and the hired police.

Accordingly, alienation is the norm, and crime rates have soared. The rejected, the unwanted, the landless might say with Richard T. Ely himself, "Do you want me to commit suicide?" Idle hands are not simply wasted, they steal, murder, burn and destroy. Persons and property have become notoriously insecure. The cumulative social costs of guarding against assault, theft, arson, vandalism, trespass, extortion, embezzlement – all the arts of gross and petty crime – amount to a large fraction of the national income. The combination of democratic forms with our divisive distribution of wealth, and our NCE leaders' distaste for full employment, makes crime the most attractive allocation of effort for millions of Americans, even though crime typically costs the victim much more than it gains the criminal.

A culture of individual crime easily coalesces into mob crime, triggered by some dramatic grievance, real or imagined. Now we have periodic civil disturbances and insurrections, and the cost of putting them down. In 1992 large parts of Los Angeles were torched, for the second time in a generation, pretty much as foreboded by Henry George in *Progress and Poverty*, Book X. Such colossal waste and barbarism traces right back to the NCE policies that alienate great masses of able people.

In the shadow world between crime and business there is now the vast, gray underground economy. Tax evasion is the poor man's tax avoidance, and our modern high taxes on exchange and production and payrolls and income arrange it so that many people can only survive by evading taxes. Street hawkers evade both taxes and high rents, and in some neighborhoods constitute a chronic force. Once one is outside the law, other illegal acts easily follow. The best-known of these is, of course, drug-dealing. It is now a major industry, with a major counter-industry, the "narcocracy," dependent on it. Rent-free and tax-free and highly portable, it is the natural outlet for those whom NCE policies push off the upperworld. Or did they expect them just quietly to commit suicide?

The national stature is dropping fast

The USA, once so self-sufficient, has grown dangerously dependent on importing raw materials, dependence so high that we are subject to extortion by our loyal OPEC "allies". To some extent this is based on simple gains from trade, and is so rationalized by faithful NCEists. It has some other, less creditable causes. One is that NCE policies have stamped on our country the most energy-intensive, resource-wasting land settlement pattern in the world, and in human history. This is the result of heeding R.T.Ely's admonition that land speculators "perform social service". Another cause is that our industry and farming are now folly dedicated, by ideology and tax-bias, to displace labor with capital and land. Capital and land require fossil-fuel energy as a complement, where labor substituted for such energy.

Another cause is that American-based land speculators, especially after World War II, have acquired shadowy titles to mineral holdings around the world, under the US military umbrella. Following J.B. Clark, they have created value and wealth from those otherwise worthless natural elements, recalling that Clark (1886, p. 10) taught us that wealth is created "from the mere appropriation of limited natural gifts...". The cost of the military umbrella was mainly borne by US payroll-tax payers. Having firmed up their titles, the new owners performed more social service by gaining privileged admission to the US market, thus raising our dependency on foreign sources.

The USA, recently the "arsenal of democracy" and the most efficient producer of almost every manufacture, now grows increasingly dependent on foreign manufactures. To live in our inefficient cities, and to pay several species of payroll taxes, American workers need premium wages. The burden on employers grows too great. Relieved by NCE individualism of ancient prejudices of patriotism and loyalty, they dump American workers and transfer operations abroad.

It is notorious that the USA, which once led the world in basic international comparisons of welfare and performance, is falling behind: in public health, in infant survival, in longevity, in literacy, in numeracy, in athletics, in wage raters, in mental health, and so on. To be sure, these are interpersonal comparisons, which Pareto taught are "most unsatisfactory," and are purged from NCE. Does this say they have no meaning? Perhaps, rather, it is NCE with its Paretian welfare criteria that has no meaning.

The USA, recently a metropolitan power center, is en route to becoming again what it was in the 19th century, an economic colony. Alien ownership is rising in the centers of power and culture, and wherever else land is highly rentable and lightly taxed. In the post-Progressive culture property wields more political power than citizenship, and it is becoming a question in some areas whether citizens as such carry as much weight as alien landowners. Indeed, there are now many water service districts in California, clothed with the powers and immunities of sovereign governments, in which only landowners can govern, and voting is in proportion to landowership.

Electoral setbacks in Greece, Lithuania, Poland, and Russia in 1993/94 show that the current NCE model pushed by the IMF-World Bank establishment is having trouble competing even with communism, even in nations that know the worst face of communism. No longer is the US model so attractive that desperate nations yearn for it above all else.

American education no longer leads the world. Privatized education in the form of commercial TV, given free use of the public domain to operate for private gain, has to a high degree superseded public education. NCE theorists should be pleased, but one can wonder: our culture is impoverished. The public schools encourage the reading of Jane Austen and Charles Dickens; they try, at least, to teach mathematics. TV gives us murder, rape, soaps, racing cars, alcohol, drugs, "gangsta rap," tabloid news, sound-bites, spectacles, and kinky sex. In the NCE view TV adds most to the national product, guided by consumer sovereignty. Public schools and libraries, being public, are inherently suspect. Public libraries are forced to serve as public restrooms for the homeless. Alternately starved and harassed, public institutions take the blame for all the intellectual faults generated by a society and economy dominated by NCE and its values.

Summing up, the recent harvest of NCE and its derived public policies is a worsening condition of labor, lower returns to saving, high and rising concentration of wealth and income, rising class divisions and social problems, and a fall of national stature. It should be enough to make us realize that NCE, forged as a strategem to discomfort Henry George and Georgists, is intellectually, morally, and practically bankrupt.

References

1 Patten later brought Scott Nearing to Pennsylvania, and encouraged other Progressives there. I cannot say if this means he was inconsistent, or inefficient, or genuinely tolerant, or a late convert to the single-tax. What is certain is that he bent his own academic work to accommodate the protectionist views and interests of his employers at Wharton School of Business.

2 Actually, Ely gradually shifted after 1893 from a classical definition of capital, limiting it to "products," to a Clarkian definition including land with capital (Fetter, 1927: 154). The shift was gliding and marked by ambiguities, which we will see is characteristic of Ely.

3 This is also called "the excess burden of indirect taxation," "the excise tax effect," and various epithets.

4 Laffer's invocation of George was, alas, opportunistic. When the chips were

down, Laffer fully supported Prop. 13 in California in 1978. He refused to acknowledge that half of the California property tax base consisted of land value.

5 Reagan-Bush tax policies actually withdrew preferential treatment from new investing and lowered rates on unearned income from land, while raising rates on payrolls.

6 "Trust no future, howe'er pleasant; let the dead past bury its dead. Act, act, in the living present, heart within and God o'erhead!"

7 Few recognized it at the time. A notable who did was Jacob Stockfisch, 1956, who, however, viewed it negatively. Stockfisch was a student of Earl Rolph, who had absorbed his Clark, Knight, and Seligman thoroughly. Stockfisch was a close associate of William Niskanen, adviser to President Ronald Reagan, and now head of the libertarian Cato Foundation. Another student of Rolph was George Break, whose student in turn was Michael Boskin, Chair of President George Bush's Council of Economic Advisers, where he crusaded to lower tax rates on unearned increments to land prices. Thus the lineage proceeds, generation to generation.

8 A long collection of dismal quotes from Alan Greenspan, Paul Samuelson, Henry Wallich, Otto Eckstein, Milton Friedman, and Arthur Okun is assembled in M. Gaffney, 1976: 101; and M. Gaffney, 1977: 58.

9 Such, for example, is the misleading implication of the now standard and generally excellent biography by Charles A. Barker.

10 Pacifists might question including the war years in the Georgist period, but consider this. Newton D. Baker, former single-tax Mayor of Cleveland, Ohio, was made Secretary of War. Under him the US had the most impartial, democratic draft policy we have ever known: no one could buy his way out. Baker's policies contrast with the neo-classical ideal of a mercenary army, articulated by Milton Friedman. Consider also that the original income tax details were forged by Georgists like Congressmen Warren Worth Bailey and Henry George, Jr. Rates during the war were set high enough so we paid for the war without borrowing as much as any of the other powers, and we did it *without taxing labor income* more than trivially. Consider also that in 1917, for the first time, the US Treasury sold bonds directly to the public, cutting out the Morgan-Seligman cartel of middlemen.

11 The first income tax legislation, passed by Congress in 1916, was crafted by Congressman Warren Worth Bailey, single-tax publisher from Johnstown, Pennsylvania. It exempted almost all wage and salary income. One of his many allies was Congressman Henry George, Jr. (D-Brooklyn). The story is told in W. Elliot Brownlee, 1985, "Wilson and financing the Modern State:

The Revenue Act of 1916," *Proceedings of the American Philosophical Society* 129(2): 173–210.

12 Congressman John I. Nolan of California introduced it in Congress on February 7, 1920 (H.R. 12,397). Note how its drafters copied the legal logic of the corporation income tax, rather than using the 16th Amendment.

13 Zangerle and Somers worked in Cleveland; Purdy in New York City; Babcock in Chicago.

14 The French signalize this in their inimitable style. They give two meanings to the verb *percevoir*: to perceive, and to tax.

15 Nothing could be more ironic than this happening in a State whose capitol is named for the Junker Otto von Bismarck. We see below how Bismarck's educational apparatus helped give NCE its anti-Georgist orientation.

16 Two excellent works on the venality and tyranny of college trustees and administrators during this period are Sinclair, 1923, and Veblen, 1918. Several more such works are needed today. Most academics could, if they had the will and the insight, write them from their own careers.

17 For example, Elizabeth Dilling, a leading alarmist of the 1930s, includes the following prominent Georgists and quasi-Georgists as members of "the red network": Wm. S. U'Ren; Frederic C. Howe; Newton D. Baker; Benj. C. Marsh; Upton Sinclair; Louis D. Brandeis; Louis F. Post; John Dewey; Philip Snowden; J. C. Wedgwood; "Mr. Asquith"; Sun Yat Sen; Carrie Chapman Catt; Jackson Ralston; Warren S. Blauvelt; Geo. H. Duncan; Alice Thatcher Post; Herbert Quick; National Popular Govt. League; People's Lobby; Harry Laidler; Otto Cullman; F.C. Leubuscher; Broadus Mitchell; Clarence Darrow; John S. Codman; John R. Commons; John Ise; and Helen Swift Neilson (Dilling, 1934). My father, a moderately liberal school superintendent, had to regulate his public life carefully to forefend Mrs. Dilling's fatal finger. It could cost one his job, and might have when she named him in the pages of the Chicago *Herald-Examiner*. One of his faculty, a free-spirited English teacher had assigned *The Communist Manifesto* to a class including her son, Kirkpatrick. Such unwelcome attentions intimidate many more than those actually named.

18 The writer has documented this in Gaffney 1970, 1971, and 1993.

19 This does raise another concern, whether such effects might lower the value of land as a tax base. It would be biased to debit George on this point, without crediting him for the equity and efficiency gains that lead to it. Still, it must be addressed, and we do so in a forthcoming CIT volume (*Private Property and Public Finance*).

20 George Gilder (getting a little carried away) even writes that human

intelligence is now the only limiting resource, and resource constraints are an obsolete notion.

21 They called him "The Prophet of San Francisco". He turned out to be The Prophet of Los Angeles – its riots and arson, that is.

22 Leon Walras impugned the character and motives of conservative economists of the French establishment, especially Bastiat, more savagely than ever Henry George impugned his targets, and for the same reasons. It is an interesting question why Leon was forgiven, and George was not. It is probably because Leon, like Mill, pulled his punches: he proposed compensating landowners before taxing them. One may insult the hired help so long as one does not threaten the existing maldistribution of wealth.

23 Fred Foldvary coined this apt term recently. See his contribution to *Land and Taxation* (Editor: Nicolaus Tideman), London: Shepheard-Walwyn/ CIT, 1994

24 Post was also the author of Labor Day, and Assistant Secretary of Labor, 1913–20. He was to conduct an heroic rear-guard action against the stampede engineered by Mitchell Palmer and J. Edgar Hoover to deport US labor leaders.

25 Before that Butler was Dean of the Faculty of Philosophy. I surmise that my original source, a careful scholar, has a basis for the statement, and the error is only a detail. Wall Street, New York City, and Columbia University had interlocking directorates.

26 Concerning the political ambitions, machinations, connections, and low academic productivity of Butler see Sinclair, 1923, Chaps. I–XIII. Sinclair conceived his low opinion of higher education as a student at Columbia.

27 Figures are from E.R.A. Seligman's introduction of the man he ribbed familiarly as his "benevolent despot," N.M. Butler, at a banquet in honor of J.B. Clark. Apparently he had lost the exact count.

28 *Dartmouth College v. Woodward*, 4 Wheat. 518 (1819).

29 George and Georgists regarded franchises as forms of landownership, and would subject them, like all lands, to heavy taxation. They rather quickly worked out what is now called the principle of marginal-cost pricing for decreasing-cost services, and would regulate fares at low levels, where appropriate, making up the fare-box deficit through land taxation. Cleveland's mass transit applied this system under Georgist Mayor Tom L. Johnson, 1901–10; New York City kept its subway fare at 5 cents for decades under this system. The brilliant economist Harold Hotelling rather timidly formalized this concept in 1938. Kenneth Arrow (1987) characterizes his position as "market socialism," but that is a blind spot: it is pure Georgism, restated after

the fact for the Econometric Society.

30 Some notable cases were the firing of Edward W. Bemis from Chicago, for speaking out for the strikers in the Pullman case, offending a potential donor, the head of the Chicago and Northwestern Railroad (Barber, 1988: 252–53); the dismissal of Edward A. Ross from Stanford for advocating public power and transit; the dismissal of Veblen in 1909. The overt domination of Stanford by Leland's widow, Jane Stanford, was notorious (Cookingham, 1988: 280–89; Sinclair, 1923: 152–68). Mrs. Stanford at one point put the Stanford faculty on her payroll as personal servants. It was an infighting maneuver among rival robber barons, but an accurate statement of the faculty's status. Leland and Jane Stanford had originally founded their university on the advice of a medium hired to communicate with the ghost of their deceased only child (Wallace, 1905).

31 The scenario fits almost exactly Ibsen's *An Enemy of the People.*

32 Nearing told Upton Sinclair that he commanded larger and more interesting audiences after the Pennsylvania dismissal (Sinclair, 1923: 449). In 1922 Nearing was still so dangerous that the President of Clark University interrupted and closed a visiting lecture he was giving to a student club, literally ordering the lights put out. On this occasion his offense was quoting from Veblen on *The Higher Education in America* (Sinclair: 296–97).

33 This much is from family lore (Clarke was my great-uncle). Professor John Henry (1992: 16, n.11) believes that threats to religion were seen as threats to property. I am not at all persuaded of this, considering the uses to which Darwinism was put by Spencer, Huxley, Sumner, *et al.* Clarke himself was a Roosevelt Republican, perhaps slightly to the right of J.B. Clark, a Cleveland Democrat.

34 There was little reason to suspect Ely of anything but loyalty to rent-takers, as we will see below.

35 Professor Henry's works on Clark are stimulating and well-researched. We maintain a long, friendly correspondence. Our differences stem, I believe, from the domination of modern radical scholarship by those who overestimate the role of Marx.

36 Frank Knight, 1946. The profession took this nonsense with all gravity. A Committee of the American Economic Association (Bernard Haley and William Fellner) laid on its hands by selecting this article for reprinting in its *Readings in the Theory of Income Distribution*, 1951: 384–417.

37 J. and W. Seligman Brothers had a lock on a fixed share of the distribution of US Treasury bonds, along with Belmont, Rothschild, and Morgan. In 1917 the Treasury cut out the middlemen, with no apparent loss of efficiency

(Myers, 1907: 560, n.10).

38 This is laid between the lines, as absurd points must be to get by, but it is central to the argument he makes. What he says is that a tax on housing will drive capital out of housing unless land is also taxed, which will drive it back into housing. Uniformity is thus what makes taxes neutral. The corollary is that to tax land and not capital would drive too much capital out of land and into housing.

39 McLure, then a Treasury official, gave intellectual guidance. Politically, the leaders were Congressman Daniel Rostenkowski, Chair of the House Committee on Ways and Means, and Senator Robert Packwood, head of the Senate Finance Committee. Both of the last two later achieved notoriety on other grounds. The power of those who write tax laws has led others into temptation before (like Andrew Mellon and Wilbur Mills, each in his own way).

40 Seligman repeats this point verbatim through 10 or more editions of *Essays in Taxation*, Chap. III, sect. 4. He really means it. The original phrasing actually came from Charles Spahr (1891: 632).

41 George had given most of his emphasis to the extensive margin of production. Critics of the "any-stick-to-beat-Henry-George" school accuse him of overlooking the intensive margin, but a careful reading of George shows otherwise. E.g. he writes that when wages fall, labor resorts "... to inferior lands, *or to inferior points on the same lands* ..." (1879: 169). This phraseology, repeated elsewhere, clearly refers to an intensive as well as an extensive margin.

42 George Stigler exhumed them in 1969, *J. of Law and Economics* 12:181–226. The itch to giggle at the ghost of George continues to run high, even among those who insist he is inconsequential and forgotten.

43 A Lorenz Curve is simply information organized in this manner: the top 4% of the landowners have 53% of the land, etc.

44 Ely refers only to "Mr. Sage". This would be Henry W. Sage, a resident of Ithaca who made a fortune speculating in western timberlands. By coincidence the better-known Russell Sage was, with Ezra Cornell, a major Western Union stockholder.

45 Ezra Cornell was guaranteed a 7% return on his investment before the College got its share (Gates, 1943: 35–36, 56–57). Gates, a Cornell historian, hints vaguely that E.C. may have pocketed more than he should (p.58). Sometimes he did not pay for the scrip up front. Those, however, are only incidental suspicions.

46 There are no adequate sources on this neglected era, but some usable ones are

Young, 1916; Miller, ca. 1919; Fillebrown, ca. 1901–20; Whitlock, 1925; Steffens, 1931; Geiger, 1933: 381–478; and Fels. Brownlee, 1985, is very good on its limited topic. Historians have focused excessively on George the person, to the neglect of the movement that throve for twenty-five years following his death.

47 This strange locution is repeated verbatim in Fetter, 1933: 149.

48 Genealogical evidence suggests that Ely was distantly related to the present writer: his mother was Harriet Mason from Massachusetts. His works resonate with *simpatico* old New England verities. We also share common backgrounds in western New York, Wisconsin, Chicago's North Shore, and the study of land economics. My father, like Ely, studied at Heidelberg. So much sadder the regret at our differences, which are deep.

49 Gilman and White had remarkably parallel careers. They went to Yale together; they overlapped at the University of Berlin (Barber, 1988: 210); they were attachés together in the US Embassy at St. Petersburg (*New Columbia Encyclopedia*); they exploited the Morrill Act together. White engineered Gilman's appointment at Hopkins, patronized Ely in Berlin, and then placed Ely with Gilman (Barber, 1988: 210). Later he helped Ely found the American Economic Association, although White was an historian. Another ally was Timothy Dwight, President of Yale. Many tracks lead back to Yale. Something ambitious was stirring there: this is the same Yale generation that took over the lands of Hawaii in the name of Christian conversion. To these Yale divines, Skull and Bones was more than a club, it was an ensign. Conspiracy theorists revel in the "secret society" Skull and Bones connections. This writer lacks the expertise to form any opinion on this "spooky" aspect, and finds Sutton's (1983) treatment too disjointed, even though provocative and often factual. Sutton also seems to mysticize what is more obviously explained as common class interest and clubbiness. For whatever reasons, the community of academic economists was thick as thieves.

50 In 1888 he had written tolerantly, even favorably of the results of early Ohio experience with focusing the property tax on land value (1888: 135, cit. Ralston, 1931: 155). "Ely changed his economic views upon making a fortune as a land speculator" (Ralston: 156).

51 Jackson H. Ralston wrote *The Law and Procedure of International Tribunals* (1926, Stanford University Press), based on his experience in the field. He was also attorney for the American Federation of Labor for 26 years. After 1928 until retirement he lectured at Stanford on International Arbitration.

52 Jackson Ralston was later a Judge, and visiting Law Professor at Stanford.

He was the leader of various single-tax campaigns in California. Congressman John I. Nolan of California introduced the present Bill in Congress on February 7, 1920 (H.R. 12,397). Note how its drafters copied the legal logic of the corporation income tax, rather than using the 16th Amendment.

53 Data to test and refute this lay in 1923 income tax returns. In 1923 and 1924 Congress made this information public, for the first and last time. Jorgensen uses it effectively to refute Ely, citing the *Report* of the Secretary of the Treasury, 1923: 11 (Jorgensen, 1925: 76).

54 "Colonization company" was at that time a euphemism for a land speculator.

55 Lowden's stature was such that in 1924 he declined the Republican nomination for vice-President – he evidently thought he should head the ticket. Lowden contested Hoover for the 1928 Republican nomination. Their main difference was that Lowden favored subsidies for farm landowners (Hicks, 1960: 201–202).

56 These included some of my ancestors, but that was long ago and has played only a minor role in forming my biases, such as they may appear to the reader. My Irish grandfather was a militant Fenian in the late 1860s, joining in the abortive invasion of Ontario by Irish-American veterans of the Civil War. However, he soon repudiated the leadership of that fiasco, and ended his career as a puritanical Presbyterian clergyman in upstate New York. In any event he died in 1911, well before my birth.

57 This seems inconsistent with the denial that interpersonal comparisons are valid, but untangling Edgeworth is a full career that I will not enter.

58 Better yet, let the reader consult Pareto's books and articles. The *Manual*: 349 ff., consists of disjointed misanthropic ravings. Pareto, 1893, is totally cynical and nihilistic, with no constructive end in view.

59 The unwary modern reader might assume this to refer to Tolstoy's pacifism, but Pareto himself was an anti-militarist. The context of these remarks is opposition to leveling and redistribution of wealth. Pareto favored the use of force internally, to maintain the unequal distribution of wealth. He opposed almost everything else done by governments, including international war. This is consistent with his anti-leveling spirit. International wars generally result in stronger community feelings and higher taxes. George himself was not a pacifist, but a supporter of Lincoln. He also volunteered in an abortive venture to back Juarez against Maximilian in 1865 (Barker, 1955: 70).

60 J.M. Clark was probably a good and moderating influence on J.B. Clark, all in all, but J.B. Clark was still the dominant influence on J.M. Clark: father, teacher, dissertation chair, and finally predecessor in the chair J.M. Clark got at Columbia.

61 To repeat and remind, Clark and Knight could not abide Austrian capital theory because it distinguished land from capital by stressing that each item of capital has a period of investment from birth to exhaustion.

62 This is a stylized "production function" in which output is an instantaneous function of labor and capital, each described as a quantity at a point in time.

63 This is in the oral tradition. It was told me years ago by Dr. Walter Chryst, a Brown student, now deceased. I believe the writer was King. I have not confirmed it otherwise.

64 I have not researched whether this is original with Plehn. Whoever did originate it, it surely has become a major point of rent-takers in our times.

Bibliography

Other bibliographies are in the works cited below by Bullock, Cord, Dwyer (1980), Ellickson, Ely (1938), Ely and Wehrwein, Gaffney (1982), Hollander, J.D. Miller (including a list of more bibliographies), and Skouras. Barker lacks an alphabetical bibliography, but the notes may be mined for many original references. *The New Palgrave* is essential.

Ackerman, Joseph, and Marshall Harris (eds.), 1946. *Family Farm Policy*. Chicago: University of Chicago Press

Alonso, William, 1964. *Location and Land Use*. Cambridge: Harvard University Press

Andelson, Robert (ed.), 1979. *Critics of Henry George*. London, and Cranbury, N.J.: Associated University Presses, Inc., and Fairleigh-Dickinson University Press

Andelson, Robert, and Mason Gaffney, 1979, "Seligman and his Critique from Social Utility," in Andelson (ed.), *Critics of Henry George*: 284–89

American Academy of Political and Social Science (AAPSS) 1915, *Annals* 58:149–227, March (single-tax discussion)

Argyll, Duke of, 1893. *The Unseen Foundations of Society*. London: John Murray

Arrow, Kenneth, 1987. "Hotelling, Harold". In Eatwell, John; Peter Newman, and Murray Milgate (eds.) *The New Palgrave Dictionary of Political Economy* London: The Macmillan Press, Ltd.

Babcock, Frederick, 1932. *The Valuation of Real Estate*. New York: McGraw-Hill

Bailey, Warren Worth. Bailey Collection of Manuscripts, Princeton University Library.

Barber, William J., (ed.), 1988. *Breaking the Academic Mould: Economics and American Learning in the Nineteenth Century*. Middletown, CT: Wesleyan University Press

Barber, William J., 1988a. "Political Economy from the Top Down: Brown University". In Barber, William J. (ed.), q.v.: 72–94

Barber, William J., 1988b. "Political Economy and the Academic Setting before 1900: an Introduction". In Barber, William J. (ed.), q.v.: 3–14

Barber, William J., 1988c. "Political Economy in the Flagship of Postgraduate Studies: The Johns Hopkins University". In Barber, William J. (ed.), q.v.: 203–224

Barber, William J., 1988d. "Political Economy in an Atmosphere of Academic Entrepreneurship: The University of Chicago". In Barber, William J. (ed.), q.v.: 241–265

Barker, Charles A., 1955. *Henry George*. New York: Oxford University Press

Becker, Arthur P. (ed.), 1969. *Land and Building Taxes: Their Effect on Economic Development*. Madison: University of Wisconsin Press

Black, R.D.C., A.W. Coats, and C.D.W. Goodwin, 1973. *The Marginal Revolution in Economics*. Durham, NC: Duke University Press.

Blauvelt, James G., 1936. "George L. Record, a Foreword". In Record, q.v.

Böhm-Bawerk, Eugen v., 1895–96. "The Positive Theory of Capital and its Critics". *Quarterly Journal of Economics* 9:121 ff.

Böhm-Bawerk, Eugen v., 1907–08. "The Nature of Capital: a Rejoinder". *Quarterly Journal of Economics* 22:30 ff.

Bogart, William T., David F. Bradford, and Michael G. Williams, 1992. "Incidence and Allocation Effects of a State Fiscal Policy Shift: The Florio Initiatives in New Jersey". Working Paper No. 4177, National Bureau of Economic Research, Cambridge, MA. Rpt. *National Tax Journal*, December, 1992

Bowles, Samuel, and H. Gintis, 1976. *Schooling in Capitalist America*. New York: Basic Books

Bracewell-Milnes, Barry, 1993. Review of Burgess, *Public Revenue without Taxation*, in *Business Economist* Vol. 25, Winter 1993: 52. Cites *Land and Heritage*, Hobart Paper 93, Inst. of Ec Affairs, 1982

Bronfenbrenner, Martin, 1971. "The Theories of Rent" Ch.14, in his *Income Distribution Theory*. Chicago: Aldine.

Brown, Harry G., 1932. *The Economic Basis of Tax Reform*. Columbia, MO: Lucas Bros.

Brownlee, W. Elliot, 1985. "Wilson and Financing the Modern State: The Revenue Act of 1916," *Proceedings of the American Philosophical Society* 129(2):173–210.

Bullock, Edna, 1917. *Selected Articles on the Single Tax*, 2nd Ed. New York: H.W. Wilson Co.

Cannan Edwin, 1907. "The Proposed Relief of Buildings from Local Rates". *Economic Journal* 17:36–46

Cirillo, Renato, 1980. "The 'Socialism' of Leon Walras and his Economic Thinking". *American Journal of Economics and Sociology*, July: 294–303

Cirillo, Renato, 1981. "The Influence of Auguste Walras on Leon Walras". *American Journal of Economics and Sociology* July: 309–16

Clark, Colin, 1965. "Land Taxation: Lessons from International Experience". In Peter Hall (ed.), *Land Values*. London: Sweet and Maxwell

Clark, J.B., 1886. *The Philosophy of Wealth*. Boston: Ginn & Co.

Clark, J.B., 1888. *Capital and its Earnings*, Publications of the American Economic Association vol. III, no. 2, May

Clark, J.B., 1890a. "*De l'influence de la terre sur le taux des salaires*". *Revue d'Economie politique*, tome 4, Mai-juin: 252–71. Extrait, Paris, Larouse.

Clark, J.B., 1890b. "The Ethics of Land Tenure". *International Journal of Ethics*, October. Reprinted, 17 pp.

Clark, J.B., 1890c. "The Moral Basis of Property in Land". *Journal of Social Science*, October: 21–28. (This is Clark's paper at the Saratoga "Single Tax Debate" with Henry George, q.v.)

Clark, J.B., 1890d. "The Law of Wages and Interest". *AAAPSS* l(1):43–65

Clark, J.B., 1891a. "Distribution as Determined by a Law of Rent". *Quarterly Journal of Economics*, April: 289–318.

Clark, J.B., 1891b. "Marshall's Principles of Economics". *Political Science Quarterly* 6Pp. 125–51. (*PSQ* was ed. at Columbia, by its faculty, including Seligman, who was its founder. It would be fair to call Seligman a patron.)

Clark, J.B., 1892. "The Theory of Rent". *The Christian Register*, Jan. 7.

Clark, J.B., 1893a. "The Genesis of Capital". *Yale Review*, Nov.: 302–15.

Clark, J.B., 1893b. "The Surplus Gains of Labor". *Annals* of the AAPSS, v.3, no.5: 607–17. Rpt. *Publications of the AAPSS*, no.85

Clark, J.B., 1895a. "The Origin of Interest". *Quarterly Journal of Economics*, 9(3):April, 24 pp. Reprinted.

Clark, J.B., 1895b. "Real Issues Concerning Interest". *Quarterly Journal of Economics*, Oct.: 98–102

Clark, J.B., 1899. *The Distribution of Wealth*. New York: Macmillan.

Clark, J.B., 1903, The Cooper Union debate on the single tax between Louis F. Post and John B. Clark. *The Single Tax Review*, April 15: 1–16.

Clark, J.B., 1907a, *Essentials of Economic Theory*

Clark, J.B., 1907b. "Concerning the nature of capital: a reply to Dr. Eugen von Böhm-Bawerk". *Quarterly Journal of Economics*, v.21: 351–70, May. Transl. to German by Dr. Josef Schumpeter. *Zeitschrift fur Volkerwirtschaft*, v. 16: 426–40, 1907.

Clark, J.B., 1911a. "Land and Building Taxation". *New York Tribune*, Dec. 1.

Clark, J.B., 1911b. "Taxation on Buildings". *New York Tribune*, Nov. 21.

Clark, J.B., 1913a. "Proposed Surtax Erroneous in Principle". *Real Estate Record and Builder's Guide*, Feb. 1.

Clark, J.B., 1913b. "Shall we Tax the Unearned Increment?" *Globe and Commercial Advertiser*, Feb. 1

Clark, J.B., 1914a. "Concerning Wealth that Resides in Land". *Globe and Commercial Advertiser*, Jan. 24

Clark, J.B., 1914b. "Dangers of Increased Land Tax Pointed Out by Noted Economists". *Globe and commercial Advertiser*, Jan. 17.

Clark, J.B., 1914c. "Realty Experts Warn Against New Tax Bill: Summary of Professor Clark's Views". *New York Press*, Feb. 1.

Clark, J.B., 1914d. *Social Justice Without Socialism*. Boston and New York: Houghton, Mifflin Co.

Coats, A.W., 1987a. "Seligman, Edwin R.A". In Eatwell, John; Peter Newman, and Murray Milgate (eds.) *The New Palgrave Dictionary of Political Economy* London: The Macmillan Press, Ltd.

Coats, A.W., 1987b. "Ely, Richard T". In Eatwell, John; Peter Newman, and Murray Milgate (eds.) *The New Palgrave Dictionary of Political Economy* London: The Macmillan Press, Ltd.

Coats, A.W., 1988. "The Educational Revolution and the Professionalization of American Economics". In Barber, William J. (ed.), q.v.: 340–75

Collier, Charles, 1976. "Henry George's System of Economic Analysis and Criticism". Ph.D. thesis, Duke University

Collier, Charles, 1979. "Clark and Patten: Exemplars of the New American Professionalism". In Robert Andelson (ed.), *Critics of Henry George*. Rutherford, N.J.: Fairleigh-Dickinson University Press

Collier, Charles, 1991. "Henry George's System of Political Economy". In Lissner and Lissner (eds.), q.v.: 413–42

Commons, John R., 1893. *The Distribution of Wealth*. New York: Macmillan

Commons, John R., 1922. "A Progressive Tax on Bare Land Value". *Political*

Science Quarterly 37:41–68

Cookingham, Mary E., 1988. "Political Economy in the Far West: The University of California and Stanford University". In Barber, William J. (ed.), q.v.

Cord, Steven B., 1965. *Henry George: Dreamer or Realist?* Philadelphia: University of Pennsylvania Press, 1965

Cornick, Philip, 1938. *Premature Subdivision and its Consequences.* New York: Institute of Public Administration, Columbia University

Davenport, H.J., 1909. "Exhausted Farms and Exhausting Taxation". *Journal of Political Economy* 17:354–62

Davenport, H.J., 1917. "Theoretical Issues in the Single Tax". *American Economic Review* 7:1–30

de Mille, Anna George, 1950. *Henry George: Citizen of the World.* Chapel Hill: University of North Carolina Press

Dennett, L.L., 1916. "Irrigation District Bonds backed by Miracle Project". *The San Francisco Call and Post*, 15 January: 7

Dennett, L.L., 1916. "Irrigation District Work makes Arid Land Flourish". *The San Francisco Call and Post*, 16 January: 9

Dewey, Donald, 1987. "Clark, John Bates". In Eatwell, John; Peter Newman, and Murray Milgate (eds.) *The New Palgrave Dictionary of Political Economy* London: The Macmillan Press, Ltd.

Dilling, Elizabeth (Kirkpatrick), 1934. *The Red Network*. Published by the author, 545 Essex Rd., Kenilworth, Illinois; also 53 W. Jackson Blvd., Chicago

Dixon, Jennifer, 1994. "10th of US hungry, study says". AP. Riverside (CA): *The Press-Enterprise*, March 9: A3

Douglas, Paul, 1972. *In the Fullness of Time.* New York: Harcourt, Brace, Jovanovich

Douglas, Roy, 1976. *Land, People and Politics.* London: Allison and Busby

Dwyer, Terence M., 1980. "A History of the Theory of Land Value Taxation". Ph.D. dissn., Harvard, under Richard Musgrave. Excellent bibliography

Dwyer, Terence M., 1991. "Henry George's Thought in Relation to Modern Economics". In Lissner and Lissner (eds.): 296–306

Edgeworth, F.Y., 1879. *The Hedonical Calculus*. Rpt. *Mathematical Psychics*, 1881, London: C. Kegan Paul Co.

Edgeworth, F.Y., 1881. *Mathematical Psychics*. London: C. Kegan Paul & Co.

Edgeworth, F.Y., 1906. "Recent Schemes for Rating Urban Land Values." *The Economic Journal* **16**: 66–77.

Ellickson, Donald, 1966. "A History of Land Taxation Theory". Ph.D. dissn., Wisconsin, under Harold Groves. Excellent bibliography.

Ely, Richard T., 1885. "Henry George and the Beginnings of Revolutionary Socialism in the United States". Chapter 2 in his monograph, *Recent American Socialism*. Baltimore: The Johns Hopkins University

Ely, Richard T., 1886. *The Labor Movement in America*. New York: T.Y. Crowell Co.

Ely, Richard T., 1888. *Taxation in American States and Cities*. New York: T.Y. Crowell Co.

Ely, Richard T., 1893. *Outlines of Economics*. Orig. Meadville, PA, and New York: Flood and Vincent. Several editions and reprints, for 45 years. Orig. 1884, *Introduction to Political Economy*, Chautauqua Literary and Scientific Circle

Ely, Richard T., 1914. *Property and Contract in their Relation to the Distribution of Wealth*. New York: Macmillan

Ely, Richard T., 1920. "Land Speculation". *Journal of Farm Economics* 2:121–36

Ely, Richard T., 1922. "The Taxation of Land". *Proceedings of the Annual Conference of the National Tax Association* pp.24–54. Harrisburg, PA: National Tax Association

Ely, Richard T., 1922. *The Outlines of Land Economics*. Vols. I–III. Ann Arbor, Michigan: Edwards Brothers.

Ely, Richard T., 1924. *Taxation of Farm Lands*. St. Paul: Webb Publishing Co.

Ely, Richard T., 1927. "Land Economics". In Hollander, Jacob (ed.), q.v.: 119–35

Ely, Richard T., 1938. *Ground Under our Feet: an Autobiography*. New York: Macmillan Co. Includes complete chronological bibliography of Ely.

Ely, Richard T., and George Wehrwein, 1940. *Land Economics*. New York: The Macmillan Co. (other editions and publishers, 1928–64)

Ely, Richard T., and Edward W. Morehouse, 1924. *Elements of Land Economics*. New York: Macmillan Co.

Erickson, James H., 1989. "Memo to Faculty and Staff, from the Vice Chancellor, University Relations and Development," 27 September. Riverside: The University of California

Fabian Society, 1950. *Fabian Essays in Socialism*, Jubilee Edition. London: George Allen and Unwin, Ltd.

Fels, Mary, 1919. *Joseph Fels: His Life Work*. New York: B.W. Huebsch

Fels, Mary, 1940. *The Life of Joseph Fels*. New York: Doubleday, Doran & Company, Inc. (This work makes no reference to the 1919 Huebsch book, which I have not seen. They may be much the same, but that is not certain.)

Fetter, Frank A., 1900. "Recent Discussion of the Capital Concept". *Quarterly

Journal of Economics 15 (November). Rpt. Fetter, 1977.

Fetter, Frank A., 1901a. "The Passing of the Old Rent Concept". *Quarterly Journal of Economics* 15 (May). Rpt. Fetter, 1977

Fetter, Frank A., 1901b. "The Next Decade of Economic Theory". American Economic Association, *Papers and Proceedings of the Thirteenth Annual Meeting* 2 (February). Rpt. Fetter, 1977

Fetter, Frank A., 1904. "The Relations Between Rent and Interest". American Economic Association, *Papers and Proceedings of the Sixteenth Annual Meeting* 5 (February). Rpt. Fetter, 1977

Fetter, Frank A., 1907. "The Nature of Capital and Income". *Journal of Political Economy* 15 (March). Rpt. Fetter, 1977

Fetter, Frank A., 1917. "Landed Property as an Economic Concept and as a Field for Research – Discussion". *American Economic Review*, Supp.7, March

Fetter, Frank A., 1927, "Clark's reformulation of the capital concept," in Jacob Hollander (ed.), *Economic Essays Contributed in Honor of John Bates Clark*. Freeport, N.Y.: Books for Libraries Press, Inc.

Fetter, Frank A., 1933. "Capital". In E.R.A. Seligman (ed.), *Encyclopedia of the Social Sciences*. Rpt. Fetter, 1977

Fetter, Frank A., 1977. *Capital, Interest, and Rent: Essays in the Theory of Distribution*. Edited with an Introduction by Murray N. Rothbard. Cosponsored and Copyright by the Institute for Humane Studies, Menlo Park, CA. Kansas City: Sheed Andrews and McMeel, Inc., Subsidiary of Universal Press Syndicate

Fillebrown, Charles Bowdoin, 1907. "The Single Tax". National Tax Association *Bulletin* 1:286–93

Fillebrown, Charles Bowdoin, 1912. *The ABC of Taxation*. Garden City, N.Y.: Doubleday, Page & Company.

Fillebrown, Charles Bowdoin, 1915. *Thirty Years of Henry George*. Boston

Fillebrown, Charles Bowdoin, 1917. *The Principles of Natural Taxation*. Chicago: A.C. McClurg

Fillebrown, Charles Bowdoin, ca. 1901–20. "MS Correspondence Regarding the Single Tax Movement". This was available from bookseller Robert H. Rubin of Brookline, MA, in 1991, but escaped me. The correspondents include the leading academic economists of the era.

Flux, A.W., 1894. Review of K. Wicksell and P.H. Wicksteed. *Economic Journal* IV:305–13

Fuller, Aaron B., III, 1991. "Selected Elements of Henry George's Legitimacy as an Economist". In Lissner and Lissner (eds.): 307–23

Furner, Mary, 1975. *Advocacy and Objectivity: a Crisis in the Professionalization of American Social Science*. Lexington, KY: University Press of Kentucky

Gaffney, Mason, 1962. "Land and Rent in Welfare Economics". In Marion Clawson, Marshall Harriss and Joseph Ackerman (eds.) *Land Economics Research*. Baltimore: The Johns Hopkins University Press. Pp. 141–67

Gaffney, Mason, 1969. "Economic Aspects of Water Resource Policy". *AJES* 28(2): 131–44, April

Gaffney, Mason, 1970. "Adequacy of Land as a Tax Base". In Daniel Holland (ed.), *The Assessment of Land Value*. Madison: Univ. of Wisconsin Press, 1970: 157–212

Gaffney, Mason, 1971. "The Property Tax is a Progressive Tax". *Proceedings, NTA*, 64th Annual Conference, Kansas City, 1971: 408–26. [Republished in *The Congressional Record*, March 16,1972: E 2675–79. (Congr. Les Aspin.) Resources for the Future Inc., *The Property Tax is a Progressive Tax*, Reprint No. 104, October 1972.]

Gaffney, Mason, 1973. "Tax Reform to Release Land". In Marion Clawson (ed.), *Modernizing Urban Land Policy*. Baltimore: Johns Hopkins Press: 115–52

Gaffney, Mason, 1976a, "Toward Full Employment with Limited Land and Capital". In Arthur Lynn, Jr. (ed.), *Property Taxation, Land Use and Public Policy*. Madison: Univ. of Wisconsin Press: 99–166

Gaffney, Mason, 1976b. "The Many Faces of Site-Value Taxation". *Report of Proceedings*, 27th Tax Conference, Canadian Tax Foundation, Quebec City: 749–63

Gaffney, Mason, 1977. "Capital Requirements for Economic Growth". Joint Economic Committee, Congress of the United States, *US Economic Growth from 1976 to 1986: Prospects, Problems and Patterns*. Vol. 8: 56–75

Gaffney, Mason, 1982. "Two Centuries of Economic Thought on Taxation of Land Rents". In Richard Lindholm and Arthur Lynn, Jr., (eds.), *Land Value Taxation in Thought and Practice*. Madison: Univ. of Wisconsin Press: 151–96

Gaffney, Mason, 1987a. "Brown, Harry Gunnison". In Eatwell, John; Peter Newman, and Murray Milgate (eds.) *The New Palgrave Dictionary of Political Economy* London: The Macmillan Press, Ltd.

Gaffney, Mason, 1987b. "George, Henry". In Eatwell, John; Peter Newman, and Murray Milgate (eds.) *The New Palgrave Dictionary of Political Economy* London: The Macmillan Press, Ltd.

Gaffney, Mason, 1987c. "Land Tax". In Eatwell, John; Peter Newman, and Murray Milgate (eds.) *The New Palgrave Dictionary of Political Economy* London: The Macmillan Press, Ltd.

Gaffney, Mason, 1987d. "Single Tax". In John Eatwell, Peter Newman and

Murray Milgate (eds.) *The New Palgrave Dictionary of Political Economy.* London: The Macmillan Press, Ltd., 1987.

Gaffney, Mason, 1987e. "Wallace, Alfred Russel". In Eatwell, John; Peter Newman, and Murray Milgate (eds.) *The New Palgrave Dictionary of Political Economy* London: The Macmillan Press, Ltd.

Gaffney, Mason, 1992a. "Falling Property Tax Rates and Rising Concentration". In G. Wunderlich (ed.), *Land Ownership and Taxation in American Agriculture.* Boulder: Westview Press

Gaffney, Mason, 1992b. "The Taxable Surplus in Water Resources". *Contemporary Policy Issues*

Gaffney, Mason, 1993a. "The Taxable Capacity of Land". *Papers Presented at The Conference on Land Value Taxation for New York State,* January. Albany, New York: The Government Law Center, Albany Law School. (There is also a separate volume with the oral *Proceedings.*)

Gaffney, Mason, 1993b. "Land Reform through Tax Reform". In Riel Franzsen and C.H. Heyns (eds.), *A Land Tax for the New South Africa?* Pretoria: The Centre for Human Rights Studies, Faculty of Law, Universiteit van Pretoria: 111–26

Gaffney, Mason, 1993c. "Whose Water? Ours". In Polly Dyer (ed.), *Whose Water?* Seattle: The University of Washington

Gaffney, Mason, 1994. "Land as a Unique Factor of Production". In Nicolaus Tideman (ed.), *Land and Taxation,* London: Shepheard-Walwyn/CIT.

Gates, Paul, 1943. *The Wisconsin Pine Lands of Cornell University.* Ithaca: Cornell University Press

Geiger, George R., 1933. *The Philosophy of Henry George.* NY: The Macmillan Co.

Geiger, George R., 1936. *The Theory of the Land Question.* NY: The Macmillan Co.

Groenewegen: D. (ed. & transl.), 1977. *The Economics of A.R.J. Turgot.* The Hague: Martinus Nijhoff

Groves, Harold M., 1946. Revised edition. *Financing Government.* New York: Henry Holt and Company

George, Henry, 1871, rpt. various dates. *Our Land and Land Policy.* New York: The Robert Schalkenbach Foundation

George, Henry, 1877, rpt. 1904. "The Study of Political Economy". In *The Complete Works of Henry George.* New York: Doubleday, Vol. 8:135–53

George, Henry, 1879, rpt. 1971. *Progress and Poverty.* New York: Schalkenbach Foundation

George, Henry, 1881. *The Irish Land Question.* New York: Schalkenbach Foundation

George, Henry, 1883. *Social Problems.* New York: Schalkenbach

Foundation

George, Henry, 1886. *Protection or Free Trade?* New York: Schalkenbach Foundation

George, Henry, 1898, rpt. 1971. *The Science of Political Economy*. New York: Schalkenbach Foundation

George, Henry, Jr., 1900. *The Life of Henry George*. Rpt. NY: Robert Schalkenbach Foundation, 1943

George, Henry. *Complete Works*. Garden City, NY: The Fels Fund. Also other publishers

Goldenweiser, E.A., and Leon Truesdell, 1924. *Farm Tenancy in the United States*. US Bureau of the Census, Monograph No. IV

Goldman, Eric, 1956. *Rendezvous with Destiny*. New York: Vintage Books

Goldman, Eric, 1979. Letter to the *Henry George News*, on the Centennial of *Progress and Poverty*

Goodrich, Carter, 1960. *Government Promotion of American Canals and Railroads*. New York: Columbia University Press

Goodwin, Craufurd D.W., 1973. "Marginalism Moves to the New World". In Black, Coats, and Goodwin (eds.), q.v.

Gottlieb, Robert, 1993. *Forcing the Spring: the transformation of the American environmental movement*. Island Press

Gray, Lewis C., 1914. "Rent under the Assumption of Exhaustibility". *Quarterly Journal of Economics* 28:464–89

Gray, Lewis C., Charles L. Stewart, Howard A. Turner, J.T. Sanders, and W.J. Spillman, 1923. "Farm Ownership and Tenancy". *Yearbook of Agriculture*. Washington: US Government Printing Office

Greider, William B., 1992. *Who Will Tell the People?* New York: Simon and Schuster

Groves, Harold, 1946. *Financing Government*. New York: Henry Holt & Co.

Hacker, Louis M., 1940, rpt. 1947. *The Triumph of American Capitalism*. New York: Columbia University Press

Haig, Robert M., 1915a. *The Exemption of Improvements from Taxation in Canada and the United States*. New York: The Committee on Taxation

Haig, Robert M., 1915b. "The Effects of Increment Taxes upon Building Operations". *Quarterly Journal of Economics* 29:829–40

Haig, Robert M., 1915c. *Some Probable Effects of the Exemption of Improvements from Taxation in the City of New York*, a Report Prepared for the Committee on Taxation of the City of New York. New York: Press of Clarence Nathan

Haig, Robert M., 1917. "The Unearned Increment in Gary". *Political Science*

Quarterly 32:80–94, March

Haig, Robert M., 1926. "Toward an Understanding of the Metropolis". *Quarterly Journal of Economics*, February and May

Haley, Bernard, and William Fellner, (a Committee of the American Economic Association), 1951. *Readings in the Theory of Income Distribution*, published for the AEA by Blakiston, Philadelphia

Hampton, George P., 1917. "The Farmer and the Single Tax". In Miller (ed.), q.v.: 261–66.

Harberger, Arnold, 1968. *The Taxation of Income from Capital.* Chicago: University of Chicago Press

Harrison, Fred, 1983. *The Power in the Land.* New York: Universe Books

Hayek, Friedrich v., 1936. "The Mythology of Capital". *Quarterly Journal of Economics*, Vol. L: 199–228, February; rpt. Fellner and Haley, 1951: 355–83

Hebert, Robert F., 1979. "Marshall: a Professional Economist Guards the Purity of his Discipline". In Andelson (ed.), q.v.

Henley, Albert T., 1957. "The Evolution of Forms of Water Users Organizations in California". *California Law Review* 45

Henley, Albert T., 1969. "Land Value Taxation by California Irrigation Districts". In Arthur Becker (ed.), *Land and Building Taxes.* Madison: UW Press: 137–45.

Henry, John, 1982. "The Transformation of John Bates Clark". *History of Political Economy* 14(2): 166–77

Henry, John, 1983. "John Bates Clark and the Marginal Product". *History of Political Economy* 15(3):375–89

Henry, John, 1992. "God and the Marginal Product". Paper delivered at annual meeting of the American Economic Association, New Orleans, January. MS: 1–37

Henry, John, 1994. Book-length MS on J.B. Clark, in progress

Herford, C.H., 1931. *Philip Henry Wicksteed, his Life and Work.* London: Dent and sons

Hibbard, B.H., 1930. "A National Policy to Conserve Land Values". *AAAPSS* 148:115–19.

Hibbard, Benjamin H., 1921. *An Analysis of the Ralston-Nolan Bill.* Chicago: The National Association of Real Estate Boards, June

Hicks, John D., 1960. *Republican Ascendancy.* New York: Harper and Brothers, Publishers

Hirshleifer, Jack, James De Haven, and Jerome Milliman, 1960. *Water Supply.* Chicago: University of Chicago Press

Hobson, J.A., 1897. "Influence of Henry George in England". *Fortnightly*

Review 2, December: 835–44

Holland, Daniel M. (ed.), 1970. *The Assessment of Land Value*. Madison: University of Wisconsin Press

Hollander, Jacob, (ed.), 1927, rpt. 1967. *Economic Essays Contributed in Honor of John Bates Clark*. Published on behalf of the American Economic Association. Publication Committee, in order listed: E.R.A. Seligman, R.T. Ely, J.H. Hollander, followed by a line, then B.M. Anderson, Jr., J.M. Clark. Freeport, N.Y.: Books for Libraries Press, Inc.

Homan, Paul T., 1928. *Contemporary Economic Thought*. New York, London: Harper and Brothers

Hotelling, Harold, 1938. "The General Welfare in Relation to Problems of Taxation and of Railway and Utility Rates". *Econometrica* 6:242–69

Howe, Frederic C., 1925. *Confessions of a Reformer*. New York: Scribner's Sons

Hoyt, Homer, 1933. *One Hundred Years of land Values in Chicago, 1833–1933*. Chicago: University of Chicago Press

Hutchison, T.W., 1953. *A Review of Economic Doctrines, 1870–1929*. Oxford: Clarendon Press

Hutchison, T.W., 1969. "Economists and Economic Policy in Britain after 1870". *History of Political Economy* 1:231–55

Hyndman, Henry, 1911. *Record of an Adventurous Life*. New York: Macmillan

Jaffe, Grace Mary Spurway, 1979. *Years of Grace*. Sunspot, NM: Iroquois House

Jaffe, William, 1975. "Leon Walras: an Economic Adviser Manquee". *Economic Journal* 85:810–23

Johnson, Alvin S., 1902. *Rent in Modern Economic Theory*. AEA Publications. Third Series 3, No.4

Johnson, Alvin S., 1914. "The Case against the Single Tax". *The Atlantic Monthly* 113:27–37

Johnson, Alvin S., 1927. "The Farmer's Indemnity". In Jacob Hollander (ed.) *Economic Essays Contributed in Honor of John Bates Clark*. Published on behalf of the American Economic Association. Publication Committee: E.R.A. Seligman, R.T. Ely, J. Hollander, B.M. Anderson, Jr., and J.M. Clark. Freeport, N.Y.: Books for Libraries Press, Inc.: 215–28. Reprinted 1967

Johnson, Tom L., 1911. *My Story*. NY: Huebsch

Jorgensen, Emil Oliver, 1925. *False Education in our Colleges and Universities*. Chicago: Manufacturers and Merchants Federal Tax League, 1346 Altgeld Street

Keiper, Joseph S., Ernest Kurnow, Clifford Clark, and Harvey Segal, 1961. *Theory and Measurement of Rent*. Philadelphia: Chilton Co.

Kerney, James, 1936. *The Political Education of Woodrow Wilson*. New York: Century

King, W.I., 1921. "Earned and Unearned Income". *AAAPSS*: 251–59

King, W.I., 1924. "The Single-tax Complex Analyzed". *Journal of Political Economy* 32:604–12

Knight, Frank, 1931–36. Eight works disputing the concept of a period of investment. Itemized in Hayek, 1936: 199, and rpt. 1951: 355, q.v.

Knight, Frank, 1946. "Capital and Interest". *Encyclopedia Britannica* 4:779–801. Republished in Haley and Fellner, q.v.: 384–417

Knight, Frank, 1953. "The Fallacies in the Single Tax". *The Freeman*, 809–11.

Knight, Frank, orig. 1924, rpt. 1952. "Some Fallacies in the Interpretation of Social Cost". In G. Stigler and K. Boulding (eds.), *Readings in Price Theory*. Chicago: R.D. Irwin

Kurnow, Ernest, 1959. "Measurement of land Rent and the Single Taxers". *Commercial and Financial Chronicle* 190:834, August

Kurnow, Ernest, 1960. "Land Value Trends in the United States", *Land Economics* 36(4):341–48, November

Kurnow, Ernest, 1961. "Distribution and Growth of Land Values". Three studies in Keiper *et al.*: 155–68

Landlines, 1994. Lincoln Inst. of Land Policy (a house organ), May

Large Landholdings in Southern California (A Report on), with Recommendations, 1919. Issued by California Commission on Immigration and Housing. Sacramento: California State Printing Office.

Lawrence, Elwood P. 1957. *Henry George in the British Isles*. E. Lansing, MI: Michigan State University Press

Lindholm, Richard W., and Arthur D. Lynn, Jr. (eds), 1981. *Land Value Taxation in Thought and Practice*. Madison: University of Wisconsin Press, 1981

Lissner, Will (ed.), 1941-date. *The American Journal of Economics and Sociology*. NY: Robert Schalkenbach Foundation

Lissner, Will, and Dorothy Burnham Lissner, 1991. *George and the Scholars*. New York: Schalkenbach Foundation

Lucas, Robert, 1986, "Models of Business Cycles". Paper prepared in mimeo. for the Yrjo Jansson Lectures, Helsinki, March: 18. Cit. Howard Sherman, 1993, "The relational approach to Political Economy". *Rethinking Marxism* Vol. 6, No. 4 (Winter 1993): 105

Lutz, Friedrich, and Vera Smith Lutz, 1951. *Theory of Investment of the Firm*. Princeton: Princeton University Press. Rpt. New York: Greenwood Press, 1969

Madsen, Arthur W., 1936. "Land Value Taxation in Practice". In Record, q.v.: 178–201

Marling, Alfred E., Chairman, 1916. *Final Report of the Committee on Taxation of the City of New York*. New York: The O'Connell Press

Marsh, Benjamin C., 1911. *Taxation of Land Values in American Cities*. New York

Marshall, Alfred, 1891 and ff. editions. *Principles of Economics*. London: Macmillan

Marshall, Alfred, orig. ms from 1883. See George Stigler, 1969, "Three Lectures on *Progress and Poverty*" *J. of Law and Economics* 12:181–226

Marx, Karl, 1867, rpt. 1906. *Capital*, trans. Samuel Moore and Edward Aveling. Chicago: Charles H. Kerr

Marx, Karl, orig. 1847. *The Poverty of Philosophy*. New York: International Publishers

Mason, J. Rupert, 1942. "The California Irrigation Districts Case". *American Journal of Economics and Sociology* 2(3):393–402

Mason, J. Rupert, 1949. "Land Reclamation and Land Tenure in California". Paper #6, *Proceedings*, Seventh Annual Conference to Promote land-value Taxation and Free Trade. London: The International Union

Mason, J. Rupert, 1957–58. "On Single Tax, Irrigation Districts, and Municipal Bankruptcy". An oral history conducted in 1957–58 by Willa K. Baum. Regional Oral History Office, Bancroft Library, University of California-Berkeley

Mason, J. Rupert, 1959. "Irrigation and Land Values in California". Papers of 10th International Conference, Hanover, West Germany. International Union for Land Value Taxation and Free Trade. Bancroft Library F862.25.M246

McLain, James J., 1977. *The Economic Writings of Du Pont de Nemours*. London

McLure, Charles E. Jr., and Peter Mieszkowski (eds.) Fiscal Federalism and the Taxation of Natural Resources. (Lexington, MA, and Toronto: D.C. Heath & Co., 1983)

Metropolitan Water District of Southern California, *Focus*, (a house organ), May, 1990.

Mill, John Stuart, 1872. "Influence of the Progress of Industry and Population on Rents, Profits and Wages". A chapter in his *Principles of Political Economy*. People's ed. Boston: Lee and Shepard

Miller, Joseph Dana (ed.), 1917. *Single Tax Year Book*. New York: Single Tax Review Publishing Company (Sun Building)

Miller, M.M., 1913. *Great Debates in American History*. Vol. 10. "The Single

Tax," pp. 52–109. New York: Current Literature Publishing Company

Moley, Raymond, 1962, rpt. 1975. *The American Century of John C. Lincoln.* New York: Hawthorne Books, Inc.

Myers, Augustus, 1907, rpt. 1936. *History of the Great American Fortunes.* New York: The Modern Library (Random House, Inc.)

National Tax Association, 1915. *Proceedings of the Eighth Annual Conference,* Madison, Wisconsin. Single Tax Session: 405–69

Nearing, Scott, 1915. "Land Value Increase in American Cities". *The Public,* Nov. 26: 1151, cit. Young, 1916: 280, n.69

Nearing, Scott, 1917. Analysis of Educational Governing Boards. *School and Society,* September 8

New York City, Public Library. Henry George Collection

Newman, Peter, 1987. "Edgeworth, Francis Ysidro". In Eatwell, John; Peter Newman, and Murray Milgate (eds.) *The New Palgrave Dictionary of Political Economy* London: The Macmillan Press, Ltd.

Ormerod, Paul., 1994. *The Death of Economics,* London, Faber and Faber.

Pareto, Vilfredo, 1893. "The Parliamentary Regime in Italy". *Political Science Quarterly* 8:677ff

Pareto, Vilfredo, orig. 1906 in Italian; 1927, French; 1971 transl. Ann S. Schwier. *Manual of Political Economy.* NY: Augustus M. Kelley

Patten, Simon N., 1908. "The Conflict Theory of Distribution". *Yale Review* 17:156–84, August

Pigou, Arthur C., 1949. *A Study in Public Finance.* 3rd rev. ed. London: Macmillan

Pinchot, Amos, 1936. "George L. Record, an Introduction". In Record, q.v.

Plehn, Carl C., 1896 et seq. *Introduction to Public Finance.* New York: The Macmillan Company; London: Macmillan & Co., Ltd.

Polak, Edward C., 1915. "Reduction of Tax on Buildings in the City of New York". *AAAPSS* 58:183–88

Pollock, W.W., and K.W.H. Scholz, 1926. *The Science and Practice of Urban Land Valuation.* Philadelphia: The Manufacturers' Appraisal Co.

Post, Louis F., (ed.) 1898–1913. *The Public.* Chicago

Post, Louis F., 1903, The Cooper Union debate on the single tax between Louis F. Post and John B. Clark. *The Single Tax Review,* April 15: 1–16

Post, Louis F., 1915. *Taxation of Land Values* 5th ed. Indianapolis: The Bobbs-Merrill Company

Post, Louis F., 1923. *The Deportations Delirium of 1920.* Chicago: Charles H. Kerr & Company, Co-operative

Post, Louis F., 1930. *The Prophet of San Francisco.* NY: Vanguard Press

Purdy, Lawson, 1929. *The Assessment of Real Estate.* 4th ed. New York: National Municipal League

Quesnay, Francois, 1759. *Tableau Economique.* Paris

Ralston, Jackson H., 1931. *What's Wrong with Taxation?* San Diego: Ingram Institute

Record, George L., 1936. *How to Abolish Poverty.* Jersey City: The George L. Record Memorial Association

Reder, M.W., 1987. "Chicago School". In Eatwell, John; Peter Newman, and Murray Milgate (eds.) *The New Palgrave Dictionary of Political Economy* London: The Macmillan Press, Ltd.

Robinson, Joan, 1933. *The Economics of Imperfect Competition.* London: Macmillan

Ross, D., 1977–78. "Socialism and American Liberalism: Academic Social Thought in the 1880s". *Perspectives in American History.* 11.1.5–79

Ross, Edward A., 1893. Book review, "The Unseen Foundations of Society". *Political Science Quarterly* 8:722–32.

Ross, Edward A., 1914. In *Publications of the American Sociological Society,* IX, cit. Sinclair: 402

Rothbard, Murray N. (ed.) See Fetter, 1977.

Rothbard, Murray N. (ed.), 1977. *Capital, Interest, and Rent.* Essays in the Theory of Distribution, by Frank A. Fetter. Kansas City: Sheed Andrews and McMeel, Inc.

Rozwadowski, Franek, 1988. "From Recitation Room to Research Seminar: Political Economy at Columbia University". In Barber, William J. (ed.), q.v.: 169–202

Samuels, Warren J., 1991. "The 'Progress and Poverty' Centenary". In Lissner and Lissner (eds.): 394–401

Saratoga "Single Tax Debate," 1890. *Journal of Social Science,* no. 27, October

Sass, Steven A., 1988. "An Uneasy Relationship: The Business Community and Academic Economists at the University of Pennsylvania". In Barber, William J. (ed.), q.v.: 225–40

Sawyer, Rollin A. Henry George and the Single Tax, a Catalogue of the Collections in the New York Public Library. (NY: New York Public Library, 1926)

Scheftel, Yetta, 1916. *The Taxation of Land Values.* Boston: Houghton Mifflin Co.

Schrecker, Ellen W., 1986. *No Ivory Tower: McCarthyism and the Universities.* New York: Oxford University Press

Schuchert, Charles, 1925. "Memorial of John Mason Clarke". *Bulletin of the Geological Society of America* 37:49–74

Schultz, Theodore, 1953. "The Declining Economic Importance of Agricultural Land". Chapter 8, *The Economic Organization of Agriculture*. New York: McGraw-Hill

Schumpeter, J.A., 1954. *History of Economic Analysis*. New York: Oxford University Press

Scitovsky, Tibor, 1952. *Welfare and Competition*. London: Allen and Unwin

Scott, Anthony (ed.) Natural Resource Revenues: a Test of Federalism. (Vancouver: University of British Columbia Press, 1976)

Seligman, E.R.A., 1895, rpt. 1921, *Essays in Taxation*. New York: Macmillan

Seligman, E.R.A., 1914. "Halving the Tax Rate on Buildings: the Argument in Opposition". *Survey* 31:17 March, rpt. Bullock, comp., q.v.

Seligman, E.R.A., 1916, "Tax Exemption through Tax Capitalization," *American Economic Review* 6:790–807

Seligman, E.R.A., with J.B. Clark, Henry George, et al., 1890. "The Single Tax Debate". *Journal of Social Science*, no. 27, October

Shannon, H.L., and H.M. Bodfish, 1929. "Increments in Land Values in Chicago". *Journal of Land and Public Utility Economics* 5:29–47

Shearman, Thomas, 1889. "Who Owns the United States?" *The Forum Magazine*, November

Shearman, Thomas. *Natural Taxation*. 2nd ed. (NY: Doubleday, 1911; orig. 1888)

Shaw, George Bernard, 1889. "Bluffing the Value Theory". Orig. *Today*, May. Rpt. 1930, *Bernard Shaw and Karl Marx*. New York: Random House: 175–200

Simon, Julian L., 1981. *The Ultimate Resource*. Princeton: Princeton University Press

Simpson, Herbert D., and E.R. Burton, 1931. *The Valuation of Vacant Land in Suburban Areas*. Evanston: Northwestern University Press

Sinclair, Upton, 1923, *The Goose Step: a Study of American Education*, Pasadena, California: Published by the author

Skouras, A., 1977. *Land and its Taxation in Recent Economic Theory*. Athens: Papazissis Publishers

Somers, William A., 1901. *The Valuation of Real Estate for the Purpose of Taxation*. St. Paul, MN: Rich and Clymer. (Somers applied his method in Cleveland, just as Newton D. Baker was succeeding Tom L. Johnson as Mayor, 1910. In 1924 one could buy "Unit Value Land Maps" from the Cuyahoga County Auditor in Cleveland.)

Spahr, Charles, 1891. "The Single Tax". *Political Science Quarterly*, 6:625–34

Spahr, Charles, 1893. "Giffen's case against bimetallism". *Political Science Quarterly* 8(3):401–25

Spahr, Charles, 1896. *The Present Distribution of Wealth in the United States.* New York: Thomas Y. Crowell & Company

Steedman, Ian, 1987. "Wicksteed, Philip Henry". In Eatwell, John; Peter Newman, and Murray Milgate (eds.) *The New Palgrave Dictionary of Political Economy* London: The Macmillan Press, Ltd.

Steffens, Lincoln, 1931. *Autobiography of Lincoln Steffens.* New York: Harcourt Brace

Stigler, G.J., 1941. *Production and Distribution Theories.* New York: Macmillan

Stigler, G.J., 1947. *The Theory of Price.* New York: Macmillan

Stigler, G.J., 1969. "Alfred Marshall's Lectures on Progress and Poverty". *Journal of Law and Economics* 12:181–226

Stigler, G.J., 1987. "Frank Hyneman Knight". In Eatwell, John; Peter Newman, and Murray Milgate (eds.) *The New Palgrave Dictionary of Political Economy* London: The Macmillan Press, Ltd.

Stockfisch, Jacob A., 1956. "Capitalization, Allocation, and Investment Effects of Asset Taxation". *Southern Economic Journal* 22:317–29

Sutton, Antony C., 1983. *An Introduction to The Order.* Volume One of a Series. Phoenix: Research Publications: O. Box 39850, zip 85069.

The Freeman Book, 1924. New York

The Monthly Freeman, 1938–42. New York

The Single Tax Review (later *Land and Freedom*), NY: 1900–43.

The Single Tax. Orig. Glasgow, 1894 (later *Land Values*, 1902–19; and *Land and Liberty*, 1919-date, now pub. London, ed. Fred Harrison)

The Standard, 1887–92. Weekly. New York

Tideman, Nicolaus, 1982 "A Tax on Land Value *is* Neutral.", *National Tax Journal* 35:109–11.

Tobin, James, 1985. "Neo-classical Theory in America: J.B. Clark and Fisher," *American Economic Review* 75(6):28–38, December

Tracy, Count Destutt. A Treatise on Political Economy. (Thomas Jefferson, trans.) (Georgetown: 1817. Rpt. NY: A.M. Kelley, 1970)

Trott, Harlan, 1956. "Doing it the Wright Way". *Frontier*, August: 1–3. Rpt., San Francisco: Irrigation Districts Association

Troy, E.P.E., 1917a. "California's Irrigation Districts". In Miller (ed.), q.v.: 52–56

Troy, E.P.E., 1917b. "Land Monopoly and Taxation in California". In Miller (ed.), q.v.: 398–400

Udell, Jon, 1969. *Social and Economic Effects of the Merger Movement in Wisconsin.* Madison: Bureau of Business Research and Service, Graduate School of Business, Univ. of Wisconsin.

U'Ren, William S., 1917. "Oregon". In Miller (ed.), q.v.: 42–46

Veblen, Thorstein, 1918. *The Higher Learning in America.* New York: B.W. Huebsch, Inc.

von Wieser, F.F., orig. 1909. "The Theory of Urban Ground Rent". In L. Sommer (ed.), 1960. *Essays in European Economic Thought.* Van Nostrand

Walker, Francis A., 1883a, rpt. 1898. Letters to *Frank Leslie's Illustrated Newspaper.* Rpt. 1898 as appendix to George, Henry, *Social Problems.* New York: Doubleday and McClure. Also in later printings of *Social Problems,* New York: Schalkenbach Foundation

Walker, Francis A., 1883b. *Political Economy.* New York: Henry Holt

Walker, Francis A., 1883c. *Land and its Rent.* London: Macmillan

Wallace, Alfred R., 1905. *My Life.* London: Chapman and Hall

Walras, Leon, 1861. *Theorie critique de l'impot.* Paris: Guillomin et Cie

Walras, Leon, 1896. *Studies in Social Economics.* Lausanne: F. Rouge et Cie., S.A. (M. Gaffney transl., unpublished, 1967)

Walras, Leon, 1898, rpt 1936. *Etudes d'Economie Sociale.* 2nd ed. Lausanne: F. Rouge et Cie., S.A.

Webb, Sidney, 1890. *Socialism in England.* London: Swan Sonnenschein & Co.

Whitlock, Brand, 1925. *Forty Years of it.* NY: Appleton

Wicksteed, Philip H., 1894. *An Essay on the Coordination of the Laws of Distribution,* London: Macmillan & Co.

Wicksteed, Philip H., 1910. *The Common Sense of Political Economy.* Lionel Robbins (ed.), 1933. London: Routledge and Kegan Paul. 1944, 4th printing, George Routledge and Sons, Ltd.

Wicksteed, Philip, 1914. "The Scope and Method of Political Economy". *Economic Journal* 24, March

Yeager, Leland B., 1991. "The Methodology of Henry George and Carl Menger". In Lissner and Lissner (eds.), 1991: 185–90

Young, Arthur N., 1916. *History of the Single Tax Movement in the United States.* Princeton: Princeton University Press

Zangerle, John A., 1924. *Principles of Real Estate Appraisal.* Cleveland: Stanley McMichael Publishing Organization. 2nd Ed., 1927

Ziemba, William T., ca. 1988. *Dr. Z's Beat the Race Track.* Cited in *Bottom Line,* 15 July 1988 p. 13

The Georgist Paradigm

Fred Harrison

1

Life is coming apart at the seams. We see the disintegration all around us. The statistics on crime and deprivation justify the claim that the social institutions and processes that are supposed to unite us are in an advanced stage of decomposition. People have lost hope, which is why there has been the mass withdrawal from participation in politics. Alienation is an emotional state for a large proportion of the populations in the market economies of the West. Emile Durkheim, the French sociologist, wrote about it 100 years ago, in his classic study on suicide. Qualitatively, little changed for the better during the 20th century; the alienation remains, intensified.

We observe the manifestations of disintegration every day, in the destruction of life within the individual building blocks that make up society: the family. That is why, in trying to comprehend the social crisis, the biographical proclivities that "explain" the aberrant actions of individuals count for little. Society is failing to nurture people through the crises that must necessarily confront them throughout the process of growing, living and dying.

People are not deluded by the soporific platitudes of politicians-in-panic. They sense that the origins of the problem stem from some fatal flaw in "the system", a flaw which they intuitively believe must be fundamental because it has the power to threaten our living environment: Mother Earth.

And yet, despite the evidence, our ideology inhibits us from acknowledging the reality; which is why many of the acts of self-destruction are interpreted as failures of the individual rather than expressions of something seriously wrong with the structure and function of society itself.[1]

The thesis examined here goes beyond the claim that society is blighted by a systemic flaw. I also maintain that, during the past two centuries, western culture has also nurtured the seeds of a new type of society which is waiting to blossom forth. This view is not based on some theory of historical inevitability of the Marxist kind, however. Change in the immediate future is not a foregone conclusion, because the centrifugal forces generated by the distortions in our culture have created a strong sense of powerlessness.

I accept that the prospects for change of an epochal kind depend on the willingness of the democratic majority to exercise their will: only then will we be able to drive through the evolutionary reforms that would liberate citizens within the framework of a new set of social relationships.

That something has to give, in our society, there can now be little doubt. For while preaching the message that every person is responsible for his actions (that there is free will), we nurture our children into a dangerous world that is deliberately structured to suffocate their natural instincts to love and create; we school them in the arts of greed and destruction.[2]

The most savagely symbolic articulation of the anxiety of the citizen-in-society is the way in which we have had to transform our houses into fortresses. No longer are they homes; neighbours are separated from neighbours behind the barricades that are erected against the barbarians who may strike at any time, in any street, in any town. And nothing happens when the citizens appeal for action, because politicians are also seemingly powerless against the tidal wave of crime.

Yet we do not offer a gospel of despair. It is possible to empower people, if we enforce those primary rights that are supposedly the property of each and every one of us. But that will not happen until we correctly diagnose the nature of the disintegrative pressures which, thus far, are unevaluated, because unidentified, and are therefore allowed to operate uncontrolled, subverting the economy and society.

Social rules have to be changed, if we are to benefit from qualitative improvements that would make life in the 21st century a tolerable prospect for our children.[3] But if we are to avoid civil strife as the mechanism for effecting large-scale change, we need a thorough philosophical debate. Unfortunately, this will not even get started until we develop new perceptions of how society can and ought to "work".

The demise of communism has not helped. It has not brought with it a vigorous exploration of new forms of behaviour, but rather a naked triumphalism that has spawned an arrogant complacency about the virtues of liberal democracy. A sterile silence prevails among social scientists, the diagnosticians who ought to initiate and vigorously inform the debate about the primary problems that beset the world.

This silence is compounded by the detached state of the mainstream politicians who, in a democratic society, are under an obligation to sponsor discourse about the nature of the reforms that might be implemented. Timidly, they ask for evidence of a "constituency" (the promise of a bloc of votes) in support of a new idea, before they engage the public in a dialogue on fresh proposals.

Paradigms lost

Ultimately, however, the citizen cannot avoid his or her personal responsibility by blaming others. If we are to create a healthy society, people in general must participate in the radical reappraisal of all our futures.

Capitalism is as redundant as the social system built on the communist ideology. The world needs a new paradigm – a new conceptual framework, or model, which coherently explains how society actually works. Only then can we formulate proposals for the appropriate reforms.

Such a paradigm does exist. It has been lurking like a ghost in the literature of scholars and artists for over 200 years. It could be called by one of a number of names, but the label that economists and historians would recognise would be "the Georgist paradigm," after the American social reformer Henry George (1839–1897).

Over the past century, attempts to transform Henry George's central idea into social reality have been made by men of action like Winston S. Churchill, and sensitive artists like Leo Tolstoy; but to no avail. The force of unreason was overwhelmingly against them. Why, then, do I think the time is now ripe for the Georgist paradigm to find its expression through social evolution? The conditions that favour the advent of a new epoch do appear to be in place, for the conventional paradigms are generally perceived to be discredited by the facts of life.

Communism, which unleashed a Superpower and was the first to fire mankind into spatial orbit, has gone. In the course of five brief years, from 1986 to 1991, it was buried as an anachronism. As a practical system for shaping social institutions and individual behaviour, it is as dead as the dodo. The sun set rapidly on the Soviet Union because the ideologists who wanted to reform communism from within had not the slightest idea where to find the blind spot in their cosmology.[4]

But what of capitalism? It limps along, with its principal spokesmen – political leaders from the richest industrial nations, civil servants representing the world financial institutions – plaintively pleading for unity behind a single set of policies. They hope that these policies, an unconvincing matrix drawn from the failed experiments of the past, will bail the global economy out of the depression of the 1990s and set the world on a new course to suatainable prosperity.

The world will, once again, climb out of the economic trough, but many people will be left behind, marooned without jobs in the economic doldrums. Even as science and technology yields new secrets about how to accelerate the multiplication of wealth, millions of people will sink deeper into the state of poverty.

Yet, while few people are satisfied with the liberal democratic society and its economy, we are persistently told by the apologists that the capitalist paradigm offers the best arrangement that mankind can devise. This claim is undermined by the Georgist paradigm,[5] whose critique of the old system begins the process of illuminating the vision of a qualitatively different kind of society. But how confident can we be in the primacy of claims made on behalf of the Georgist paradigm?

Other views on how best to reorder society may be on offer, but if they are to be taken seriously they, too, must pass the tests to which we will subject the principles on which the Georgist social philosophy are based.

First, to be of value the new paradigm must be able to identify the fatal flaws in the existing systems. We discover that the Georgist paradigm's critique of both capitalism and communism flows from the logic of its principles. The strengths of the Georgist paradigm expose the weaknesses at the heart of capitalism and communism.[6]

Second, the Georgist paradigm offers an approach to life that appears to synchronise with people's overriding aspirations. For example, it rejects coercion and offers liberty, and it is able to specify precisely how this state of freedom can be achieved for everyone. In other words, it "makes sense" to ordinary folk.

Third, the paradigm specifies the mechanism for executing two crucial tasks:

(i) It explains how to facilitate the transition to a new society without the use of force. Breathing life into a new social system through the barrel of a gun atop a tank – as happened in Moscow in October 1993 when Boris Yeltsin sought to introduce capitalism into Russia – is a contradiction from which only trouble can flow.

(ii) The governing mechanism offered by the new paradigm is self-sustaining. Since the Great Depression of the 1930s, economists have been searching for the secret of how to create what they call a state of equilibrium; they have not succeeded. Ecologists also insist on the need for equilibrium (they call it homeostasis) as the precondition for the survival of our species. Ecologists, however, while correctly recognising that we have to pursue solutions in terms of the primacy of man's relationship with land, have yet to incorporate the practical lessons of the Georgist paradigm into their perspectives.[7]

Fourth, the economic pillars of the paradigm can be described in rigorously testable terms. This means (in the language of the scientist) that they can, in principle, be falsified. The paradigm, therefore, is a scientifically-based theory. In the past century, elements of that theory have been subjected to limited empirical tests; these have failed to discredit the theory.

Fifth, the foundations of the paradigm are grounded in both a morality and an anthropological tradition that are unassailable.

Despite these considerations, however, we do not smugly believe in the inevitability (as opposed to the necessity) of the Georgist paradigm. For it is a paradigm that has been well understood in Europe for 250 years, and yet – on the basis of a superficial reading of current affairs – it appears to be as far away from realisation today as it ever was.

The original economic elaboration was articulated by the Physiocrats in France in the 18th century. Their principles, which emphasised a reform of public finance, were to be echoed in the seminal treatise on economics by Adam Smith.

These economic principles were further developed during the 19th century, a process of theoretical refinement that culminated in the most comprehensive treatment from the pen of Henry George, a journalist in California who wanted to know why poverty was an endemic feature of a society that enjoyed abundance of natural resources and wealth.

In the 20th century, the economic theory was further investigated by eminent scholars. One of these, Professor Joseph Stiglitz of Stanford University, was to become a member of President Bill Clinton's Council of Economic Advisers. Stiglitz gave a name to his findings: "the Henry George Theorem".[8]

Most recently, the crowning endorsement of the economics that underpins the Georgist paradigm came in an Open Letter to Mikhail Gorbachev. This was signed by, among others, three Nobel prize-winning economists (Robert Solow, Franco Modigliani and James Tobin).[9]

Why, then, in the face of the evidence, has the economics of this paradigm not been adopted by people who are the heirs to a tradition of enlightenment? Because it was opposed by the most powerful of all vested interests: the private owners of land. They were not going to relinquish their power; and any threat to their status in society, which flowed from their command over the rental income of land, was vigorously opposed. For two centuries they have successfully fought a rearguard action in a desperate bid to avoid being consigned to the museum of social history. That defensive struggle continues today, the outcome of which will determine whether society can gain access to the promised land.

2

The Wax Works

The reason why society is not functioning properly cannot be a mystery.

The ancestors of *homo sapiens* successfully negotiated the evolutionary challenges in the course of two million years. They got here, from the slime of creation, because they learnt to know themselves and their habitat. It was that accretion of consciousness, built into the genes of the species, that transformed us into the unique bearers of culture and language. And yet, today, we find ourselves out of tune with both our fellow human beings and our living environment. In searching for the clues to this detached state of affairs, therefore, we probably need not look far for the answers.

Where do we start? The beginning is as good a place as anywhere. Let us rehearse some basic facts.

Earth is threefold: land, sea and air. Life would not have emerged, but for the appropriate combination of those three elements, the interaction of which over billions of years has come to constitute a satisfactory system for maintaining life.

Nature is threefold: animal, vegetable and mineral. It would not make sense to try and understand life by studying two of the three elements (ignoring, say, the mineral component).

Man is threefold: body, mind and spirit. His language is based on a grammar that has a classification based on sex: masculine, feminine, neuter; or first, second and third person.

We could not hope to understand how these primary systems work unless we have a grasp of reality – unless we are firmly rooted in the world of three dimensions (length, breadth and thickness). Try erecting a house on two dimensions!

In asking whether there is a basic flaw in the structure of modern society, we need to start with a definition of the constituent parts. Again, we find that the system is characterised by a trinity: the individual, the group and the habitat. A human being is a distinctive individual, but he cannot be separated from the social milieu or the natural environment that gives him meaning and the means of life. The individual is what he is, today, because he evolved – both physically and psychologically – within a community, and adapted to the habitat. The search for a fundamental flaw in the system, therefore, would be doomed to failure, if our cosmology excluded from consideration one of the three elements.

Unfortunately, social science today attempts to do just that: its practitioners search for solutions to problems without taking into account all the facts. We have learnt to view ourselves and society from a partial perspective, an approach that has had a fundamental impact on the way in which political decisions have been taken for the past 100 years. Those who had the power to shape society approached life on a two-dimensional level. They sought to control the fast-moving circumstances of industrial society as if they were living on a dualistic plane. They emphasised man and society, and ignored or disparaged the role of nature. They counterposed private life (the family) with public life (community), struggling to define a balance between the two, while for most important practical purposes excluding from consideration the ecological habitat within which people lived. Whether this was deliberate, or accidental, is for the reader to judge, after reflecting on the history of economics as presented by Prof. Gaffney. For the moment, our problem is to cast off the blinkers. We have to excavate from the past a complete appreciation of the condition of mankind.

To illuminate our problem, let us move from the broad picture to a particular case. Consider the economy, which is where problems emerge in their most vividly fractious state.

Economics is supposed to be the scientific study of three factors of production: land, labour and capital. The classical economists correctly defined the terms, but early in the 20th century the neo-classical exponents of the discipline defined away one of the factors. Land was assimilated into, as a species of, capital. So successful were they in burying land, that this third dimension to life now barely rates a mention in the most voluminous of the university textbooks that are recommended to students.

This is one of the primary causes of our state of incomplete understanding of how the economy works, a claim that can be illustrated by the way in which we classify the income of the nation.

Classical economists recognised that income must be decomposed into the returns to the three factors of production: rent, wages and interest. Today, in the national accounts, and in the analyses of professional economists, rent is not acknowledged as a unique category: it is but a part of the returns to "capital". If, therefore, there is a qualitative difference between land and capital – or between rent and interest – the impact of that distinctiveness on the economy is concealed from puzzled eyes.

In fact, there is something fundamentally different between land and capital, in terms of both their nature and in their operational impact on human behaviour.[10] By telescoping these differences into the stratosphere of incomprehension, economists successfully deny themselves the practical understanding of how the economy really works. We know they do not know how the economy really works, because they always evince surprise when the economy changes gear!

An analogy may help to clarify the point. Reflect on why a system is likely to malfunction if the conditions appropriate for its optimum effectiveness are not preserved. Consider, for example, a car, the engine of which receives power from two sources: electricity from the battery, and the combustion power generated by the injection of petroleum (Figure 1). Is that all you need for a lively engine? Hardly; the machine won't function without the interaction of a third element, which does not come from either the dynamo or the petrol tank: oil.

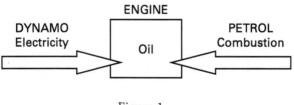

Figure 1

If the engine seized up, we would be poor mechanics if we did not question the possibility that the oil had dried up! No amount of power from petrol, or electricity from the battery, will turn that engine if the oil has leaked out of a broken gasket.

Now, return to the economy. Wages and profits are the rewards for the injection of labour and capital into the productive process. Rent is the reward to land – the measure of the beneficial use of particular sites, or natural resources, which have no cost of production, and which are literally provided free by nature. Unfortunately, every now and again that engine of the wealth-creating process – the market – seizes up (Figure 2). People lose their jobs. Obviously, we want to know why. Economists do not have much of a clue as to the reason why the economy is afflicted by the business cycle. If they did, the cycle would have been eradicated long ago! There appears to be a simple explanation for this puzzle. What we discover is that economists turn a blind eye to the special role of land.

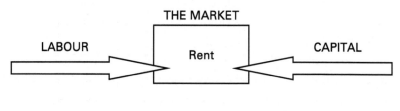

Figure 2

Rent serves the function of oil. Properly deployed within our social system, it is the fluid that lubricates the working environment: the public sphere of life. Rent is thus distinguished by its social character. It is income that is not created by particular workers or particular pieces of capital equipment. It is the product of the union between the community and nature.

Now the probable reason for the cyclical breakdown of the economy becomes apparent, once we incorporate into our investigation the flaws that have been built into the modern market in land. Industrial society was built in such a way as to allow rent to leak through the financial gaskets. That is the essence of the problem. The income flows are not in harmony. Now and again, the liquid dries up in some sections of the market and there is overheating of the working parts, and seizure. We express astonishment, we appeal to the mechanics – who scratch their heads in puzzlement – and then, blindly, we jab at the parts that ought to be working. Eventually, unexpectedly, something happens – we do not quite know what – and the engine splutters back into life. We breathe sighs of relief, and drive on ... until the next time the engine seizes up! And so on, a bizarre cycle of stop-go sequences that have blighted every generation for two centuries.

We may now begin to appreciate why neither of the alternative ideologies that were developed in the 19th century – capitalism and communism – could sustain themselves for long. They generated social systems that were detached from people's roots on earth, thereby creating an artificial state of affairs that could only be preserved – against all the instincts of mankind – by wrapping a conceptual blindfold around society.

Those with most to lose by the solution to this problem were alert to the threat posed by the penetrating analysis in *Progress and Poverty*, which Henry George published in 1879. He toured the world on lecture engagements that commanded mass audiences. His philosophy inspired land leagues from Ireland to Scotland and Australia. Yet the people who manipulated the levers of power were unyielding.

One man who spent years reflecting on this tragedy of history was to record his explanation. Leo Tolstoy campaigned for the policy in Russia, carefully studying the social response to the wisdom of the Georgist paradigm. In an interview with Herman Bernstein which was published in the *New York Times* on July 20, 1908, Tolstoy said:

> As I have pointed out in my introductory note to the Russian version of 'Social Problems,' Henry George's great idea, outlined so clearly and so thoroughly more than 30 years ago, remains to this day entirely unknown to the great majority of the people. This is quite natural. Henry George's idea, which changes the entire system in the life of nations in favor of the oppressed, voiceless majority, and to the detriment of the ruling majority, is so undeniably convincing, and, above all, so simple, that it is impossible not to understand it, and understanding it, it is impossible not to make an effort to introduce it into practice, and therefore the only means against this idea is to pervert it and to pass it in silence. And this has been true of the Henry George theory for more than 30 years. It has been both perverted and passed in silence, so that it has become difficult to induce people to read his work attentively and to think about it. Society does with ideas that disturb its peace – and Henry George is one of these – exactly what the bee does with the worms which it considers dangerous but which it is powerless

to destroy. It covers their nests with wax, so that the worms, even though not destroyed, cannot multiply and do more harm.

The wax worked. For 100 years, people groaned under the injustices of the social systems, without seeing the source of their suffering.

But then, in the late 20th century, Earth hit back: hard enough for some people to begin searching for fundamental answers. The wax has begun to melt.

3

Paradigm Unearthed

Order is an essential ingredient of any dynamic system that is capable of sustaining its momentum.

Order comes in many forms, but the essence of that order can be instantly recognised: there is something beautiful about the proportions, the locomotions, the relationships, which define that orderliness.

When we recognise something as being "true" – whether in literature, engineering, town planning – we have little difficulty in articulating the principles that shaped the structural order.

In architecture, for example, we continue to marvel at the proportions of the villas built in the Venetian hinterland by Andrea Palladio (1508–1580), who remains the most famous architect in the western world. What is it about Palladio's methodology which "in diluted form affected Western architecture for four hundred years, and seems especially potent today"?[11] It is the order of his designs which he believed he derived from nature, and which he was able to translate into terms that made it possible to erect buildings that have stood the test of time and place. He imposed a rigorous control over the three dimensions, to ensure proportionality in both the functional and aesthetic characteristics of his walls, rooms and buildings.

One type of proportionality was called "harmonic", which was translated into numbers: 6:4:3, or $\frac{6-4}{6} = \frac{4-3}{3} = .333$. The significance of these 3-

term formulas has been uncovered: we now know that they enable the architect to design not only rooms and facades, but even whole plans.[12]

Modern architects are not mechanically bound by formulae developed in Italy in the 16th century, of course; it is possible to vary the proportions and still construct a building that is aesthetically pleasing. But no matter what the variations in design, the architect is still bound to conform to certain principles if his structure is to remain upright for as long as it takes the materials to deteriorate naturally.

The challenge is to find the correct relationship between the strength and combination of materials. Penalties are paid for incorrect solutions. A builder can compensate for a poor design by committing additional materials to make sure that the structure remains upright, but the price of poor design is a heavy one. By over-investing in one building, fewer materials are left to be deployed elsewhere (which means fewer buildings) and there is a loss in aesthetic and functional satisfaction.

And so it is with social systems. Because of poor design, they can be here today, gone tomorrow. The social superstructure that was developed out of the communist ideology was evidently a very fragile one: the Soviet Union lasted just over 70 years – a flicker in time! The stresses that flowed from the flaws in the superstructure were too great even for the intense coercion that was brought to bear to create and sustain the collectivist society.

Nevertheless, intrinsically unstable systems can be preserved for long periods of time, without resorting to the use of naked coercion. This has been the case with the market economies of Europe and North America, where governments have used what John Kenneth Galbraith calls compensatory power.[13]

The social reforms of the early 20th century in Britain, which led by osmosis to the welfare state, were an attempt to fine-tune an unstable system that was ready to explode at the seams if strenuous efforts were not made to ease the points of stress. The process was one of apparent incorporation: of setting up a structure of rights for those who appeared not to be able to meet their own needs, independently. Those who controlled the system were obliged to pay the price by buying a kind of stability.[14] This amounted to a political confession that society carried an outclass in its interstices which, ultimately, could not be ignored. Action that recognised the needs of this outclass, however, was not based on the desire to empower the individual. Rather, the solutions created a state of dependency.

Something had to be done, because the design of the 19th century capitalist system was a poor one. Governments had to wrap scaffolding around the market economy, to hold up the structure for a little longer. This response of the political system was motivated by the overriding need to preserve some of the fictions that underpin liberal democratic society.[15]

But the welfare state offers no more than a stay of execution. For as the needs of the outclass multiplied – as they were bound to do – a point had to be reached where the productive capacity of the economy would be stretched to breaking point.

Governments, such as the one over which Margaret Thatcher presided during the 1980s, may say they want to cut back on public spending; but confronted by social and economic realities, they end up spending ever more of the nation's income. In 1993, the British state and its bureaucracy spent 46% of gross national income, which was much more than when Mrs Thatcher came to power in 1979.

Disorderly conduct

It is not surprising, therefore, that, in the final years of the 20th century, the very tenets on which the welfare state was built have been called into question, suggesting that the eclipse of capitalism might not be far behind the fate of communism.

Neither capitalism nor communism could be expected to transform themselves from within, for transformation spelt liquidation! But doomed they were from the outset, for they were set in motion without an earthly anchorage. How did that happen?

The industrial mode of production came into existence on sufferance. The arrival of the new system was conditional on its acceptance of the social rules already established by the landowners, who had consolidated their private power over the public purse – and therefore the political process – during the centuries since Magna Carta. The two rules of relevance for present consideration are these:

(1) At the dawn of what was to be the post-feudal era, entrepreneurs were left in no doubt that they were outsiders. If they wanted to locate factories on land, they had to pay for the opportunity of creating jobs and wealth for the nation. There was nothing in Britain's unwritten constitution that gave

them an automatic, equal right of access to the benefits of the resources of nature which had already been privatised. So access to land was subject to negotiation with the private owners, who insisted on money up-front: future rental income had to be capitalised and paid to the current owners now, before the first brick of the factory was laid.

(2) The factory system was urban-based; and to flourish, it needed a massive enlargement of the social infrastructure – roads, safeguards for public health, and so on. Who was going to pay? These were public services, and they ought to have been funded out of the public revenue – the rent of land. But that was unacceptable to the landowners! The rent of land was implicitly sacrosanct. The process of shifting responsibility for public services onto the private incomes of labour and capital began in a most determined fashion in 1799. Thus began the retardation of the potential of the new mode of production. Taxes pushed up the price of goods, which curbed consumption and investment, but that was not the landowners' problem!

If the capitalist wanted recognition of his services in the form of an elevated social status, he had to ape the country landowner by buying a large estate. The result was the birth of a crippled social system that was periodically prevented from literally delivering the goods.

Communism was no more than the mirror image of capitalism. Karl Marx did not like what he saw, so he postulated the need for the opposite: collective action and social ownership of the means of production. The opposite of an unearthly social system was another unearthly social system!

Over the decades, social scientists tried to develop the conceptual apparatus to reflect the facts: sciences which, as they evolved, were parodies of reality. The results can now be seen in the failure to provide solutions to crying contemporary problems. Consider, for example, the need to remedy dereliction in the city.

Because "land" has now been assimilated into "capital," for conceptual purposes, nature is treated as just another marketable commodity. Its characteristics are assumed to be identical to those of an office building or a lathe. Thus, owners of urban land are free to exercise their monopoly power. Result: land speculation is the primary cause of the collapse of the urban economy and the built environment. And yet, social scientists remain silent about this process, which to this day remains free to wreak havoc.

Communism fared no better. Regimented production and marshalled labour (the dictatorship of the proletariat was deemed to be necessary to oppose the individualism of capitalism) produced grotesque cities of conveyor belt monotony. The built environment of the USSR was a social desert.

The same ideological sterility produced the ecological crisis. Communism could not respect nature, because its guiding theory – on labour value – encouraged the administrators to turn a blind eye on nature. Land, after all, could have no value, because it was not made by labour! The Soviet Union's legacy to the world is a wounded environment that will take generations to heal.[16]

Capitalist societies, while marginally better in their treatment of nature, were also compromised, in their case by the formative mentality that was forced to focus on spatial mobility and the depletable, reproducible characteristics of capital. The unique characteristics of land, defined to include all of nature, were just not allowed to intrude into the equation.

The self-financing system

We can now develop a picture of the social framework prescribed by the Georgist paradigm.

The principles of proportionality can be highlighted by examining an economic relationship that offers a striking contrast with capitalism: income distribution and public finance.

We are not claiming that, in a Georgist society, the proportions are rigidly enforced: a healthy society is a dynamic, ever-growing organism, in which the numbers adjust according to particular conditions. Nonetheless, they do cluster closely around the long-run average.

Recall that wealth is produced by three factors of production: land, labour and capital, each of which receives income: rent, wages and interest. A society that had preserved the integrity of its evolutionary roots would be able to sustain itself in a harmonious manner without the stresses that are associated with the maldistribution of income: envy, greed, despair, and so on. But in an unnatural society, such as the one that was to emerge in Western Europe at the end of the Middle Ages, governments had to intercede in the distribution of income to buy some kind of stability.

There is no ambiguity about what went wrong. Traditionally, the primary functions of society – territorial defence, political leadership and the administration of justice – were funded out of the income that we now call the rent of land. With cultural evolution, however – in the direction of the formation of the nation-state – those who were responsible for discharging the social functions were threatened with redundancy. In a nutshell, their jobs were being professionalised (standing army, bureaucracy and circuit judges). To preserve their status and income, they had to do something desperate: they stole the public purse. Public servants of the Middle Ages, who knew their redundancy notices were in the mail, shrewdly privatised the public revenue. They became the great landowners of enclosure fame: no social functions to perform, but a lot of rents to enjoy.

The greatest fraud in history remains undetected, transmuted into a lawful pastime by the skilful manipulation of historical documents: See Kenneth Jupp's contribution to *Private Property and Public Finance*, another volume in this series. The beneficiaries can today be counted not in their few thousands – the major landowners – but by the million: homeowners fail to pay – directly – for the full benefits of the location of the land they occupy. And by the "trading up" process they participate in the game of land speculation.

The outcome of this feat, of transforming public revenue into private income, is that modern governments continue to be obliged to tax the wages of labour and the profits of capital. Thus was born a system of politics based on class and conflict rather than consensus. Politics became a process dominated by two overriding dynamics:

(1) Rent-seeking: the manipulation of politics by the landowners, who by virtue of their control over land were the most influential class in society; and

(2) The desperate needs of the underclass, which could only be assuaged by appropriating part of someone else's earned income.

This was an unstable system: people resent having to pay taxes out of the income that they earn. And the social, economic and personal costs of financing government out of taxes on wages and interest are enormous.

There is a superior approach to regulating social and economic activity, and it is most fully elaborated by the Georgist paradigm. If we want to move in the direction of a rational social system, we need to retrieve the philosophy of public finance which, from time immemorial, served mankind so well. This will not happen, however, until there is a thorough debate about the philosophy of public finance.

One of the first questions that we need to ask is this. What, in a tax-free society, would be the distribution of income between the three factors of production?

In present conditions (i.e., in societies whose governments take anything between 35 to 50 per cent of national income), the imputable rental income of land is of the order of 22 to 25 per cent. This is the conservative estimate for both the UK[17] and the USA.[18]

Empirical research and scholarly reflection by economists who have studied the Georgist paradigm suggests that the share of rent in the modern society, if the current system of taxation were abolished, would be about 35% of national income. The figure may be higher, in the view of Mason Gaffney, a Professor of Economics at the University of California (Riverside), who has spent a lifetime investigating this question. He believes that, in a tax-free society, the rent of land might be as much as 40%.[19]

What of wages in a tax-free society? In Britain, according to Ronald Burgess, the author of *Public Revenue Without Taxation*, income from employment net of taxation has been stable at 50 per cent of national income for the past 100 years.[20] The figure fluctuated up or down by about 5 per cent, but it returns to the long-run average of half the total income of the nation. Adding up rent and wages provides us with the figure that rewards the owner of capital. The distribution of income between rent, wages and interest, then, in a tax-free society, may be approximately this:

$$35 + 50 + 15$$

These figures, if they are validated by further research, yield an important conclusion: taxes on wages and interest can be abolished, to leave the income to land free to discharge its traditional role, that of underwriting the costs of public services. Our confidence in this conclusion is heightened when we take into account three facts:

(1) If the social system were a rational one, a large slice of the existing financial commitments of the state would evaporate. The public provision of certain services of a welfare character would be eliminated, once the obstacles to employment and decent wages were removed. Poverty would be diminished, if not abolished, so dependency on the welfare state would be voluntarily reduced.

(2) The state, which must necessarily provide some services that cannot be more efficiently provided by the private sector, is entitled to charge users for the services rendered. This revenue, however, takes the form of fees from customers, not across-the-board taxes imposed on every member of the public.

(3) For social reasons – such as health – it might make sense to retain certain taxes: for example, on tobacco.

When the revenue from these three sources are added up, we could abolish the existing system of taxation and rely on the rent of land as the major source of public revenue. This thesis is fully elaborated in *Private Property and Public Finance*, a companion volume in this series.

The beauty of treating rent as public revenue is that it sets up a virtuous circle: public investments become self-financing. A new highway or public amenity adds to the rental value of land, which feeds back into an increase in public revenue!

The Physiocrats spotted this truth. They explained that all the public expenses of the French state could be met out of a Single Tax – the *Impôt Unique* – on the rent of land. They developed the first body of economic literature, and they were praised by Adam Smith who acknowledged that the rent of land was indeed the distinctive source of public revenue.

The significance of the work by the Physiocrats is that they assembled their economic theories, including the role of public finance, into a vision of the total system. As a mark of the poverty of modern economic philosophy, however, they are now criticised for a single nebulous reason.

The Physiocrats based their doctrine on the contention that all wealth was derived from land. To reject this statement out-of-hand is facile. The objection disregards two facts: first, that they lived in an agricultural society; and, second, that their primary concern was with public finance. If we focus on the second issue, and recall that rent is the measure of the locational value or the fertility of land, the statement by the Physiocrats is not, after all, as outrageous as modern scholars would have us believe.

So the correct fiscal principles for the modern nation-state were enunciated in the 18th century, in good time to be incorporated into the foundations of industrial society. A soundly-based system of public finance would have made it possible to avoid the most traumatic of social and economic disruptions that are inevitably associated with the transition from one social system to another.

Adam Smith, in *The Wealth of Nations* (1776), alerted Britain's parliament to the ideal system of public finance, but the aristocrats who dominated politics were no more interested in yielding the rent of land than were their cousins in the *Ancien Régime*. Thus was established the conditions for misaligning the distribution of income, which was to disfigure the wealth-creating enterprises of the 19th century. Society was misdirected along a path of institutionalised poverty even as new techniques for the mass production of wealth were being invented.

4

A Philosophy for a Fair Society

Does the Georgist paradigm offer the promise of a unique social system, or one that is no more than a variation on the capitalist theme?

It could be argued that, had the recommendations of Adam Smith been consistently adopted, the transformation from feudal to industrial society would have been in the direction that was to be visualised by Henry George. This argument collapses when we note that Adam Smith, while clearly acknowledging the unique attractions of rent for public revenue purposes,[21] championed the landlord class. He explicitly justified the maldistribution of land. In *The Theory of Moral Sentiments* (1759) he argued:

> When providence divided the earth among a few lordly masters, it neither forgot nor abandoned those who seemed to have been left out in the partition. These last, too, enjoy their share of all that it produces. In what constitutes the real happiness of human life, they are in no respect inferior to those who would seem so much above them. In ease of body and peace of mind, all the different ranks of life are nearly upon a level, and the beggar, who suns himself by the side of the highway, possesses that security which kings are fighting for.[22]

One doubts that the beggars who live underneath the arches in London's Charing Cross, or who huddle in the corners of the New York subway, would share Adam Smith's characterisation of the life of the landless.

It is Adam Smith's wish to protect the landlord class that divides him from Henry George. This is dramatically emphasised by his fiscal stricture that "The ground-rents of uninhabited houses ought to pay no tax".[23] Thus, the landowner is not to pay for the privilege of monopolising urban land, even while homeless people wander the streets. The landowner is rewarded with a persistent increase in the value of the land he occupies, thanks to the growth of the community and the expenditure of government on social services, even while he withholds land from use. Thus was the land speculator enriched in the burgeoning cities of early industrial society, even as the freeborn Englishman was dispossessed of his farm and expelled to the cities.

We do, then, have before us three distinct social paradigms, each apparently distinguished by the emphasis it places on one of the three factors of production.

Land ↔ Georgism

Labour ↔ Communism

Capital ↔ Capitalism

In fact, the symmetry is not a perfect one. For while the ideologies of capitalism and communism accord primacy to one of two factors of production, the Georgist framework does not assign pre-eminence to land (which would downgrade the importance of labour and capital). The distinctiveness of the Georgist conceptual framework is that it synthesises all three factors of production into a holistic system.

Nonetheless, given the intellectual record of the last century, the primary function of the Georgist paradigm, today, must be the rehabilitation of the importance of land in the economy and society.[24] This would recalibrate the roles of capital and labour. This, in turn, would strike a new balance between the private and public sectors of life, and open up the prospects for cultural evolution and individual liberation of the kind that are not currently within the realms of admissibility.

Some of the distinctive characteristics of the Georgist paradigm are displayed by the facility with which it addresses seemingly intractable problems. Its tenets identify the source of the problems while simultaneously offering solutions. To see how the paradigm works, we will briefly review the two crises to which we have already alluded: the urban and the ecological.

The social city

The great cities of the 19th century were largely built to suit land speculators; the result was overcrowded Dickensian hell-holes for large numbers of people.

In Britain, a comprehensive solution was offered by Ebenezer Howard, who had been inspired by the writings of Henry George. He developed a scheme for what he called the garden city: a new town built on a greenfield site, the first of which was to be Letchworth, in Hertfordshire, just north of London.

In the social city, the citizens demonstrate the feasibility of social ownership with private use of the land, to harmonise the mutual interests of the community and of the individual. In his book, Howard presented a diagram which he called "The Vanishing Point of Landlord's Rent". Rent would not disappear, of course; it would be transformed back into public revenue and used to defray the expenses of society.[25]

The relationship between private poverty and social decay was stressed by Howard. Ray Thomas, in his introduction to the 1985 edition of *Garden Cities of Tomorrow*, examined the contemporary relevance of Howard's insight:

> The theory of income distribution which underlies Howard's advocacy of social cities postulates that land ownership in old cities is the principal way in which inequalities in income are established and perpetuated. The maintenance of high urban land values in Britain over recent decades in spite of recessions in the economy, and the maintenance of high land values in Britain's old cities in spite of the exodus of population, is consistent with Howard's theory. It is also consistent with Howard's theory for inequalities in the distribution of wealth to be greater than inequalities in the distribution of incomes – a pattern which is very marked for Britain. It is unfortunate that Howard's theory has yet to be seriously considered by economists.[26]

Despite the example of Letchworth and the New Towns that were to be built in Britain in the postwar years, however, the need to treat rent as a social revenue that would solve major social problems was no longer part of the public dialogue. Why? Thomas suggests one reason:

> Howard's ideas in this area are sketchy in comparison with those provided by theoretical frameworks such as exist in the Marxist tradition. But it is not easy to identify any other contribution since that of Henry George

which relates the problem of material inequalities so clearly to the structure of cities and the pattern of land ownership.[27]

The link between land, rent and the social environment of the city has not been altogether lost, however. The connection was reiterated by the United Nations' Habitat Conference in 1976, at which a resolution was passed which declared:

> ... the unearned increment resulting from the rise in land values resulting from ... public investment ... or due to the general growth of the community must be subject to recapture by public bodies (the community).[28]

Ebenezer Howard knew that his experiment in public finance, if applied to the extensive areas of dereliction in the great cities of the nation, would transform society.[29] Unfortunately, that vision was to be betrayed by successive generations of scholars who detached themselves from the lessons of the land. Finally, under Margaret Thatcher's programme of privatisation, the property of the New Towns (Letchworth, for legal reasons, was an exception) was sold off. Thus was terminated a symbolic experiment in the Georgist paradigm.[30]

Habitat as home

We turn, now, to the environmental issue.

The depletion of natural resources and the despoliation of nature is due to a single reason: the failure properly to measure the rental value of all of nature's resources, and to make the users pay the community for the benefits they receive.

Since the dawn of the industrial era, factory owners have been allowed to belch damaging effluent into the atmosphere or rivers and seas without paying rent for occupying those precious spaces. If the users had been obliged to pay rent, they would have nurtured nature; they would have calculated carefully before abusing her. The Georgist paradigm sets in motion a sophisticated drama that prevents the exploitation of nature. This is achieved on the basis of a correct distinction between public and private property; and insistence on the principle that users should pay for the benefits they receive. Rent is the measure of those benefits.

There can be no solution to the environmental crisis until this principle is clearly established. This has not yet been achieved, despite an enormous amount of research into the problem, because the original environmental concerns were formulated from a mainly ecological perspective. This is illustrated by Gaia (the name of the Greek mother god of earth), the most popular paradigm in the field of ecology.

The Gaia hypothesis, which was developed by John Lovelock, postulates that the world is a single complex living entity that is capable of regulating and sustaining itself.[31] The hypothesis is attractive for its holistic qualities, but it cannot offer specific economic solutions for society at any particular stage of development. For example, we need to know what type of system of public finance is necessary if mankind is to work with, rather than against, Gaia.

A variety of schemes have been proposed by environmentalists, but they are generally hostile to the market economy – that is, the monopoly-inspired capitalist version.[32] The Georgist paradigm, because it is earth-based and culturally comprehensive, provides the answers to the hard practical questions; and it can smoothly embrace the Gaia paradigm as one of its components.[33]

We begin to see that the Georgist paradigm, if it were to be adopted as a guide to policy formation, would ultimately yield a unique social system. Cultural evolution would have, as its starting point, the principle that anyone who wants to have exclusive use or occupation of land would be obliged to pay to the community the full annual rent – as measured in the competitive market – for the privilege. Once the obligation is accepted, the user is then free to deploy land to realise the best results within the limits set by a democratic system of law-making. From this would spring a fruitful partnership between the public and private sectors in place of the tensions that exist today between the two spheres of life.

5

A Question of Power

The debate about "the end of history"[34] flushed out the poverty of the philosophy of the liberal democratic age.

We are told that the western approach to politics is the best model that can be devised. In the marketplace of ideas, the free market and liberal ideology have certainly outgunned the creed of the communists. And yet, the United States counts its malnourished citizens by the million. And then there is the federal deficit: the fiscal ballast, measured in trillions of dollars, that keeps the ship of state afloat even while threatening to sink it, a legacy of debt that future generations will have to finance without enjoying the benefits.

Something is wrong, and yet social scientists, with a few exceptions, are complacent. This is understandable; they are creatures of their time and place (the product of socialisation). So it is difficult for them to be objective. This, in part, explains why the social sciences have failed to match the great advances in the natural sciences. The astronomer has no difficulty in separating his personal objectives with the exercise of objectivity in his discipline. This reality will be explored in relation to the concept of power. Its centrality in our lives – and in everyday discourse – is commonplace. Yet few scientists have accorded it the investigation that it warrants. Melville Ulmer's observation is justified:

> Perhaps no subject in the entire range of the social sciences is more important, and at the same time so seriously neglected, as the role of power in economic life.[35]

Curiously, the Left has failed to fill that void, as Christopher Lasch, a Professor of History, has noted:

> It seems to me that what's really at stake here is a discussion about authority, and ultimately I think a discussion about politics, and the nature of power. This, incidentally, is astonishingly a kind of vacuum on the Left. So much attention has been devoted to the realm of production, and proportionately so little to politics and authority....[36]

The nature of power is by no means unambiguous; much remains to be done, to clarify its roots. Until that task has been undertaken, knowledge and political activity will remain distorted and ineffective.

I acknowledge that social scientists are fallible, products of their cultural environment. They are "involved": not deterministically "conditioned" in the way that Marx would have us believe, but anchored in the prejudices and needs of family, community, nation-state. The mind does permit imaginative leaps out of our present condition, but this exercise is easier for the Hollywood scriptwriter who is churning out another Star Wars fantasy; more difficult when we try to visualise a different kind of society, a process made more difficult if our vision threatens an accelerated pace of change for our community, which poses difficult questions about the reallocation of power.

Occasionally, however, there comes along a man who is able to abstract his thinking from his personal circumstances and develop a high degree of objectivity about the nature of his society. Such a man was Henry George, the journalist from San Francisco whose critique of society led to the elaboration of a new social paradigm.

Any attempt to challenge the ruling order has to offer a viable alternative. If this can be accomplished, we have at our disposal a fruitful theory, one that may be capable of yielding greater benefits than the obsolete paradigm. The role of the social scientist is to subject that theory to close scrutiny, to test its integrity and help to formulate practical solutions to ease the transitional phase to a new social system.

One approach is to analyse the distribution of power, for when the old gives way, it is because it has degenerated; it has become unsustainable because the power that holds it together is dissipating. We begin our analysis with a sketch of the power structures that distinguish the Georgist paradigm from the capitalist and the Marxist models.

The capitalist paradigm

The system that was to emerge in western Europe owed much to its two principal theorists, John Locke (1632–1704) and Adam Smith (1723–1790). They were the philosophic craftsmen who searched for the keys that would unlock the secret to a post-feudal society based on individual liberty and material prosperity, the nexus of which was private property and the interactive process that we call the market.

John Locke clarified the foundation principles with his deliberations on property. He articulated the need for private ownership, which was necessary to liberate the individual. But what of the healthy interaction of the social system? Locke's failure was in not being able to formulate a practical solution to his crucial proviso: the private possession of land should be upheld insofar as it was possible to ensure that there was sufficient for everyone to enjoy access to land of equal value.[37]

But what if there was not sufficient good, vacant land to allocate to newcomers? Unless a solution was found, the power to regulate society would fall into the hands of those who controlled the means of life: the land. Here we have the origins of a lopsided power structure and of class conflict, for which Locke offered no answer.

The second pillar of the new system was Adam Smith's defence of free enterprise. *The Wealth of Nations, inter alia,* was a treatise against government involvement in the market; the mercantile approach to economics, warned Smith, was an impediment to the creation of wealth for the benefit of the consumer.

This critique opened up the debate about the correct division between the public and private spheres of life, but it did not go far enough. As we have noted, Smith, ultimately, defended the preservation of the rights of land owners. Their power, as Winston S. Churchill was to note in one of his 1910 campaign speeches, was "by far the greatest of monopolies – it is a perpetual monopoly, and it is the mother of all other forms of monopoly". Adam Smith, in advancing the cause of market economics, failed to specify the primary condition for denying one class of people the power to manipulate the market to their unequal advantage. He sought to undermine the manipulative power of the state over the economy; but instead, was to substitute the equally uncompromising power of the landowner over the economic fate of the nation.

We have already noted why it is in the interests of a class of people to diminish awareness of the centrality of land as a factor of production. The answer is grounded in ideological roots. Professor Gaffney has offered his account.[38] For present purposes, it is sufficient to note the striking identity of perception between the capitalist and communist paradigms: in conceptual terms, they both operate on the basis of a conflict of interests between two power blocs: labour and capital.

The Marxist paradigm

The defining feature of Marx's paradigm was the dictatorship of the proletariat within a system in which land and capital were conflated into a single category – "the means of production" – and property rights were nationalised. To remove the risk of a dilution of this form of property ownership, political power was vested in the hands of the proletariat, represented by their vanguard – the Communist Party.

The Marxist model over-simplified anthropological reality. Through evolutionary timescales, culture-bearing humans had devised complex property rights that facilitated the adaptation of social arrangements to ecological niches of the richest variety. These solutions had to balance the needs of individuals with the welfare of the community. This was successfully achieved, until modern times.

Industrialisation dictated the need for a recodification of property rights. The social reformers of the 19th century, however, failed to define a structure for property rights that was capable of accommodating historical imperatives with the needs of the new mode of production. Marx fared no better, and added to the damage with his alternative paradigm. By his pronouncements on the need for dictatorship of the proletariat, he encouraged an approach to politics that was to place totalitarian authority in the hands of a few people; with the majority at the mercy of the whims of a Stalin or Brezhnev.

But there is no historically valid alternative approach, according to spokesmen for the Austrian school of economics. Ludwig von Mises, in his discussion on capitalism and socialism, asserts that "there is no compromise possible between these two systems," and "no third system".[39]

His verdict was most recently echoed by *The Financial Times*, the London newspaper whose reassuring Christmas editorial to the worlds of finance and industry on December 24, 1993, was: "No known alternative stands ready for the choosing." Yet, after recounting the fate of the lowest 25% of income earners in the developed world (income had continued to trickle up from them to richer people) and the two-thirds of the world's population which "have gained little or no substantial advantage from rapid economic growth", the voice of the capitalist world opined:

> Christmas is a time when sentimentality may be guiltlessly enjoyed. But the true spirit of the festival requires that those who desire an economic success built upon something other than foundations of much misery and deprivation engage in the search for policies which are both hard-headed and ethical. Human economic history has not ended with the triumph of the free market. It has hardly begun.

Conceptually, alas, such policies cannot be developed within the capitalist version of the market. *The Financial Times* may urge politicians and economists not to be deterred from "seeking to ensure that the fruits of capitalism do indeed reach the lower quarter of western society, as well as the global two-thirds," but such exhortations are empty: capitalism is a paradigm that is as played out as communism.

Fortunately, a third paradigm does haunt the realm of ideas, and it "stands ready for the choosing".

The Georgist paradigm

The Georgist model displays a distinctive matrix of characteristics that constitute a viable and unique social system. The reforms to institutions and processes that flow from it would emancipate every individual within a healthy community that was intrinsically biased in favour of preserving the habitat.

Henry George built his socio-economic framework on a sophisticated concept of property rights. Capital was privately created, and ought to be owned by the individual. This was a practice employed by *homo sapiens* in the hunting phase of cultural evolution, when bows and arrows and other artefacts were the property of individuals or families. Private property in those artefacts was not at variance with the welfare of the community;

indeed, it was a necessary feature of a viable social system.

Land, defined to include all the resources of nature, was different: its possession was diffused in the group (family, clan, tribe, etc). There had to be private possession, if land was to be used effectively by releasing the creativity of the individual. But the usufruct – what we now call rent – was the result of interaction and growth of the community: rent was a public revenue, therefore, which ought to be reserved for socially-necessary expenditures.

Henry George saw that the treatment of rent as public revenue was the essential device for enshrining the conditions for cultural progress in the industrial era. Civilisation, he pointed out, was made possible by cooperation and equality. Other factors were necessary, if people were peacefully to co-operate with each other; but a precondition for such progress was the social collection of rental income.[40]

Was he overstating his case? Was he doing no more than declaring a subjective preference? This is the argument of neo-classical economists, who (like the Marx of Vols. I and II) do not recognise substantive differences between land and capital. The operational consequences are discussed by Kuhn in his attempt to reconstruct social sciences in what his publisher calls "a new, single form".[41] He states:

> Most market systems operate under the private ownership of land, so that landowners are among the factor suppliers who receive income ... One of the outstanding questions of economic justice is whether any private person or organization should receive payment for land, since human beings do not produce it. We will not go into the controversy here, which is essentially a value judgment with relatively little logic to assist it. We can observe, though, that private ownership is a technique of administering the use of land as well as of distributing income.[42]

Kuhn offers no objective method for testing whether private ownership of land is appropriate within the market system of production, and yet he presents as a key test of the functional performance of the market his assumption that "equal payments to factors represent equal costs to factors". He illustrates his point thus:

> That is, if two men receive the same hourly wage, we must assume that they both suffer the same cost, opportunity plus disutility, of providing the hour's labor.[43]

On the basis of Kuhn's objective test, then, it seems that land is peculiar: it has no cost of production – it is supplied free. So for any one individual to appropriate the rent of land must mean a dysfunctional situation has been created. In Kuhn's terms, then, we are able to declare that capitalism fails to "satisfy the greatest total desires".

There is, of course, an opportunity cost of using land: this cost is paid even when land is socially owned, as Kuhn acknowledges:

> The scarcity cost of digging coal from the ground is that it is not available to be dug out again a year or a generation hence. This scarcity cost prevails just as much in a socialist as in a capitalist nation.[44]

But this cost does not fall on the individual owner; it falls on society.

Henry George analysed the tensions at the interface between the public and private spheres of life, and he was able to propose a matching solution. His prescription was perfectly synchronised with the need to optimise the allocation of resources to produce the maximum welfare for both the individual and society: people should pay the full market rent to society for the exclusive use of a natural resource.

For Henry George, rent was the integrating principle of the system, the third dimension that synchronised labour and capital into a symbiotic order. In this way, the triadic relationship of man, society and nature was enshrined in a fully functional system. The power structure was a balanced and fair one. People derived their share of power on the basis of their contribution to the welfare of society rather than the monopolisation of a scarce natural resource. No matter what unique contribution a person made (for which he was individually rewarded), everyone shared equally in the creative power that was brought to bear by the community, through the natural right of equal access to the resources of nature. Not everyone could have land of equal size and quality: but everyone could share equally in the total rental value of a nation's land and natural resources. This was the principle of social integration that was, and remains, absent from the two systems that came to dominate the past two centuries.

The Soviet experiment failed because Marx's heirs did not pay attention to the imperatives of land.[45] It would be fair to acknowledge that Marx did succeed, in Vol.III of *Capital*, in identifying the differential power of capital and of land.[46] His acolytes, however, failed to follow through with the analysis. As a result, therefore, a society modelled on the primary Marxist constructs was untenable.[47]

That the capitalist system has succeeded in maintaining itself tells us something important about the power that was deployed; and we are obliged to reflect on the nature of that power, to assess its apparent resilience and prospects.

6

Reform or Revolution?

The Georgist paradigm was not developed in a reading room; it was the creature of the sweaty imperatives of everyday life.

Henry George did not have the anthropological and biological knowledge which is now at our disposal, so he drew heavily on theological perspectives. Land, for example, could not be privately owned, for it was given by God to everyone. Working within this cosmology, Henry George conceptualised a social architecture that was culture-specific, one that suited the needs of industrial society. He elaborated, in varying degrees of detail, the concrete solutions to match the pillars of that system – the liberty and equality of individuals. George did not have to resort to the language of the revolutionary; for he was not advocating a complete rupture with the past. His cosmology precluded the use of violence, which was why it was acceptable to Leo Tolstoy.[48] His was the advocacy of reform, for his institutional solutions could be teased out of the existing order.

This is a claim that invites scrutiny. We will examine it in terms of the seemingly intractable problem of poverty in the Third World, in the course of which we can test the claim that the fate of a community is inextricably bound up with the system of public finance.

We can approach our analysis by asking: why did the "Green" revolution – the cultivation of high-yield seeds – fail to abolish hunger in the so-called "under-developed" parts of the world?

The answer cannot be sensibly elaborated without first taking into account the spatial context within which wages are determined. People labouring at the margin of cultivation set the benchmark for wages. If monopoly power is exercised, that margin – and therefore the level of rents and wages – is distorted, to the advantage of the landowner. If workers are progressively pushed out to ever-poorer soils, they have to accept lower incomes; these levels, in turn, feed back to depress the wages paid to labourers on more productive land, which leaves (other things being equal) a larger sum to be collected as land-rent.[49]

The scientists who bred new strains of high-yield seeds for wheat and rice production in the 1950s did so ostensibly to put more food in the stomachs of the hungry millions in the Third World. They certainly succeeded in increasing output, but to whose advantage? Had the policy-makers and economists used Georgist insights to reflect on the impact of scientific innovation on income distribution, they would have instantly realised that rental incomes would rise. They would have also worked out that, under conditions where the monopoly power of land was privatised, there would be a downward pressure on wages. Unfortunately, there was no inter-disciplinary approach; and even if there had been, the capitalist ideology would have blocked the relevant forecast.

Labour displaced

What are the facts, based on the history of the use of these seeds in India, Pakistan and Bangladesh?

Cultivation was biased in favour of extensive methods of production. Tractors were bought to replace labour. The sacked workers migrated to the cities, where they directly applied downward pressure on the level of urban wages, and to the foothills of the Himalayas, to scratch out a living which also applied downward pressure on wages.

The social price of the miracle seeds was matched by an ecological price. The seeds required the application of increasing quantities of imported chemical-based fertilisers. Small farmers could not afford these fertilisers, so they lost out in the competition with the large landowners. There was, as a result, a twofold effect:

(1) The large farms, which commanded the highest rents, grew larger, which meant that even more workers were displaced onto the urban labour market; and

(2) The quality of the soil deteriorated, because of the over-exploitation as cultivation was intensified.

The result was a predictable process of impoverishment of both the population and the habitat – the tragic, malevolent and uncontrolled side-effect of humanitarian research. This was due solely to the failure of the policy-makers to take into account the workings of the land market in which rent was privately appropriated. Thus did the influence of the scientists reach beyond the laboratory, to deepen the condition of powerlessness of the peasants and redistribute income in favour of those who were already well-fed – the landowners.

Beyond the personal tragedies, of course, was the larger story: the progressive disintegration of those myriad bonds that hold society together, as the affected population is displaced from the land, expelled into alien social environments where poverty encourages anti-social behaviour. This, in turn, compels governments to employ increasingly coercive methods to contain the discontent. None of this was intended by the scientists, who were ignorant of the dynamic consequences of their pure research.

Dr. Norman Borlaug earned a Nobel prize for his work in the laboratory. Out in the fields, however, something happened of which he had no comprehension. His vision was framed within the capitalist paradigm; his understanding could not penetrate the economic process. When questioned about the social effects of his work, he had to resort to concepts that commend the industrialisation of Third World countries along lines experienced in Europe and North America. Of the farmer whose livelihood was threatened by the arrival of bags of Borlaug's seeds, the scientist said:

> The small farmer is a dilemma and his social/economic situation, as long as fragmentation of land properties continues, becomes progressively worse. It is my hope that with industrialisation taking place in many of these developing countries, that many of these small farmers, or rather the descendants, can be absorbed off the land into industrial employment.[50]

Men working on the land are a "dilemma". Not to themselves, of course, for theirs was a rational preoccupation that we trace back over 10,000 years. And not a dilemma for the soil, either, which, traditionally, the peasants have lovingly nurtured. They are a dilemma to those who perceive the world through the prism of the capitalist paradigm, and the only solution is to *hope* that they can be absorbed into factories. Meanwhile, the land is fed the fertilizers that are required by the seeds cultured in the laboratory, which nurtures the parasites that can only be removed by increasing doses of herbicide.

The chemical impact on the soil is acknowledged by scientists like Dr. R. Hardy, president of the U.S. institute that discovered the first commercially-available herbicide, 24D. Scientists like Dr. Hardy are well-qualified to explain the chain-reaction that follows the introduction of factory-processed nitrates to soil that has been nurtured by hand and humus over millenia. But when it comes to the social impact of the latest laboratory advances, Dr. Hardy is coy. When he was asked by a TV interviewer: "Have you looked into any of the social relations which need to be changed for adoption of new technology, like land reform?" Dr. Hardy raised his right hand, to protect his face from the lens of the camera, and replied:

> That is a complex area that you are raising there, can we cut this? That is a question we haven't talked about.[51]

In the fields, where the human and ecological price is paid for the flaw in the system, the farmers know exactly what is going on. One Indian farmer put it this way:

> The land is like an opium addict. A man who takes opium can do twice the work. The same applies to the land. Just as men become addicted, so land is addicted.[52]

To pay for the increasingly expensive fertilizers and pesticides, farmers have to fire labourers and borrow money with which to buy tractors and combine harvesters. Field hands turn to the brick kilns for work, expanding that dependent workforce in which, according to the London-based Anti-Slavery Society, indebtedness has created a new class of urban slaves.

The law of rent
This analysis is not intended to suggest that the "green" revolution should never have occurred; rather, it obliges us to ask what would have happened if the scientific progress had been associated with the Georgist approach to public finance.

Recall that a rise in land rents, as a result of an increase in productivity, could be predicted on the basis of the theory of rent. That much has been simply evident for over 200 years, ever since the theorising by David Ricardo in England (who stressed soil fertility) and, in Prussia, Heinrich von Thunen (who stressed location). They demonstrated that rents rose to mop up the surplus income after the costs of production (in terms of labour and capital) have been met.

This effect was either good, or bad, depending on the nature of the social system – and, most specifically, the system of public finance. In the capitalist system, this was a disaster: the privatisation of rent provided the leakage that guaranteed that the economic mechanism would, at some point in time, seize up. The consequence is quite the reverse in the Georgist system.

The first step associated with a rise in land rents, as one of the "externalities" of the skills of the scientist, would be the sharing of that revenue on a social basis. So if there was a downward effect on the wages of the individual, the opportunity existed for compensation through the rise in public revenue without having to burden productive enterprise with higher taxes.

It is that flow of additional revenue to the community that provides the key. In the case cited above, for example, the rise in public revenue would have provided the finance for additional investment in the infrastructure that would have opened up new employment prospects for displaced farmhands. General living standards would have risen, as workers were absorbed into higher productivity jobs. And the pressure to use soil-damaging methods of growing food would have been reduced.

It is the failure to incorporate the theory of rent into their thinking that has allowed policy-makers and the world's financial institutions to wreak havoc. Every day, we see enacted before us the bizarre theatre of good intensions with bad results. One example, again ostensibly intended to solve poverty in the Third World, is the attempt to improve the quality of water. The World Bank, in documenting its investments in water projects (in its policy paper *Water Resource Management*), acknowledges that much more needs to be done if suffering is to be alleviated among the poor people of the world. An estimated $700 billion, invested over a 10-year period into the first decade of the 21st century, would be needed to produce comprehensive water management strategies.

But what is the use of such investment, if the poor do not benefit? Under present tax-and-tenure arrangements, there can be no doubt that the economic benefits of such an investment would be capitalised into higher land prices. These would then lead to a further displacement of people from the land, as the larger property owners deepened their control over the tracts that benefited from the new supply of fresh water.

But what would happen if the World Bank's money was invested in a social system that employed the Georgist system of public finance? Why, in that case, the increase in land rents that would flow from the influence of the new supply of water would be the fund out of which to repay the World Bank while maintaining a stable social system!

It is this comprehensive problem-solving capability that makes the Georgist paradigm relevant for today, faced as we are with impoverished people in the Third World numbering in the hundreds of millions.[53]

7

Behind the Veil

If the capitalist paradigm is obsolete, society faces two choices. One is for a helter-skelter rush into any change, for the sake of change; which implies a philosophical vacuum within which there is an absence of agreement as to the direction for the constructive renewal of society. Or: the demand will emerge for controlled change in the direction of a more fulfilling system.

The demise of the Weimar republic and the rise of Hitler during the 1930s was one example of the former process. The serious prospect of a return to this option surfaced during elections in 1993 in both Russia and Italy, in which fascists captured the allegiance of a significant proportion of populations that were sceptical about the viability of the existing social philosophy.

Constructive reforms cannot occur without solid consensus support for a new paradigm; and new visions cannot flower in the public consciousness until obsolete perceptions are consigned to history. We can hint at the obstacles to the cultural evolution of society by reviewing some contemporary problems where the demand for change is being forcefully advocated, but in which the "solutions" appear to be unsatisfactory. We bear in mind that the primary need is the reintegration of society into a wholesome system based on cooperative association and virtuous personal behaviour.

Devolution of Political Power
One of the major geopolitical exercises of the 20th century was the attempt to aggregate power into super-states. Despite some startling successes, this appears to have failed. The most notable example was the USSR. The failure of the more recent attempt by Europe to create a superstate through

the Maastricht agreement is an example of democratic politics inhibiting the aspirations of politicians who are not in touch with ordinary folk. Replacing the notion of the super-state is the concept of "subsidiarity", which expresses no more than the need to devolve powers back to the old nation-state. This return to square one, however, whether through the Balkan solution or peaceful agreement, will not satisfy the imperatives of the 21st century.

The world needs a new political matrix based on horizontal cooperation and vertical differentiation based on the devolution of political power and cultural diversity. We are one world; a global economy, facing common problems on a worldwide scale. But in addition, there is an equally urgent need to provide the flexibility that is necessary for the revival of locally-based ethnic identities built on respect for diversity.

Culture is inextricably fused with territory. There can be no renewal of cultural identity without a corresponding recognition of the need to define a new set of rights. In fact, the quest for land is the single most important issue at the peace conferences in all the trouble spots of the world. Yet the bargaining over new social and political structures proceeds outside the framework of a land ethic that is validated by anthropology and morality. Deals are struck on the basis of exhaustion from wars of attrition, and the agreements are all executed in terms of property rights that were the original cause of the conflicts.

The Georgist paradigm does not prescibe the precise nature of new social and political linkages. In fact, there can be no one solution; cultural diversity dictates the need for a variety of approaches that are capable of coexisting. The Georgist paradigm, however, facilitates their emergence through the stress on the primacy of individual liberty and communal integrity through a rational system of public finance.[54]

The Rights of Women

The debate about personal freedom is currently most sharply focused on the demands for the empowerment of women. There is an increasingly confident assertion, forcefully expressed by Rosalind Miles, that their case for power comparable to that of men is unanswerable:

> For patriarchy has run its course, and now not only fails to serve the real needs of men and women, but with its inalienable racism, militarism,

hierarchical structures and rage to dominate and destroy, it threatens the very existence of life on earth.[55]

The debate is a clouded one, stemming in part from the bias against patriarchy in an influential study by Frederick Engels. Because of his ideological preconceptions, Engels sought to link the loss of women's ancient rights to the emergence of privately-owned capital. Yet he was frank enough to admit: "As to how and when this revolution took place among civilized peoples, we have no knowledge".[56]

Feminists are now using psychoanalysis as a tool for exploring the origins of their condition. These begin with parenting which, of course, directs the initial focus onto women as mothers. The maternal role is being explained in terms of an analysis of "capitalism" – that is, that set of values assigned by Marx and Engels to that concept. Intuitively, approaching the problem from the Georgist perspective, one wonders whether "delineating the forms of psychological damage characteristic of contemporary capitalism"[57] is the appropriate starting point for an analysis of gender conflict.

An issue that warrants exploration is the value-system embedded in matriarchal society. Feminists display an ambivalent attitude towards the concept of matriarchy. Some of them argue that matriarchal society/power, as a system which pre-existed patriarchal power/society, is a-historical, a myth which they regard as part of a plot by the apologists of patriarchalism; while at the same time being attracted to the myth as supporting their onslaught on the family as the oppressive institution that must somehow be abolished.

Unfortunately, this confusion leads to an underestimation of the anthropological realities that underpin the role of women in pre-historical societies. There is adequate evidence to show that, in the earliest societies, women were at the heart of a clearly-defined set of rights to land, the purpose of which was the advancement of both the biological unit and the community. Those rights established a relationship between the sexes based on reciprocity, co-operation and respect. This is a vision that contradicts Simone de Beauvoir's conclusion that "in truth that Golden Age of Woman is only a myth ... Society has always been male; political power has always been in the hands of men".[58]

One suspects that feminists would do more to advance the cause of their gender if they abandoned the language of socialism (with, for example, the socialist's focus on "commodities") in favour of Georgism (and a consideration of the role of land rights in society). Might a redefinition of personal rights recast society in terms of equality and justice for all, irrespective of gender?

Threat to the Biosphere

Concerns such as those to which we allude above, however, will count for little unless mankind develops a new ethic for his habitat. A seemingly voracious appetite and the values and institutions which are not calibrated with the welfare of the biosphere, are now generally recognised as unsustainable. Something needs to be done, but the debate is stumbling at the first fence over two basic issues.

George Bush's intervention in the proceedings of the Earth Summit in Brazil in June 1992 usefully highlighted the poverty of philosophy and of politics. He declined to sign life-conserving protocols because (he claimed) he was concerned for the jobs of US citizens. Yet, even as the president spoke, his statisticians in Washington, DC, were preparing to announce that the system which he was championing had cast 10m people out of the jobs market, an achievement accomplished without the assistance of measures to defend Mother Earth. And then there was the problem of money. Why should the rich industrial nations pay a disproportionate amount towards the cost of changes that would help to heal the wounds of nature?

According to the Georgist paradigm, there is no problem. People do not need the president's paternal concern for their jobs. Change the system of public finance, and people will get on with the task of earning their daily bread. Within that framework – surely the rental income of land is the appropriate source from which to draw the funds to heal nature? Surely it would not take too great a leap of the imagination to see that a global development fund financed out of rent would be both equitable and efficient? Furthermore, such a strategy would be self-financing. Enhance the quality of the environment, and people will be willing to pay higher rents for the benefits of access to the improvements! In other words, the revenue base expands to meet the global clean-up challenge which will face mankind in the 21st century![59]

Issues such as these require extensive discussion, if we are to take action of the kind that can ensure that life in the 21st century is not to be punctuated by wars which, shrouded as they usually are with talk of religion, ethnicity or whatever, are, at their heart, about access to land.

8

Strategic Thinking

The fact that the Georgist paradigm is once again within the realms of the possible has awesome significance for citizens and scientists.

A new paradigm is a frontal challenge to the Old Order. It threatens to rearrange the distribution of power and disturb the expectations of people who had assumed a continuity of privileges. The new paradigm courts hostility.

It is therefore necessary to embark on a radical public dialogue, to elucidate the means by which change might be effected; and, as a priority, to discuss whether the proposals in this essay do, indeed, offer the benefits that are claimed on behalf of the Georgist paradigm. In other words, we need some fresh strategic thinking. This is a sobering challenge. For it confronts us with the realisation that there will have to be a powerful demonstration of collective moral regeneration: a determined application of our sense of fairness, and a sensitivity to the needs of the community, rather than merely the pursuit of self-interest. The Georgist paradigm presupposes general participation in the process of change, for this is a necessary condition of a shift towards moral elevation. Rights prescribed in the model entail corresponding duties to be discharged by the individual; in other words, we are not visualising a social transformation that can be entrusted to an elite vanguard.

This leads to a consideration of the specific duties of scientists.

We have to sympathise with social scientists who have vested their careers in the study (and, even, the promotion) of the capitalist paradigm. But this does not mean we can relieve them of the duty to unfurl an understanding of the features of a competing model. I propose to pursue this issue by reflecting on one feature of the capitalist model which is directly challenged by the Georgist paradigm.

It is a cherished belief that we can have both a free market and also privately appropriate the beneficial interests in land (rent). Enormous amounts of scholarship have been invested in enquiries into the conditions for establishing and defending the workings of the "free" market, all of which take for granted the private appropriation of land rent.

The Georgist paradigm, however, embarrasses this model. Insights it offers lead to the following conclusion: you can have either a market that meets the test of economic freedom, or you can retain the private appropriation of rent; but you cannot have both of them. One or the other of these cherished notions has to be abandoned.

If this statement is correct, it wreaks psychological havoc; most obviously, on those who have a vested interest in the private appropriation of rental income, but also on the rest of us who have promoted the virtues of the market economy. We can illuminate this dilemma by reference to a key sector of the industrial economy: transportation.

Henry George argued that the private appropriation of rent introduces fatal distortions in the economy. Among economists, this argument is generally restricted to a superficial discussion of how the taxation of land-rent may, or may not, lead to the misallocation of resources (general conclusion: there are no distortions). Rarely do they venture much beyond that. When they do, it is to note that land is sometimes held idle in urban areas, but this under-use is rarely evaluated for its implications for either the economy or the larger social issues (such as the displacement of people from the most efficient central-city locations).

In the context of the provision of systems of mass transportation, where does "land" figure? Almost not at all; it may surface in academic or professional research in a limited way (through discussions on how to resolve competing uses for land), but never are the key assumptions of the capitalist paradigm questioned. Could this be because there is no problem? Why investigate the spatial context of transportation, if such effort yields little of interest so far as investment is concerned?

The issue is crystallised in the words of John Hibbs, the Emeritus Professor of Transport Management at Birmingham Polytechnic Business School. In a monograph published by the Institute of Economic Affairs, a

British think-tank that advocates market solutions to economic problems, Hibbs stated:

> The problems of transport in our large cities have been so acute for many years that it is doubtful whether an ideal solution exists. The reason for this intractability is the inevitable scarcity of urban land. The result is such a degree of competition for the scarce land that the market alone cannot bring about an acceptable allocation.[60]

In fact, the ideal solution does exist. It has been elaborated by William Vickrey, Professor of Economics Emeritus at Columbia University and the 1992 President of the American Economic Association. He investigated the proposition that optimum efficiency is achieved when the rent of land is taken as revenue to subsidise the transport system. Prof. Vickrey stated in a summary of one of his studies:

> Full efficiency thus requires that all such land rents be devoted to the subsidy of these decreasing-cost industries, and the appropriation of these rents by landlords for other purposes precludes the achievement of full efficiency.[61]

A further elaboration of the attractions of the Georgist paradigm has been offered by Professor Stiglitz. He wrote:

> Not only was Henry George correct that a tax on land is nondistortionary, but, in an equilitarian society, in which we could choose our population optimally, the tax on land raises just enough revenue to finance the (optimally chosen) level of government expenditures.[62]

Thus is the social scientist brought into confrontation with political ideology. Objective analysis of the facts now presents him with a traumatic choice. If he skates over the fact that the private appropriation of rent is a fatal obstacle to efficiency in the market, he abandons all pretence at wanting to improve the workings of the market; the freedom within which must necessarily remain limited. But if he condones inefficiency as a systemic feature – where does that leave the defence of capitalism?

Political leadership

The comprehensive nature of the vision exposes the paradigm to powerful opposition from vested interests. Politicians, for example, who are supposed to offer leadership, can be expected to deny "fair dealing" to the policy because they draw financial support from the real estate industry that would fear a loss of income if they were denied the opportunity to speculate in the future increase in land rents. Why, for example, should we expect President Bill Clinton to throw his weight behind the policy? As governor of Arkansas, he and his wife participated in a land speculation deal in the Ozark mountains that was supposed to net them an unearned profit (in the event, according to the president's testimony, they suffered a loss).[63]

Under pressure from the vested interests, today's politicians will voice objections to the Georgist paradigm; answers will have to be provided. One question, for example, which ought to inspire research, is this: if Georgism really is so wonderful, why have some of its principal tenets not been adopted? As an "objection", such a statement is facile; nonetheless, it raises interesting questions which need to be addressed. For example:

• Why was Henry George so successful in attracting into reformist politics people like George Bernard Shaw, only to lose them to a lifelong infatuation with socialism? Many eminent artists and scholars of the 1880s were captivated by the Georgist vision, but only as a staging post in their journey (we now know) to socialism.

• What was it that made the 1880s fertile ground for Henry George, whose devoted audiences spanned the globe? There may be little to be gained from lamenting the past in an "if only" mode, but historical reappraisal does offer the prospect of a deeper appreciation of the state of the world today.

No matter how instructive the past, and necessitous the present, there is no guarantee that people will adopt the theoretically most satisfactory solution for the future. When people are free to exchange ideas, the prospect exists for the irrational to surface and command attention. This is most likely to occur in periods of deep-seated social instability, such as we are now experiencing.[64]

In the past, the irrational could be contained – even if, as finally occurred in the 20th century, to do so entailed Wars of global proportions. Now, however, with the demise of the USSR and of communism, and the emergence of a market in hand-held nuclear weapons, military conflicts assume a new dimension in destruction. This, together with the Balkanisation of the nation-state system and the disintegration of cultural bonds, transforms the nature of the problems confronting social scientists. We have already witnessed the state of unpreparedness of economists who were invited to offer advice on how to transform a command economy to a market system. Strategic thinkers, using the Georgist paradigm as a tool, could develop a substantial list of problems of equal significance, the solutions for which would be all the easier to elucidate.

On social scientists, then, falls an enormous responsibility. They have to restore a balance between the knowledge of human behaviour with the vast amounts of information accumulated about the "natural" world. The task is made all the more difficult because society itself is now a fast-moving "target"; there has been an acceleration in the rate of change of our cultural context, which renders measurement and quantification increasingly difficult – which, if correct, commends the virtues of quality thinking by philosophers.[65]

In their role as citizens, social scientists have a moral obligation to provide us with intellectual leadership. They are not obliged to accept any one research-guiding paradigm; but they do have to acknowledge that "science has, so to speak, a soul which lives in the conscience of scholars".[66] As scientists they are obliged to try their best to detach themselves from present commitments, the better to serve the interests of humanity in the 21st century. If the outcome of debate is the adoption of the Georgist paradigm, so be it.

9

Cloning the Failures

The assumption of responsibility by the citizen and the social scientist diminishes the risks associated with the elitist approach to political change. Nonetheless, there is a need for statesmanlike leadership, and it is to this, and the geopolitical implications, that we now turn. My analysis will employ two examples to dramatise the responsibility of governments in the process of social evolution.

A central feature of the Georgist paradigm is the specification of the conditions for taking control over one's destiny. How this might be applied is illuminated by the complaint from Third World countries that the rich industrialised nations are failing to provide leadership to abolish poverty (through appropriate changes to the world trading system) or for protection of the environment. In fact, those countries are not as helpless as they suggest. Let us return to the problem of hunger in India, Pakistan and Bangladesh.

Critics of Western economic hegemony complain that the multinational agrochemical corporations, through the protection of rights to intellectual property, are diminishing the capacity of the Third World to relieve hunger. This complaint is designed to shift responsibility onto others, and it explicitly abandons responsibility over one's fate. It is an argument that stems from an acceptance of the capitalist paradigm.

The primary source of relief from hunger will be found in changes to systems of public finance that operate at the level of the village. Third World nations have (or ought to have) total control over the implementation of institutional and legal reforms, which would do more for the production of food than all the fertilizers and pesticides that could be imported from the

West.

In other words, responsibility for hunger must be returned to the leaders and voters of the Third World. The so-called "under-developed" (they are, in fact, mis-developed) countries ought to reflect on the possibility of paradigmatic alternatives (as they did with socialism, which failed them).[67]

But I do not want to underplay the ideological influence of the rich nations. This brings us to our consideration of evolutionary change on a global scale. The world is in a mess, whichever way we look at it, but leaders of the industrialised countries are determined not to work outside the parameters of the existing order. These two related points suggest the makings of a crisis of geopolitical enormity at the turn of the century.

The disarray in which the world found itself in 1992 was summarised by *The Financial Times*, following the meeting of the leaders of the G7 countries (the most powerful of the capitalist nations) in Munich.

> The G7 failed to rekindle the flame of global macro-economic co-ordination; it failed to promise anything new for Russia and the rest of the former Soviet Union; it failed to bring urgency to the task of rendering the nuclear plants of the former Soviet Union any safer; and, despite Mr John Major's creditable efforts, it failed to bring a resolution of the impasse in the Uruguay Round of multilateral trade negotiations closer ... the leaders have not shown the needed ability to lead.[68]

But the statesmen of the richest nations could not have provided leadership, even if they had wanted to; for they were blinkered by the precepts of the capitalist paradigm, as a result of which they were unable to formulate constructive solutions to the global economic crisis. They did, finally, sign a new world trade agreement in December 1993, but that was achieved on the basis of severe compromises of the kind that are likely to deny people the full benefits of free trade. Whatever the agreements being made, these have to be compressed within contemporary modes of thinking. Consider, for example, the need to construct a new framework for the former Soviet-style economies.

In July 1992, the Secretariat of the OECD (Organisation of Economic Cooperation and Development, which represents the leading industrial countries) censured Poland for failing to define appropriate property rights for a market economy. But what are the appropriate principles of property in a market economy? Surely not the ones that have failed the economies of

Europe and North America?

Yet the statesmen and their experts who presume to instruct the citizens of the formerly socialist countries do not attempt to re-evaluate their assumptions. This was reflected in the writings of some of the officials and economists of the OECD, who distilled their wisdom in a 431-page study[69] which was hailed as "A blueprint for policymakers in a world of change".[70] This "blueprint" offered an exhaustive study of the labour and capital markets, but remained silent about the land market, which might just as well not have existed!

It gets worse. The authors of the OECD study conclude that supply-side shocks should be treated as a rule rather than an exception. In other words, they wish to build instability into the system, for managerial purposes, even though the managerial approach has been tested and has failed in the command economies, which is why it was abandoned.

And what if one of the former Soviet-style economies decided that, theoretically, it was possible to escape those shocks? What if it selected a fiscal structure which could smooth out the business of production? The prospects for such an economy making headway – given the dependence on institutions like the IMF for funds – are not good. And, indeed, we read the following strictures in another OECD manual:

> Relying on the experience of developed countries means that central and east European countries must take over from the west the basic types of taxes, such as personal income tax, corporation tax, sales tax and contributions for social security, and the basic principles on which they were formed.[71]

Yet the western economies that employ these policies have failed lamentably to find the formula for economic stabilisation, despite two centuries of practice and theorising. Nevertheless, the desire to clone more failures is powerful.

> Thus, economies in transition should take over the leading tax forms and principles underlying those established in developed countries ... It would be harmful and inadmissible ... to initiate unfair tax competition among the countries in transition, or to transform them into tax havens, or for them to become a bridge for various forms of tax evasion on an international level ...[72]

Capitalism rules, to the point where it wishes to deny the right of countries to evolve in different directions. This was what Boris Yeltsin discovered, when he sought to retain Russia's land in the public domain. The International Monetary Fund made it clear that its financial aid was conditional on progress in the cloning process. President Yeltsin signed his Decree on Land in October 1993, in which he legalised the private ownership, mortgage and sale of land.

That cloning process is advocated to the democratic leaders of the post-socialist countries as if it were the only option open to them. One adviser, Jeffrey Sachs – a professor of economics from Harvard – has helped a string of governments to restructure their economies. He has no doubt about the strategy that they ought to adopt. In his study of the changes in Poland, over which he exercised considerable influence, he was to write:

> Although there are many submodels within Western Europe, with distinct versions of the modern welfare state, the Western European economies share a common core of capitalist institutions. It is that common core that should be the aim of the Eastern European reforms. The finer points of choosing between different submodels – the Scandinavian social welfare state, Thatcherism, the German social market – can be put off until later, once the core institutions are firmly in place.[73]

There is little to choose between these submodels: they all end up in the same place – mass unemployment! That palsied condition is the result of a flaw somewhere in those core institutions which the professor has so successfully helped the politicians to bury in the fertile soil of their post-communist countries.

It thus seems unlikely that a competing paradigm will be accorded fair treatment even at the theoretical level by the official organs of the nation-state. It will take considerable courage for a statesman to break through the ideological constraints and associate himself with a formal review of the foundation tax-and-tenure principles of the capitalist model of society.

Under the pressure of persistent failure, however, this radical review will one day have to take place.

10

From Chaos to Cosmos

An orderly society is not, by itself, sufficient to satisfy human needs. Tyrants have a knack for enforcing order, but they exact a price that many people would rather not pay. Most of us expect the rules that establish order to be synchronised with the principles of justice.

The concept of justice receives legal affirmation in all societies, including those (such as Brazil) that employ policemen who shoot children in the ghettoes. Why is there often a yawning gap between theory and practice? Because the political philosophy is not tied into legal principles that a citizen can enforce in the courts.

In the Georgist paradigm, the right of every man, woman and child to an equal share in the benefits that they collectively create, in the community, constitutes the moral basis for society. Land, whether viewed as given by God or just treated as a free gift of nature, is deemed to be the sacred inheritance of each generation; passed on in as good a state as it was found by the last occupants of Earth, a rich legacy for the further evolution of the individual in society.

Capitalism lacks that moral basis, for its emphasis on self-interest, and the rights of the individual, are not properly balanced by the collective rights of the community. Justice, therefore, was something that reformers had to struggle to graft onto the outer skin of the system, for it had not been built into the foundations.

The scope for the eventual improvement of the condition of the disadvantaged in 19th century society did exist. Desperate circumstances forced governments to pile one set of remedial laws on top of another. But these were not designed to alter the foundations of capitalism; merely – much to the chagrin of Marxists – to prevent its early eclipse by communism.

But the result has been a fossilisation of the 19th century system in 20th century garb. The price has been a heavy one. To finance the alleviation of individual deprivation and social despoliation, the burden of taxation had to be increased year after year. The three classes – landowners, workers and capitalists – struggled over compensation for the negative influences generated by the system's intrinsic flaw.

The dyke was constantly springing leaks. Instead of building a new wall, to avoid being engulfed by the seas, governments kept calling for more boys to plug their fingers in the holes.

There was going to come a time when citizens had to sit back, take stock, and start to unravel the whole mess. That time seems to have come, for the weight of the state has become intolerable. In Britain, government spent 46% of gross national income in 1993, one measure of the erosion of the freedom of the individual; it is also a measure of the incapacity of the market economy – as presently constituted – to deliver services direct to the citizens without the intervention of the bureaucratic apparatus.

The welfare state, the 20th century's valiant attempt to offset the shortcomings of capitalism, is now struggling to maintain its financial commitments, and the poor, old and sick are the first victims of plans to prune public spending. The financial crisis in the public sector comes at a time not only when the integrity of the markets has been undermined by the business cycle; the moral basis of capitalism itself is also being roundly condemned by the keepers of our collective consciences, from the Pope[74] to sundry protestant bishops.

Capitalism still has its champions, including a former British chancellor of the exchequer,[75] but most people know that something is seriously wrong. Unfortunately, because the source of the stresses is not correctly identified, there is no debate about the fundamental reforms that would correct the system-by, for example, abolishing involuntary unemployment.[76] Where did it go wrong?

Constitutional foundations

The trouble originated with the constitutions on which the modern nation-state was built. The statesmen who drafted the fine words – more often than not, rallying calls to revolution – failed to match the rhetoric with the practical principles. Constitutions can, of course, be amended; but in the process, a heavy price is paid, as we can see in the case of the American Constitution.

The Founding Fathers were intoxicated with high ideals, by notions of the Rights of Man. In the course of their deliberations, however, they made two fatal mistakes, both of them the result of prejudice over property rights.

The first error was one of commission. In the Preamble to the Constitution, the Founding Fathers declared their goals to be a "perfect Union, establish justice, insure domestic tranquility, provide for the common defense, promote the general welfare, and secure the blessings of liberty to ourselves ..."

Fine, reassuring words, except for the black slave who (in Article 1, Section 3) was counted as three-fifths of a white man. In this "land of the free", half-a-million Americans had to die in a civil war before that prejudice on property rights was expunged from the Constitution.

The second error was one of apparent omission. The Founding Fathers – most of them large landowners, a good proportion of their leaders active land speculators[77] – failed to articulate a philosophy on property that matched the words about equality and social justice. How do we account for this?

The Founding Fathers treated John Locke as their philosophical guide, but not without equivocation. For Locke had insisted, in his *Treatise on Government*, that every person had the right to "life, liberty and estate" – estate being the word that was used, at that time, for land. Now that declaration – *everyone*, argued Locke, had the natural right to life, liberty and land – was awkward. For if the Constitution was to be enforceable at law, any man or woman could claim, as a constitutional right, a piece of American real estate; which might have threatened the basis on which the Founding Fathers laid claim to large tracts of land in the New World.

So how was this problem resolved? In the Declaration of Independence, the Founding Fathers edited the key phrase. They abandoned the word "estate". Now, the phrase became "Life, Liberty and the Pursuit of Happiness".

> We hold these Truths to be self-evident, that all Men are created equal, that they are endowed by their Creator with certain unalienable Rights, that among these are Life, Liberty, and the Pursuit of Happiness.

Every American was equal (apart from slaves, who were three-fifths of a white man); and every American could claim the constitutional right to the pursuit of happiness, so long as he did not also claim the constitutional right to the piece of land that he needed to sustain his life!

It is not surprising, therefore, that the Constitution, as originally enacted, was silent on property rights. As a result, the law-makers in Washington were free to develop a system of public finance that shifted taxation away from land, and on to labour and capital. And today, on the streets of America, people – many of them children – are paying with their lives for that constitutional error.[78] The victims do not know that, for many of them, the source of their fate can be traced back to the misappropriation of public revenue by private individuals; Henry George is not required reading in the schools of America.

Is this an unfair assessment of the American Constitution? The record is clear enough. James Madison, one of the Founding Fathers, was emphatic about their ulterior motives. He wrote that

> In England, at this day, if elections were open to all classes of people, the property of landed proprietors would be unsure ... Landholders ought to have a share in the government, to support these invaluable interests ... They ought to be so constituted as to protect the minority of the opulent against the majority.[79]

Madison voiced a general concern among those who sought to establish the rules that would guide life in the "land of the free". He realised that the unequal distribution of property was the most serious cause of social division, and he wanted to alert others to the risk that the landless people – who were in the majority – might use government to redistribute property. Thus: "To secure ... private rights against the danger of such a faction ... is then the great object ..."[80]

The contemporary significance of these reflections is evident. In Russia, the constitution prepared by Boris Yeltsin, which was endorsed by the slimmest of majorities in a referendum in December 1993, was ill-conceived. This was to be expected, for the President had imported his economic philosophy from Harvard University and Washington, DC. Unless the Russian people fill the void that divides their social philosophy from the new constitution, many of them will pay as fatal a price, in terms of deprivation and exploitation, as the crimes that are claiming the lives of the citizens in the New World.

Philosophy of Public finance

If the principles of the Georgist paradigm were to be enshrined in a new constitution, there could be no question of forcing particular forms of social behaviour on people.

The one principle on which there can be no compromise, however, concerns the nature of public finance: the rent of land (which excludes the undepreciated returns to improvements on the land) belongs to everyone, equally. If this principle were to be enshrined in law, one of the major sources of social discontent would immediately be abolished: resentment towards taxes. For the payment of rent is not a tax, but a payment for benefits that are received by the possessor of land (the tenant does not claim that he is being taxed, when he pays rent to the private landlord!).

This single reform would abolish the chaos that is the result of misaligned economic relationships. In doing so, it would institute a new cosmological order. The rent-as-public-revenue policy would be industrial society's improvement on the practice of Bronze Age kings, whose Clean Slate edicts periodically redeemed people's access-rights to land (a policy that was to find its expression in the Bible's Jubilee Year).[81]

Thus would be created the conditions in which a democratic people would be free to establish whatever kind of post-industrial society they wished for themselves and their children.

The citizen would be liberated: the value that he created, with his labour and capital, he would keep.

The city would flourish: no longer disfigured by the land speculator, who carves up the territory to suit his long-term capital gains.

Politics: consensus rather than conflict would be the overriding dynamic. And the freedom to disagree would be protected by the economic independence that would be enjoyed by every citizen.

Ecology: the natural environment would be lovingly nurtured. Anyone wanting to deplete or pollute would have to pay rent for the privilege, a price that would induce conservation.

A social renaissance would follow. Society would no longer be disfigured by the logic of the nation-state, which is motivated by territorial aggrandisement along the path of war and destruction and sustained by the ideologies that are the outgrowths of the capitalist version of industrial society.[82]

The business cycle as we know it, with its frenetic land-led booms and family-wrecking slumps, would be abolished.

This was the prospectus held out by Henry George, over a century ago, and it remains valid. The essential difference, today, from the conditions of the 1880s, is that the people whom Henry George rallied under the banner of social reform were able to flirt with the utopian visions of Marxism. Today, the Marxist paradigm is dead.

As for capitalism, it is one of history's walking wounded. It may not die immediately. But at the same time, capitalism is incapable of healing itself. For if it is to remain faithful to its foundation principles, it must resist root-and-branch reform of the tax-and-tenure system. And yet, the moral bankruptcy of the system must surely encourage demands for a better social order? For how can we continue to preserve a way of life that actively turns honest citizens into criminals. I am thinking of the tax system that encourages people to spend fortunes to avoid the payment of taxes. This is a system that compels people to turn to "illegal" activity, as characterised by the so-called "black economy". In Britain alone, this economy is worth between £36 and £48 billion, according to the Inland Revenue (whose estimate was recorded in the 1993 report of the National Audit Office). Many of the participants in this "illegal" trade turn themselves into outlaws as the only alternative to being consigned to economic inertia – the victims purely and simply of a system of public finance that is self-serving.

But there is now real hope for social evolution. For people are not comfortable with an absence of choice. They will now search for an alternative vision of society to replace Marxism. The Georgist paradigm will need to be tested, if people are to be convinced, postulated against the great tragedies of our time to see if it can perform better than the remedies of capitalism.

Let us return, finally, to the problem of poverty. Worldwide, about 1.1 billion people live in absolute poverty, and about 30% of the world's population faces hunger as a daily reality. What would it take to solve this problem?

In 1993, the International Monetary Fund, representing the rich capitalist nations, was reported to be offering $2 million (£1.36m) to reduce poverty.[83] This compares with the billions of dollars extended by the IMF every year to governments to be spent on projects that consolidate the power that creates the poverty in the first place. Conventional strategies are no more than cruel band-aids, barely able to cover the wounds, certainly incapable of stemming the loss of blood.

Would the Georgist philosophy fare better? Its advocates argue that nothing short of the transformation of the system of public finance, to reflect a new philosophy of property rights, will unshackle people from the conditions that generate poverty. Which approach can abolish intergenerational poverty – the IMF's hard-faced dispensation of charity, which reflects an attitude that can be traced back to the Victoria era? Or a radical restructuring of society, to liberate every person along the lines proposed by Henry George?[84]

It does not take a genius to work out which is the superior approach, but one genius did comment on the Georgist analysis – Albert Einstein himself. In a letter dated October 8, 1931, Einstein wrote:

> I read the largest part of the book by Henry George with extraordinary interest, and I believe that in the main points the book takes a stand which cannot be fought, especially as far as the cause of poverty is concerned.[85]

But the appropriate remedies will not be instituted unless people insist on a public debate on the philosophy of public finance. Such debate as is sponsored by governments is directed at the "efficiency" of specific taxes – a discussion designed to make life easier for the tax collector rather than the tax payer.

This attitude was well expressed by Kingsley Wood, a British Chancellor of the Exchequer who – in presenting his Budget in 1941 – spoke glowingly of the Englishman's "genius for co-operating with the tax collector"! As for the collection of public revenue from the rent of land – alas, Mr Wood had told the House of Commons, there were administrative difficulties with this fiscal policy. So, once again, he would have to increase the taxes on people's earned incomes. Overcoming the alleged administrative problems was not something with which the government would concern itself: an easy life for the tax collector was what it was all about![86]

Adam Smith, in itemising the canons of taxation that are even today cited with approval by economists and politicians, did not deem it necessary to highlight norms of social justice. It was, apparently, a privilege to be paying taxes:

> Every tax ... is to the person who pays it a badge, not of slavery, but of liberty. It denotes that he is subject to government, indeed, but that, as he has some property, he cannot himself be the property of a master.[87]

By such talk was the freeborn Englishman turned into a slave – by hoodwinking him into believing that he had to pay for the privilege of being governed. By such analysis was he encouraged to bear with pride the loss of his earned income, even while the unearned income – the public revenue, the rent of land – was being siphoned off by those who reserved unto themselves the right to make the laws.

Utopian?
Society's crying need is for its institutions to be rebased on a realistic footing.

Is the vision that I have offered a utopian one – outside the realms of practical politics? Some will say so. Such an attempt to dismiss the Georgist paradigm, however, would not work in China and Russia, for without the ideological interference of the landowning class. And what would happen if China and Russia were to adopt the rent-as-public-revenue policy – a policy that was first offered to them 80 and more years ago by Leo Tolstoy and Sun Yat-sen? Other nations would have two options. Either they would have to abandon the philosophy of free trade, to which they penned their names under the General Agreement on Trade and Tariffs in 1993, and retreat into autarky; or they would have to abandon the present system of taxation.

Why? Because the economic consequences of such a decision by China and Russia, for the exporting nations, would be traumatic. Russia and China, two nations rich in scientific know-how, people and natural resources, would come to dominate the global markets within a decade. This would happen for one simple reason: by not having to carry the burden of taxes on labour and capital, the prices of their manufactured products would be too low for the European and North American nations to compete.

And so we begin to glimpse the reality – that it was communism and capitalism that were impossible dreams. No sooner did they come into existence, than it was necessary to sustain them by a system of carrot-and-stick.

In the 20th century, the genius of *homo sapiens* was expressed in the discovery of the means to soar beyond Earth's gravity, to begin the odyssey into the heavens. But this was not the dawning of a Brave New World. The astronomic feats of communism and capitalism symbolised the tragedy of rootlessness that had befallen the people of the world. By the millions they died in defence of land that did not belong to them – deceived by the ideology of nationalism. By the million, they starved to death for want of access to the soil – while being admonished as slothful. By the million, they wandered the world for the want of homes of their own – refugees in a world that begrudged them.

If, in the 21st century, there is to be a resolution of the crises that afflict people in their daily lives, it will not be found in an escape into the heavens. Peace and prosperity for everyone will remain beyond our reach until the day we find our way to '*A Philosophy for a Fair Society*'.

References

1 The capacity for self-delusion, while frustrating for some, actually helps to sustain a malfunctioning system until the time has come to implement radical changes. For example, our political leaders find it difficult to admit that the economy which they claim to "manage" deprives people of the freedom to work. Who is to take the blame, for example, for the fact that, throughout the years of growth in the 1980s, 12% of US males aged 25–54, and 14.9% of UK prime-age males, were out of work? (Edward Balls, "Missing the unemployment-deregulation link", *The Financial Times*, London, Sept.6, 1993). This record is glossed over by emphasising that many more women were now in employment (albeit in largely low-pay, menial jobs): women were being "emancipated", even while their children were necessarily neglected, deprived of the contact they need with their mothers.

2 The horror in which two 10-year-old English boys battered to death a three-year-old child made headlines around the world, in December 1993; yet we

ignore the routine homicides in the United States, where the killing of
children by children is a daily occurrence.

3 The urgency of such a debate is emphasised by the findings of a research
project in Britain by the Children's Society. Its report, *Hidden Truths*
(1993), revealed that one in seven teenagers in Leeds runs away from
home. The report suggests that the police estimate that 100,000 children
in Britain become fugitives every year understates the reality.

4 I was able to test this proposition in 1986, at a Press conference in Moscow,
when I questioned Abel Aganbegyan, the economic adviser to Mikhail
Gorbachev during the crucial early phase of perestroika. It was apparent
from his answers that perestroika was an empty concept; the Soviet Union
under communism could go nowhere except oblivion. See Fred Harrison,
"Post socialism and the Single Tax", in Richard Noyes (editor), *Now the
Synthesis: Capitalism, Socialism and the New Social Contract*, London:
Shepheard-Walwyn/New York: Holmes & Meier, 1991, pp.82–85.

5 This exercise in social criticism is not particularly difficult, as any alert
reader of the daily newspaper can testify. Take, for example, the corruption
that has been traced right up to the top in Italy and Japan, two democracies
with contrasting cultural backgrounds. In both countries, the democratic
parties that governed for decades were unceremoniously ditched during
elections in 1993. This rejection by the electorate, however, occurred
outside the framework of a debate about how to improve the qualitative
state of society. Not surprisingly, therefore, the electoral outcome was
unstable rule by a multiplicity of parties representing minority interests.
In Italy, in the municipal elections in November 1993, the demise of the
Social Democrats exposed the nation to the mercies of just three new
parties: the former communist PDS, the fascist Italian Social Movement
spearheaded by Alessandra Mussolini, the Duce's granddaughter; and the
separatist Northern League. None of these groups could provide Italy
with a viable approach to consensus politics or institutional reform.

6 My first attempt at such a critique appears in *The Power in the Land*,
London: Shepheard-Walwyn, 1983.

7 The British Green Party is an exception to this observation. But see David
Richards, "The Greens and the Tax on Rent", in Noyes, *op. cit.*, pp. 160–163.

8 Anthony B. Atkinson and Joseph E. Stiglitz, *Lectures on Public Economics*,
London: McGraw Hill, 1980, p.525.

9 The Open Letter is reproduced in Noyes, *op. cit.*, pp. 225–230.

10 Harrison, *op cit.* See also Mason Gaffney and Fred Harrison, *Land
Speculation & the Business Cycle:* Shepheard-Walwyn/CIT, London, 1995.

11 James S. Ackerman, *Palladio,* London: Penguin, 1991, p. 182.

12 *Ibid.,* p. 162.

13 John Kenneth Galbraith, *The Anatomy of Power,* 1984, London: Hamish Hamilton.

14 They did not do so willingly, however. See Roy Douglas, *Land, People & Politics: A History of the Land Question in the United Kingdom, 1878–1952,* London: Allison & Busby, 1976.

15 In Britain, the Left's poverty of philosophy is illustrated, in the post-Thatcher era, in the attempt to define the future of individual welfare in legalistic and income-redistribution terms, rather than the empowerment of the individual through a fluid system of wealth creation. See, for example, Anna Coote (editor), *The Welfare of Citizens,* London: Institute for Public Policy Research/Rivers Oram Press, 1992.

In America, "progressives" have a similar conceptual problem in the post-Reagan era. Frustratingly, one of them, Gar Alperovitz, comes tantalizingly close to the Georgist paradigm, with this kind of statement: "A public trust to establish community ownership of such wealth (and natural resources) – at the national, regional, state and local levels – could in turn produce a stream of income, part of which might be used by the community as a whole to offset taxes and provide needed services, and part of which might be allocated to provide direct economic stability and security to individuals in the interest of a new structural basis for human liberty and democratic participation" (Gar Alerpovitz, "Beyond Socialism and Capitalism", in Chester Hartman and Pedro Vilanova (editors), *Paradigms Lost: The Post Cold War Era,* London: Pluto Press, 1992, p.198). In the end, his perceptions on property rights stem from the socialist paradigm. Alperovitz, therefore, like his British counterparts, cannot see beyond legalism, and the need for a system of planning, despite the unambiguous lessons of the Soviet Union.

16 Murray Feshbach and Alfred Friendly Jr., *Ecoside in the USSR,* London: Aurum Press, 1992.

17 Ronald Banks (editor), *Costing the Earth,* London: Shepheard Walwyn, 1989.

18 Steven Cord, *Incentive Taxation,* August 1986, Center for the Study of Economics, Columbia, MD.

19 Prof. Gaffney offered this estimate during a seminar in St. Petersburg, January 1993, in answer to a question from the present author. For his definitive judgement, however, see his contribution to Ronald Banks and Kenneth Jupp (eds.). *Private Property and Public Finance,* London: Shepheard-Walwyn/CIT, 1995.

20 Ronald Burgess, *Public Revenue Without Taxation,* London: Shepheard Walwyn, 1993. The 50% figure was a personal communication to the present author.

21 Adam Smith, *The Wealth of Nations,* Bk V, Ch.II, pp.370–371. Page references are to the 1976 edition by Edwin Cannan, The University of Chicago Press.

22 Adam Smith, *The Theory of Moral Sentiments* [1759]; page 304–205 in the edition published by Liberty Classics, Indianapolis, 1969. For a fuller treatment of the moral flaw in Smith's philosophy, see Harrison, *op. cit.,* Ch.2.

23 *The Wealth of Nations, op. cit.* p.370.

24 The necessity of this task is illustrated by the work of an international team of distinguished scholars, which was collated in a volume called *The Crisis in Economic Theory* (editors: Daniel Bell and Irving Kristol, New York: Basic Books, 1981). The index lists 19 references to wages, 11 references to profits/interest; and not a single reference to rent. Land does, in fact, make an appearance in the book, but not as a subject worthy of separate treatment. "Wealth, we assume, is land, machinery, goods," wrote one of the editors (Bell, p.59).

25 Howard's book was first published as *Tomorrow: A Peaceful Path to Real Reform* (1898). It was reissued in 1902 as *Garden Cities of Tomorrow,* the revised edition was published in 1985 by Attic Books, Eastbourne.

26 *Ibid.,* pp.xxiv–xxv.

27 *Ibid.* For a recent review of the garden city concept, and an exposition of what the author views as a conspiracy to bury the land-rent issue, see ColinWard, *New Town, Home Town,* London: Calouste Gulbenkian Foundation, 1993. In *A New London* (London: Penguin, 1992, p.xxxii) architects Richard Rogers and Mark Fisher affirm the need to revive the Howard/Habitat plan for reconstituting the modern city on the basis of a reform of the system of public revenue.

28 Conference on Human Settlements, 31 May–11 June, 1976, New York: United Nations, A/CONF. 70/15, p.65.

29 *Op. cit.,* Ch.12.

30 A similar vision was elaborated by architect Frank Lloyd Wright in the United States. He, too, was a devotee of Henry George's land philosophy. Alas, his Broadacres – unlike Howard's Letchworth – was not to leave the drawing board.

31 John Lovelock, *GAIA: A New Look at Life on Earth,* Oxford: Oxford University Press, 1982.

32 There are exceptions to this stricture in the voluminous literature on environmental issues. One such is M.D. Young, *Sustainable Investment and Resource Use,* Paris: UNESCO, 1992.

33 See Paul Downing, (Editor), *Poverty and the Bounty of Nature,* another volume in this series.

34 Francis Fukuyama, *The End of History and the Last Man,* London: Hamish Hamilton, 1992.

35 Melville J. Ulmer, "Economic Power and Vested Interests", in K.W. Rothschild (editor), *Power in Economics,* Harmondsworth: Penguin, 1971, p.245.

36 Christopher Lasch, "Family and Authority", in Barry Richards (editor), *Capitalism and Infancy* (1984), London: Free Association Books, p.29.

37 Richard Noyes, "Dialectics and the Millennium: emergence of the Synthesis", in Noyes, *op. cit.*

38 M. Gaffney, "Two Centuries of Economic Thought on Taxation of Land Rents", in Richard W. Lindholm and Arthur D. Lynn, Jr. (editors), *Land Value Taxation,* Madison: University of Wisconsin Press, 1992, and his contribution to this volume.

39 Ludwig von Mises, *Bureaucracy* [1944], New Haven: Yale UP, 1962, p.10. Frederick von Hayek adopts a similar view; the reason why this school of economics did not see the prospect of a qualitative transformation of "capitalism" is that it was locked into the Lockian system of property rights in land. Hayek, for example, informed the present author that the concept of land monopoly did not make sense, given that land was owned by so many people. This revealed a surprisingly superficial understanding of what is meant by land monopoly.

40 Henry George, *Progress and Poverty* [1879], New York: Robert Schalkenbach Foundation, 1979, Bk.X, Ch.3. A close reading of *Progress and Poverty* repays with a rich set of hypotheses, such as the ecological theory of international trade, which Henry George recognised as an inducement to peaceful co-operation and therefore the advancement of civilisation (*ibid,* p.512).

41 Alfred Kuhn, *The Study of Society,* London: Tavistock Publications, 1966.

42 *Ibid.,* p.582. In this statement Kuhn smuggles in a justification for private ownership in terms of the administrative function. But land can be equally well administered by people who do not enjoy ownership rights (tenant farmers, for example).

43 *Ibid.,* p.587.

44 *Ibid.,* p.743.

45 Fred Harrison, "Post-socialism and the Single Tax: a holistic philosophy", in Noyes, *op. cit.*

46 Although Marx called his book *Capital,* the posthumously published Vol. Ill provided the corrective analysis. In the end, Marx *did* perceive the difference, but the significance ofhis insights escaped the attention of his adherents. See Fred Harrison, "Gronlund and other Marxists", in Robert V. Andelson, *Critics of Henry George* (1979), Cranbury, NJ: Associated University Presses, pp.206–213.

47 Henry George certainly thought so, 100 years ago. He analysed the prospective failure in terms of the organisational impossibility of commanding an economy to deliver the goods. See Henry George, *The Science of Political Economy* (1898), New York: Robert Schalkenbach Foundation, 1981, pp.394–6. His prediction has proved to be correct.

48 David Redfearn, *Tolstoy: Principles for the New World Order,* London: Shepheard Walwyn, 1992.

49 In Latin America, the vast abundance of vacant or under-used farmland is associated with starvation-level wages. Why? Because the *latifundistas* earn higher rents if they keep land out of use. This forces labourers to migrate to the margins of society – which, in Brazil, is the Amazon basin, where they proceed to wreak ecological havoc in their battle for survival.

50 *Seeds of Plenty, Seeds of Sorrow,* BBC2 television documentary, June 4, 1992.

51 *Ibid.*

52 *Ibid.*

53 It is the failure to comply with the precepts of the Georgist paradigm which permits institutions like the World Bank to finance the wrecking of the environment. For a review of the impact on the rainforests of the World Bank's Tropical Forestry Action Plan, see Susan George, "Managing the Global House: Redefining Economics", in Hartman and Vilamora, *op. cit.,* pp.121–124. Miss George, a passionate critic, alas fails to redefine economics, beyond suggesting the need to return to its classical forms – which is, admittedly, a start in the correct direction.

54 Henry George argued that cooperation and equality dictated severe constraints on the size of the political entity, "... when large bodies come to act together, personal selection becomes more difficult, a blinder obedience becomes necessary and can be enforced, and from the very necessities of warfare when conducted on a large scale absolute power arises." *Progress & Poverty,* op. cit., p.517.

55 Rosalind Miles, *The Women's History of the World* (1988), London: Michael

Joseph.

56 Frederick Engels, *The Origin of the Family, Private Property and the State*; Introduction and Notes by Eleanor Burke Leacock, London: Lawrence & Wishart, 1972, p. 120.

57 Barry Richards, "Introduction", *op. cit.*, p.18.

58 Simone de Beauvoir, *The Second Sex* [1949], translated and edited by H.M. Parshley, London: Pan Books, 1988, p.102. This judgement warrants further scrutiny. We need to know, for example, about the status of women in tropical Africa, where societies were largely matrilineal until the change to patrilineality sometime during the past 500 years. *Ancient Civilizations of Africa* (editor: G. Mokhtar), Paris: UNESCO, 1990, p.388.

59 I proposed such a development fund, financed out of the rental value of land, for the former Soviet countries, in Noyes *(op cit*: pp.99–100). The "external diseconomies" of modern methods of production now transcend continents, let alone the territorial borders of nation-states, so nothing short of a global strategy will meet the demands of either ecology or equity.

60 John Hibbs, *Transport without Politics . . .?* London: IEA Hobart Paper 95, p.56.

61 William Vickrey, "The City as a Firm", in Martin S. Feldstein and Robert P. Inman, *The Economics of Public Services*, London: Macmillan, 1977, p.334.

62 Joseph E. Stiglitz, "The Theory of Local Public Goods", in Feldstein and Inman, *op.cit.*, p.282.

63 They speculated $69,000 in the Whitewater deal, and lost nearly all of it. "All the Pieces Fit to Puzzle", *Time*, January 17, 1994.

64 In California, for example, which suffered grievously from the riots in Los Angeles in 1992, citizens are so anxious about their welfare – and are resigned to living in a community incapable of enforcing acceptable standards of civic behaviour – that private security guards outnumber policemen.

The cost to society of lawlessness is phenomenal. Firearm injuries alone, for example, cost the US economy over $20 billion a year, according to a study at the University of California at San Francisco (published in *Health Affairs*, January 1994). This includes $1.4 bn in medical costs, $1.6 bn in lost productivity and $17.4 bn in lost productivity due to premature death.

65 Durkheim analysed the role of specialisation in science in the creation of anomie. "... science, parcelled out into a multitude of detailed studies which are not joined together, no longer forms a solidary whole. What best manifests, perhaps, this absence of concert and unity is the theory, so prevalent, that each particular science has an absolute value, and that the scholar ought to devote himself to his special researches without bothering

to inquire whether they serve some purpose and lead anywhere". Emile Durkheim, *The Division of Labor in Society* (1893), New York: Free Press, 1933, p.357.

66 *Ibid.*, p.362.

67 Mark Gallagher, *Rent Seeking and Economic Growth in Africa*, Boulder: Westview Press, 1991.

68 "G7 poverty", *The Financial Times*, London, July 9, 1992.

69 John Llewellyn and Stephen J. Potter, *Economic Policies for the 1990s*, Oxford: Blackwell, 1991.

70 Peter Norman, "Economic Notebook", *The Financial Times*, London, July 6, 1992.

71 P. Jurkovic, "Designing a Tax System to Promote Structural Change", in *The Role of Tax Reform in Central and Eastern European Economies*, Paris: OECD/Centre for Co-operation with European Economies in Transition, 1991, p.48.

72 *Ibid.*, pp.48–49.

73 Jeffrey Sachs, *Poland's Jump to the Market Economy*, Cambridge, Mass.: The MIT Press, 1993, p.5.

74 Jas Gawronski, "States of savagery, seeds of good", *The Guardian*, London, Nov.2, 1993. John Paul II characterised the failure of capitalism in terms of its failure to recognise the significance of the spirit of community, which was a feature of communism. The problems of capitalism stemmed from the emphasis on individualism.

75 Lord Lawson, "A paean of praise to capitalism", *The Financial Times*, London, Sept.4, 1993.

76 The dominant outlook, indeed, was one of pessimism; this was reflected in the view, expressed by a British government minister, that to expect the abolition of unemployment was "fantasy".

77 Daniel M. Friedenberg, *Life, Liberty and the Pursuit of Land*, Buffalo, NY: Prometheus Books, 1992.

78 Over 60 children were murdered on the streets of Chicago alone in the first eleven months of 1993. "Many of the killers, usually with guns, are other children," reports Paul Barker in "Street violence for export?" *The Guardian*, London, Dec.4, 1993.

79 Quoted in Louis Hacker, *Triumph of American Capitalism*, New York: Columbia University Press, 1947, p.187.

80 The Federalist No.73, cited in Charles Beard, *An Economic Interpretation of the Constitution*, New York: Macmillan, 1935, pp.156–158.

81 Michael Hudson, *The Lost Tradition of Biblical Debt Cancellations*, New

York: Henry George School of Social Science, 1993. See also his contribution to *A Philosophy for a Fair Society,* a companion volume in this series.

82 Michael Howard, *The Lessons of History,* Oxford: OUP, 1991.

83 "World Bank aims to halve global hunger", *The Guardian,* London, Nov.30, 1993.

84 The Georgist philosophy is presented in the Latin American context by Robert V. Andelson and James M. Dawsey, *From Wasteland to Promised Land,* Maryknoll, NY: Orbis Books/London: Shepheard Walwyn, 1992.

85 Quoted in *Land and Liberty,* London, March–April 1932, p.35.

86 B.E.V. Sabine, *A History of Income Tax,* London: George Allen & Unwin, 1966, p.199.

87 *Op. cit.,* Bk.V, Ch.II, p.384.

Postscript on neo-classical economics
South Africa 1994: Countdown to Disaster

Kris Feder and Fred Harrison

Apartheid South Africa was in turmoil in 1990. Nelson Mandela dreamed of a free country, and his African National Congress was in the throes of the struggle for the right to vote.

In that year two white South Africans published a manifesto for a fair society. *The Trial of Chaka Dlamini* was constructed in the form of a platonic dialogue by Stephen Meintjes, the managing director of a Johannesburg investment management company, and Michael Jacques, a chartered accountant. The sub-title, *An Economic Scenario for the New South Africa,* indicated the sweep of their proposals. They had come to realise that political rights that were not matched by economic rights were of little value. And they had concluded that Henry George's Single Tax strategy was what a multi-racial South Africa needed. The pre-condition for economic freedom, they explained, was the abolition of the tax burden on production and consumption -- on wages and profits – while treating the rent of land and natural resources as the appropriate source of public revenue.

Four years later, in April 1994, the racist order was swept away and the people received the opportunity of a fresh start. The political slate was wiped clean. Nelson Mandela became the popular president of a multi-racial government of national unity. The ANC shed its "communist" aura and became a party of reasonableness. It committed itself to working with the International Monetary Fund to restructure the economy, while declaring the need to correct the injustices – the black man's burden – of the 20th century.

Conflict over the possession of land was the most vexatious problem. The Mandela government determined to tread a difficult path to meet the aspirations of both its black and white citizens. Here, surely, was the laboratory for the Single Tax? This simple-to-understand policy would encourage investment, create jobs, and enable those who possessed land to choose: either use the land properly – and pay the community for the benefits received – or release it to others.

The Mandela government lost no time in establishing a Tax Commission that would investigate all options. This time round, one would have thought, the Single Tax strategy would not be patronised and sneered out of the realms of political debate. For one of the first lines of attack on the policy – the claim that there are practical problems of implementation – could not possibly be raised in the South African context. For nearly all the municipalities of South Africa directly levied a tax on the value of land (i.e., excluding the value of buildings): the principle of treating land different from capital was an established fiscal fact! The bureaucratic infrastructure that is required to assess the taxable value of land and collect the revenue was in place. All that South Africa needed was an imaginative redesign of the architecture of public finance, building a system that would liberate the talents and savings of people (fair to all) while raising revenue from the rental value that was created by the community (fair to all).

Although the site-value property tax has an established history in South Africa, the tax rates are so low that the country has not enjoyed the macro-economic benefits that flow from the Single Tax. Nonetheless, a crystal-clear hint of the dynamic benefits of this approach to public finance was visible in the economic record. Godfrey Dunkley, an advocate of the Single Tax policy, had analysed the data and published the results.

He found that, between 1951 and 1984, there had been a shift among municipal authorities in favour of raising local revenue from the value of sites alone (the "site value" approach), rather than from the total value of land-plus-buildings (the "flat rate") or the "composite value" (a higher rate of tax on land than on the value of buildings).

Analysis of data in the South African Municipal Year Book revealed that the towns that raised revenue from site value increased from 11% to 38% of the total cities; the flat-rate towns declined from 58% to 24%. The composite rate towns increased from 31% to 38%. The trend was unmistakable. Property owners, through their democratic representatives, favoured the exemption of the value of their improvements on the land; while raising an increasing proportion of municipal revenue from the rental value of the land they occupied. One of the economic consequences of this transformation is traced in the table. This reveals the growth in the value of improvements on land over a 10-year period. The top 48 towns are included, each with a total value of over R200 million.

Table 1
48 South African towns
Value of improvements on land

Tax base	No.of towns	Improvement value (Rand: millions)		Growth %
		1974	**1984**	
Flat	2	1412	4080	189
Composite	13	1856	7085	282
Site value	33	5084	26084	413
Total	48	8353	37250	345

Source: Godfrey Dunkley (1990: 124).

Among the largest towns of South Africa, only the two ports of Cape Town and Port Elizabeth had failed to adopt the more sophisticated property tax – the one that acknowledges the need to differentiate between land and buildings. They levy a tax at a uniform rate on both components of property. Logically, these two towns – one of them the legislative capital, the other a commercial nerve-centre – ought to have kept pace with the average rate of growth of investment enjoyed by the other major towns. In fact, their percentage growth has been less than half that of the towns that exempt buildings from the tax base.[1]

But while the picture at the municipal level is unambiguous, the benefits of the Single Tax could not be fully enjoyed until the policy is adopted as the central feature of national government strategy. The Mandela government, before it could contemplate a radical shifting to an entirely new approach to fiscal policy, had to be sure that there would be no loss of desperately-needed revenue. Would a Single Tax strategy meet the fiscal needs of the new South Africa? Meintjes and Jacques had little doubt that it would, and they submitted their proposals to the Tax Commission in July 1994. In proferring figures, they confidently explained the philosophy that underpins the Single Tax – a policy of fairness, and one that just might succeed where others had failed:

> The inability of all developing and developed economies to eliminate poverty is due to the failure to recognise that locational advantage is the natural source of revenue for the community.

Their analysis was starkly simple:

> In South Africa, of all places, where only 15% of the surface area is arable [and] the overwhelming bulk of secondary industry is restricted to a handful of metropolitan areas it is, or should be, an axiom of taxation, that the greater part of the surface area of the country has little or no taxable capacity, i.e. locational advantage. Failure to recognise this leads to under-recovery of natural rent and underutilisation of land and natural resources on prime sites, and futile attempts to raise revenue from sites at the margin. Such attempts include not only the heavy incident of indirect taxation in outlying areas but also PAYE. Since the latter can only be derived from value added by the enterprise it is in effect a payroll tax which eliminates employment opportunities in these areas by preventing businesses from achieving the necessary minimum returns on capital. Such attempts are therefore directly responsible for the uprooting of rural communities and the flood of squatters to metropolitan areas. (Meintjes & Jacques 1994: 2)

Here, in a nutshell, was the exposition that the neo-classical economists had sought to shroud in metaphysics. It exposed the destructive dynamics of taxation on wages and profits, which destroyed jobs and reduced living standards; taxation that inhibited investment and fostered social conflict.

For generations the people of South Africa had been denied the full benefits of the rational system of public revenue. Added to the tax burden were the other economic weapons against freedom – monopolies, subsidies, tariffs – which, as Meintjes and Jacques put it, had been "giving rise to substantial artificial rents".

A switch to the Single Tax strategy would channel the "artificial rents" into the public purse. Meintjes and Jacques listed some of the dynamic benefits for the benefit of the Tax Commission:

• Economic activity on sites of marginal value, including less valuable sites in metropolitan areas, would become viable.

• The development and efficient use of natural resources would be encouraged, and the hoarding of land by those who were enriched by systemic inefficiency would be deterred.

• Land reform would be facilitated on an equitable basis.

• Capital cost of access to land – one of the major obstacles to starting new businesses and creating jobs – would be eliminated.

• Site values would no longer serve as collateral, because the bulk of natural rent would be treated as public revenue. Banks would therefore be deterred from fuelling speculation: they would become more feasibility-oriented in their lending criteria, i.e., they would be more concerned about the viability of projects and management rather than mechanically counting on collateral to rescue them from poor lending decisions.

In the course of phasing in the Single Tax policy over (say) 10 years, explained Meintjes and Jacques, people in the metropolitan areas would become richer and the profitability of enterprises would increase. This would result from

• Creation of additional markets for output;

• Reduction of problems that result from the inward flood of impoverished squatters; and

• Stimulation of the whole economy on a win-win basis for all.

Meintjes and Jacques emphasise that this process would be guided by market mechanisms, including the use of auctions to ensure that prospective users – not civil servants – determined the rental value of land. The new system would have to be transparent: the fullest information provided to the public, to eliminate one of the obstacles to the pricing mechanism that characterises most of the market economies of the world – the concealment of information, particularly in the land market. And aware of the need for an optimum financial system for the mining industries, they also explained how the Single Tax would stimulate new investment in the gold mines.

This, surely, was a prospectus that would appeal to the Mandela government as it deliberated on the need for revisions to the South Africa constitution in 1994? The alternative – retaining the core institutions of the western market economy – was surely not a serious option? For was it not those core institutions that had escorted – if not engineered – the world economy into the greatest depression since the 1930s?

Cry economic freedom

Enter the Free Market Foundation of Southern Africa. This organisation, headquartered in Johannesburg, is patronised by some of the leading entrepreneurs in the diamond cartel. It advocates "economic freedom". That philosophy of freedom, however, does not have universal application. The freedom championed by the well-financed Foundation is the freedom of those who already control the property of South Africa. And they were determined to nail the ghost of Henry George before anyone started talking about the need to depart from the tax policies of the neo-classical economists!

Henry George had suspected that the emerging neo-classical school of economics was designed to silence the single tax movement by crippling the language of the land question. [George, 1898:200–209] As Mason Gaffney documents in this volume, George was at least partly correct. Moreover, the "neo-classical stratagem" of suppression continued to be pursued many years after George's death. (Feder 1994a)

Lest it be supposed that Prof. Gaffney has rewritten history to boost Henry George – or, that economists today have finally put aside politically-motivated resentments, and are prepared to confront Georgists with unassailable logic – the attack by The Free Market Foundation bears witness to the current state of debate in economics.

Its study was prepared by Richard Grant, the Foundation's former Director of Research who received his doctorate from George Mason University in the United States, before moving to South Africa where he was to lecture on economics at the University of the Witwatersrand. [Grant, 1994] Referring to the current dialogue in South Africa regarding the use of taxation as a tool of land reform (Franzsen and Heyns 1992), Grant disparages the Georgist proposal as merely another dangerous scheme to nationalise land. The "single tax on land rent," he pronounces in *Nationalisation: How Governments Control You* (1994: 51) is unjust and confiscatory; it flagrantly disregards legitimate property rights; it compels arbitrariness in assessments, inviting collusion and corruption in government. Worst of all, it is inconsistent with the operation of a market system, and leads inevitably to socialism. Grant reinforces his position with frequent appeals to the authority of Frank Knight, the Chicago School economist who, according to Gaffney, "probably produced more neo-classical economists and neo-classical economisms than anyone in history." As Gaffney observes, Knight's treatment of the land question "reads like a caricature of Chicago." Grant's assault, in turn, reads like a caricature of Frank Knight – like a silly spoof of the neo-classical paradigm. Grant has assembled two dozen of the most transparent single-tax fallacies, throwing in a couple more of his own devising. What is frightening is that uninformed readers, concluding that the single tax is a hoax, may give it no further consideration. Some, though not all, of the efficiency advantages of taxes on rent or land value are widely recognised by mainstream economists. According to Grant, however, the single tax is as inefficient as it is as inequitable. A tax on rent, he believes, is just like any other tax: all have unfortunate consequences for economic incentives; they should be applied at low rates, and only as necessary to raise revenue. There is nothing "magical" about a special tax collecting all of land rent. On the contrary, if applied at rates approaching 100%, as single-tax advocates insist, it would cripple land markets, paralysing their inherent tendency to allocate land to its most productive uses. Grant opens with the assertion that "the distinction between man-made and natural factors of production – that is, between capital and land ... is irrelevant when discussing intervention and taxation: the consequences will be the same for any asset." (p.51)

Nothing could be further from the truth. Taxes are, or ought to be, predictable long-term arrangements; so the long-run supply conditions of productive factors are critical to the effects of taxes upon them. A tax on the ownership of capital will, in the long run, discourage the production of new capital. A tax on the ownership of non-produced land has no such disincentive effect. Grant does not consider this, however; he takes a different angle. "Rent," he writes, "is a general phenomonon that applies to all assets, not only land." (p.52) The implicit suggestion is that one can refute George by redefining terms – the standard neo-classical stratagem. Henry George followed Ricardo in defining rent as the amount by which the product of a land parcel exceeds that of the best available no-rent land. Rent, in other words, is the minimum amount which a prospective user would have to pay, in a competitive market, to outbid all others for the use of land. As we now say, rent is the opportunity cost of land use. Grant, however, defines "economic rent" as "the difference between the return to one asset and the return to the poorest asset being used for the same purpose." Thus, presumably, the rent of a car used in transportation is equal to the difference between its return and that of the least efficient bicycle, or pair of feet, used for the "same purpose" – however narrowly or broadly that phrase may be interpreted.

The definition given any term is neither right nor wrong; it is simply more or less useful in facilitating thought. Now, George's classical definition of rent is intelligible and eminently useful, particularly for analysis of the issue at hand. Grant's definition, by contrast, is plagued by ambiguity, and serves little function in economic inquiry. It matters not that Grant's definition of "economic rent" differs subtly from the usual, equally problematic, neo-classical definition, because he takes it nowhere. It is as though economists have redefined "rent" in a manner calculated to dispose of the term altogether. Grant's next argument is novel. He says that a 100% tax on rent would, through tax capitalisation, "make the price of land the same everywhere, regardless of location or quality." True enough – the selling price of all unimproved land will be zero. But Grant draws the surprising conclusion that "this artificial levelling of relative prices" would "leave no differential rent for purposes of economic calculation," "blinding" the land market "with respect to quality." (p.52)

Grant seems to mean that, since all land bears the same (zero) price, users are indifferent among land parcels of different qualities. Plainly, however, if all items of a kind are priced equally, buyers will hardly be blinded to quality; quite the contrary, they will choose among them on the basis of qualitative and locational differences alone. Just as obviously, a uniform (zero) price for title to land does not mean that the cost of land to buyers is the same for all land. The high or low purchase prices paid for good or poor land are simply commuted into high or low annual rent payments. Rents continue to perform their function of allocating scarce land to its highest-yielding uses. If bidders for land have different preferences for land consumption and/or different comparative advantages in production, land subject to rent taxation will also be allocated efficiently among users.

In fact, as Georgists have shown, a high tax on rent causes land markets to operate more fluidly, competitively, and efficiently. By slashing start-up costs, the tax makes it easier for productive users to acquire land. It improves efficiency by bypassing the distortions introduced by inherently imperfect capital markets. The annual tax also functions far better than once-for-all prices to signal landowners information on the current opportunity cost of holding possession. (Gaffney 1992)

The source of Grant's confusion emerges in his next two paragraphs. He interprets the Georgist position to mean that "any benefit that a landowner derives from land that is better than the worst land in use is to be taxed away." (p.52) He asks: "What good are title deeds if the government takes all the net income ...? How long would you want to hold an asset from which the income is expropriated?" (p.53) Grant evidently supposes that the tax assessment on a particular parcel of land would depend upon how productively the current owner is putting it to use – so that the harder and smarter he works, the higher go his taxes, leaving him no reward for superior effort.

This does not describe the Georgist tax on land rent, which is a market-determined measure of the annual opportunity cost of land possession, i.e., of its potential productivity as estimated by market participants. The true Georgist tax is a fixed charge from the point of view of the individual title-holder; it leaves to the owner the full wages and interest of the labour and capital which he contributes to production, plus any entrepreneurial profit or loss. Economic incentives are channelled in the right direction. Ironically, Grant's criticism correctly applies, not to the Georgist proposal, but instead to traditional taxes based on income or production. A second error is operative here. "How long would you want to hold an asset from which the income is expropriated?" In other words: how long would you want to hold an asset for which you must pay the opportunity cost on an annual basis? The answer is: as long as the value of the asset to you continues to meet or exceed the value of the asset to others. The point holds no mystery for anyone who has ever leased a car, rented an apartment, or borrowed money at interest.

Turning next to the issue of land speculation, Grant objects to the single tax on several ethical and efficiency grounds. He fumes: By what standard do the Georgists and other interventionists label someone an "idle hoarder" or "speculator"? And by what right would they penalise these people? Doing so would require some standard superior to the market, but they cannot demonstrate what that is. (p.53)

Quoting Frank Knight, Grant observes that in competitive markets, buyers pay, in the purchase price of land, the entire present value of expected potential future net land income, land speculation is risky and expensive; speculators do not, on average earn undue profits. Moreover, if society proposes to confiscate the gains of the winners, it ought to compensate the losses of the losers – not only to meet the demands of justice, but also to preserve entrepreneurial incentives. Yes, it ought! And it does, automatically, under the single tax. When land values rise, so do payments to the community – and symmetrically, when land values fall, payments fall proportionately. The risk of appreciation or depreciation caused by events outside the landowners' control are borne by society as a whole, not by individual landowners. Pooled, the risks decline. Gains and losses resulting from private entrepreneurial activity, on the other hand, are untaxed.

On the subject of economic efficiency, Grant works both sides of the street. He argues inconsistently that it is undesirable to use rent taxation to discourage speculation since speculators "provide a valuable service" – but that, anyway, the tax will not succeed in forcing marginal land into use. (pp.54–55)

The Georgist position on land speculation may be summarised as follows. When neighbourhood land uses are changing, it is occasionally efficient to postpone land development or redevelopment until a new use becomes remunerative. This occurs when no potential interim use can be expected to yield revenues sufficient to amortise sunk capital before the optimal time of redevelopment. A tax on land rent or land value does not disturb such efficient land speculation, since the owner can reduce only his net income – not his fixed tax burden – by developing the land prematurely. (Feder, Tideman) Thus, insofar as speculators do "provide a valuable service," rent taxation will not disturb their choices. Marginal land bears no tax, so it will not be forced into use, just as Grant says. With respect to efficient land use, rent taxation is neutral. On the other hand, there are a host of reasons why inefficient land speculation frequently occurs. As noted above, rent taxation corrects inefficiencies arising from capital market imperfections, and the annual charge reminds inattentive owners of the income forgone when land is underused. Georgists have shown that rent taxation systematically penalises at least some forms of inefficient speculation, thus intensifying market pressures to use land productively.

(Brown 1927; Gaffney 1992; Feder 1994b) One writer calls this characteristic of rent taxation "superneutrality." (Dwyer 1981: 128ff)

In short, the standard to which Georgists hold the speculator is the standard of social efficiency. The single tax does not necessitate "some standard superior to the market": it makes the market operate better, closer to the competitive ideal.

Nor is the single tax motivated by envy, a scheme to strip successful businessmen of their hard-earned wealth. The aim of the single tax is to distribute the value of natural and social resources fairly among all, while leaving producers the full earnings of their labour and capital, untaxed. Henry George wrote: "We must make land common property" (1879: 328) and erected a lightning rod which has attracted unending criticism. Few terms have engendered more confusion in economics than the phrase "common property." It is no surprise that Grant manages to muddle the issues as thoroughly here as elsewhere.

> The Georgists have apparently forgotten that we are no longer a hunter-gatherer society ... Even though all land may once have been common "property," this does not give to every newborn today a share in everyone else's property. The whole meaning, and practical virtue, of private property is that it is privately owned and controlled ... The collective farms of the old Soviet Union prove this ... A drive through the tribal land of (the now former) Lebowa is very instructive on the issue of common property ... The grass has been overgrazed and the trees are steadily disappearing ... It is in those regions where property rights are suppressed or undeveloped that no one laughs at Malthus. (pp.55–56)

Grant nowhere explains what Soviet collectives and Lebowan tribal commons have to do with the single tax; he trusts the reader to accept thoughtlessly the implicit analogy. It is false.[2] The subterfuge relies on the merging of concepts three distinct concepts. Soviet collectives were state-owned and state-controlled *government property*, not common property. With no exclusive rights of tenure, workers had little incentive to concern themselves with productivity, lands (also air, water, or biological species) that are freely accessible to all comers, with no regulatory mechanism to ration their use, are not common property (*res communis*) but "nobody's property" (*res nullius*). When human populations are relatively large, such a resource is characterised by over-exploitation and depletion. Users have no direct stake, individually, in maintaining the asset value of the resource, since they possess only rights of extraction and use, not exclusive rights of ownership. Trees left standing, or fish left swimming, are resources ceded to competitors. All of this was recognised by Henry George.

The function of the single tax is to strengthen, not weaken, the legitimate property claims of labour and capital – while guaranteeing the equal right of every person to the use of the primary, non-produced resources necessary for all production. Without access to natural opportunities, after all, the celebrated right to enjoy the product of one's labour, thrift and ingenuity becomes a cruel joke. We have never heard anyone openly reject the ethical proposition that all human beings ought to be accorded equal opportunity to avail themselves of what nature provides. Even Grant falls short of this; he twists away by pretending that the Georgist ethical premise implies a free-for-all.

This, indeed, is the puzzle: how can equal rights to land be assured in an industrial and service economy, where an equal physical division of land among individuals would be hopelessly inefficient? Those unfamiliar with Georgist thought typically accept the existing system of fee simple land tenure despite its evident inequities, presuming that land cannot be made common property without creating economic and political chaos. The core contribution of Henry George lies here: in a monetary market economy with democratic political institutions, natural resources can be fairly shared by the device of collecting rent – all of it – by taxation, using the revenue (along with that from other user charges and taxes) for the support of government. (Part of the rent could be simply paid out as an equal cash dividend to each citizen. The dividend would operate like the personal exemption credited to taxpayers in the U.S. personal income tax system – except that it would be enjoyed even by those with little or no taxable income.)

> The tax upon land values falls upon those who receive from society a peculiar and valuable benefit, and upon them in proportion to the benefit they receive. It is the taking by the community, for the use of the community, of the value that is the creation of the community. It is the application of the common property to common uses. (George 1879: 421)

The genius of the single tax is that it allows rents to be shared without disturbing the system of private, exclusive land use which is indispensable for harnessing productive incentives and exploiting the advantages of specialisation and scale economies. Society need not alienate the common property to individual ownership in fee simple to enjoy the benefits of a market system. Equity need not be compromised in the name of efficiency, nor efficiency compromised for the sake of equity. We can have both. Under the Georgist system, everyone willing to pay its opportunity cost to society can get title to as much land as he likes; and he may, within reasonable bounds, do with it what he will. If government expenditures are optimal, an individual who happens to take title to his equal value-share of land will receive, in the value of public goods and transfers enjoyed, an amount exactly equal to the rent he pays to the community for his land title. An individual who takes more than his equal share of land will, on balance, just compensate the community for encroaching upon others' shares. An individual who chooses not to own any land still receives his equal share of rent, in consideration of the fact that his abstention leaves all the more land for others to use.

Under the single tax, everyone is a rent-taker. Ultimately, of course, everyone also pays for the productive contribution of natural resources in proportion to his consumption.

> The value of land expresses in exact and tangible form the right of the community to land held by an individual; and rent expresses the exact amount which the individual should pay to the community to satisfy the equal rights of all other members of the community. (*Ibid.*: 34)

The value of a plot of land reflects not only the value of the natural resources it contains, but also its location with respect to markets, people, jobs, schools, recreational areas, and all manner of public goods and services, such as police and fire protection, schools, and infrastructure. When private activities incidentally enhance or depress neighbouring land values, economists speak of positive or negative spatial externalities. If I plant a cool orchard where once bare terrain burned under the sun and eroded in the rains, my neighbour's land rises in value; if I erect a noisy, smoky factory, my neighbour's land value falls. Similarly, the benefits of access to local public goods lodge in land values. For example, many families prefer to live in communities where the public schools have a good reputation; so the demand for – and price of – land in these districts is higher than elsewhere, *ceteris paribus*.

Ideally, perhaps, individuals should be compensated for emitting positive externalities and penalised for emitting negative ones. A set of so-called Pigouvian taxes and subsidies could, in principle, "internalise" externalities to achieve efficiency, essentially by creating quasi-markets. Economists love these. They are, of course, just Georgist taxes on rent, applied to fluid (air and water) resources which had been previously treated more or less as *res nullius*.

Unfortunately, for most everyday spatial externalities, it is prohibitively expensive, if not impossible, for a tax assessor to measure the aggregate net external impact of any one individual's activities. Without this information, the theoretically optimal tax for that individual cannot be found, and supply incentives for externalities will fall short of ideal. Fortunately, however, markets can, on the demand side, effectively ration scarce access to spatial externalities and public goods. The rationing mechanism is rent, and it works fairly well even when land is subject to private property in fee simple. It will work magnificently under the single tax, designed to include effluent fees and related environmental-use charges where feasible.

Georgists have said the single tax is best conceived as a "user charge." Grant disparages the phrase, but its rationale is easy to see. Taxes proper are involuntary payments, owed by virtue of residence in a given geographically-defined political jurisdiction. The taxpayer enjoys the benefits of public expenditure, of course, but he has no choice (except as one voter among many) about the level of taxes; anyway, there is little correlation between the amount of his tax and the value to him of the benefits he receives. User charges, by contrast, are prices, paid voluntarily in exchange for benefits received. There can be little doubt, then, that taxes on the rents arising from government expenditure are equivalent to user charges.

If the Georgist ethical principle is accepted, and natural resources and privately-generated (but unattributed) externalities are treated as common property, then all rent taxes (in a society with just and democratic political institutions) may be conceived as user charges. Grant strays from the point with several remarkable complaints. First, he writes that a tax on land rent "lower[s] returns to all capital and labour used on that property." Surely it is plain that taxes on capital and labour, which Georgists yearn to abolish, are considerably more likely than land taxes to lower the returns to labour and capital! The fact is, tax capitalisation, which Grant elsewhere accepts, implies that a tax on pure rent does not lower the returns to labour and capital.

Incredibly, he next uses the notion of spatial externality to argue that a rent tax is really a tax on labour and capital – since "whenever they tax one person's property, they are in fact taxing everyone else's labour and capital that have contributed to its value." (p.56) It does not take an economist to see that the persons responsible for emitting externalities which affect a given property do not pay the land tax on that property, directly or indirectly. The person who benefits from their activities, by virtue of his possession of well-situated land, pays the tax, ensuring that private individuals do not receive windfall gains or suffer windfall losses merely by virtue of their location with respect to external influences out of their control.

Grant goes on to accuse Georgists – targetting the two South African's, Meintjes and Jacques – of "methodological collectivism ... They fail to see that their 'community' is an abstraction, not an acting entity that can create value." (p.57) In fact, the community is not a vacant abstraction but a collection of real individuals, institutions, and capital.

Though he is shooting blanks, Grant has no shortage of ammunition. His next angle is to argue that rent takers receive no unearned income because they pay for the land which yields them rent! Again he quotes Frank Knight: "[T]he value alleged to be socially created is always paid for before it is received – as far as the parties most interested are able to predict its arising." (p.57, from Knight 1953: 809) There is no denial, only neglect, of the fact that market expectations of the future are frequently and understandably wrong, so windfall gains and losses accrue to landowners. The benefits of government projects are particularly difficult to foresee many years in advance. The question is: should the land gains resulting from proximity to government services and other community activities accrue to private landowners individually, or should they be pooled, and used for the support of the government and the citizenry?

Grant's confusion, inherited from Knight, runs deeper than the convenient fiction of perfect foresight. Because land has an opportunity cost to the firm or household, they deny that rent constitutes a social dividend. Their fallacy of composition has been exposed by Gaffney in this volume. Wages are the earnings of human effort in production. Interest is the reward for thrift and foresight in accumulating and employing capital. Rent is the payment for the use of land, with consideration for the value of natural resources, government services, and net private externalities (insofar as these cannot be internalised in markets or quasi-markets). For economic efficiency, rent must be paid by users to allocate scarce land among competing demands. But there is no efficiency requirement for rent to be paid to landowners; they do not produce land. Efficiency is achieved as well – better – when rent is collected by the community.

Grant's next argument is that the separate values land and improvements cannot be measured, since "economic rent is an abstract concept that does not appear separately in the market." (p.58) It is true enough that rent seldom "appears separately." Neither do wages: most products result from the commingled input of several factors of production. Yet markets do value factors separately, according to the familiar principle of marginal productivity. Tax assessments follow the market (assisted by computer-generated cadastral maps, which plot sales and interpolate surrounding values), land values are easier to assess than incomes, which can be concealed, and also easier to assess than building values, which require on-site inspection.

But Grant has a further, and novel, reason for insisting that land rents cannot be measured. The very imposition of the single tax itself, he says, destabilises the land market: "Any buyer knows that the more he pays for any property, the more rent he will be forced to pay." (p.59) Since the present value of his future taxes rises in lockstep with the price he pays for the land, a potential land buyer is indifferent about the price agreed upon. However, the Georgist tax on rent is assessed on the basis of current market valuation, not the historical price of the parcel under consideration. An individual's bid for land influences future assessed land values only indirectly and marginally, as one bit of market data among many. Unless regional land markets are characterised by significant monopoly power (which Grant would surely deny), an individual would ignore, as negligible, the influence of his own revealed demand upon his future land taxes. There is neither evidence nor theoretical justification for Grant's startling claim that "[t]he formal land market would largely break down." (p.59)

Unsettled questions

Can it be that, of Dr. Grant's many objections to the use of rent as the primary source of public revenue, not one withstands inspection? After all, plenty of genuinely unsettled questions and difficulties do remain in the economic theory of land and rent. If he truly wished to educate himself and others on the issue, Grant could have found them. One of his comments does carry weight: the puzzling thing is that he makes little of it. His readers will have noticed the point, however, so a few words are due. He notes:

> At the time of its imposition, there is no escape from the tax. The owner at that time will suffer a once-off capital loss on the property value and there is unlikely to be much shifting of ownership. (p.59)

We suspect that the reason he has not emphasised the point is that Grant believes, erroneously, that only part of the burden of the rent tax falls on current owners, and that future workers, capitalists, and landowners also bear a large part. In truth, the theory of tax capitalisation suggests that all of a rent tax (or tax increase) on land rent falls directly on those who own land at the moment the tax (increase) is announced: other things equal, the selling price of a plot of land falls by the full present value of all future taxes on that land. Afterward, a new buyer of the plot gets a reduced stream of after-tax rent, but pays a proportionately reduced land price, so that the rate of return is unchanged, and equal to the unchanged rate of return on other assets. This is the property responsible for the celebrated neutrality of land taxation. It is precisely because landowners can do nothing to escape it that the rent tax does not "distort" markets.

Ironically, the very efficiency of the land tax raises the problems of distributive equity and political acceptability – though only during the period of transition to the new tax structure. Inefficient taxes are popular in part because, through tax shifting, their burden is spread around in invisible and untraceable ways. Why should current landowners, whether they inherited their holdings or bought them yesterday at premium prices, be forced to bear the whole burden of the single tax? There are good answers, answers which do not depend upon painting innocent investors as sociopathic criminals.

First, not even the most impatient of Georgists suggests that the single tax system should be imposed all at once. Tax rates should be altered gradually, according to an agreed schedule. This allows individuals time to adjust their land holdings and their investment plans in order to take best advantage of the reform. In addition, the more gradually a rent tax increase is introduced after it is announced (the further in the future is the anticipated tax increase), the lower is the present value of future land taxes at the date of announcement, so the smaller is the decline in after-tax rents, and the smaller is the burden on current landowners. In effect, the burden of tax reform is shared among all taxpayers, who are compelled to endure the pre-existing system of distortionary taxation so much longer.

Second, the accompanying reduction or elimination of taxes on labour, capital, and exchange offsets the increase in the rent tax—in the aggregate— more than offsets it in fact, since the excess burden of taxation is reduced as the overall efficiency of the tax system is improved. The average household is better off, on balance. The significance of this is not merely that most landowners are also capitalists and wage earners too, and thus enjoy direct tax cuts.

It is a fundamental point of tax theory that taxes on production and wealth are generally shifted forward to consumers insofar as demand is relatively inelastic, and/or shifted backward to owners of resources insofar as factor supplies are relatively inelastic.

In an economy like that of South Africa, where real wages approach subsistence and can be forced no lower, both labour and capital are highly elastically supplied – so, most kinds of taxes on production are ultimately shifted largely to immobile land, which can neither starve nor flee. The converse of this is that when these taxes are reduced, the primary result of tax un-shifting is an increase in the gross rent of land. A moderate dose of single tax therapy will, in all likelihood, actually increase net (after-tax) rents received by landowners. As the rent tax rate approaches 100%, the effect of the increase in the rent tax must eventually overtake the contrary effect of the decrease in other taxes; land prices will approach zero. Still, if the single tax program is installed gradually, there is no undue burden on current landowners.

Third, some degree of shifting of the rent tax onto capital may occur after all, although only as the result of healthy, growth-producing wealth and liquidity effects, not from any distortionary tax "wedge." As Henry George emphasised and as Mason Gaffney has rigorously shown (for a review, see

Gaffney 1992), by reducing land prices and bypassing credit markets, the single tax makes it easier for cash-poor new producers to acquire land. At the same time, by raising holding costs, the tax makes it harder for unproductive hoarders to hold their savings in idle land, anticipating so-called "capital" gains and confident that any reversal in the upward trend of land prices can only be temporary. The consequence is an increase in the intensity with which land is used, which necessarily raises the demand for labour and capital. Even if credit markets were perfect, the single tax would stimulate capital formation. A rent tax reduces or eliminates private savers' option of holding land as an asset: the asset value of land (or some proportion of it) is now public property. Savings are thus redirected from land into produced capital, stimulating investment and (depending on the supply elasticity of capital) possibly lowering the marginal rate of return to capital. Furthermore, wages again tend to rise, not fall, as workers are employed to produce and use the new capital. All this, of course, is to the good. (Feldstein 1977; Gaffney 1992)

A false accusation

Grant's foremost charge against the single tax is his most desperate and far-fetched, but also the one that promises the greatest shock to conservative readers. This is the charge that Georgism is really a dangerous formula for repressive socialism, masquerading as benign free-market economics.

> In adopting the term "user charge", [Georgists] seem to have been ... taken in by the Marxist approach, which holds that the state is the true owner of the land. (p.61)

As we have noted, Grant confuses the concepts of *government property*, *res communis*, and *res nullius*. In the Georgist approach, natural resources are owned, not by the State, but by all the people in common. True, some public authority – a government – must collect and distribute the rent. But land is held in private title; markets operate freely; individuals manage their own affairs.

> Society would thus approach the ideal of Jeffersonian democracy, ... the abolition of government ... as a directing and repressive power ... We should reach the [egalitarian] ideal of the socialist, but not through government repression. Government would change its character, and would become

the administration of a great co-operative society. It would become merely
the agency by which the common property was administered for the
common benefit. (George 1879: 455–457)

But Grant's accusation of single-tax socialism is more than a matter of
philosophical language. "Professor Knight," he writes, "puts it bluntly:"

To collect such rent, the government would in practice have to compel the
owner actually to use the land in the best way, hence to prescribe its use in
some detail. (Knight, 1953: 809; quoted in Grant: 62)

Now, in a single-tax world, rational individuals who bid successfully for title
to land are generally able to pay the 100% rent tax and still earn a market rate
of return on their labour and capital. If no one volunteers to take a certain land
parcel and pay the assessed tax, this constitutes direct and publicly-available
evidence that the assessment on that parcel is too high; it overestimates the
value of the land. Why, then, would a tax on rent entail central planning?
Knight's only explanation is that "some official, some 'bureaucrat' with power,
would have to appraise it" (Knight 1953: 809), an observation that does not set
rent taxation apart from many other, apparently unobjectionable taxes. Grant's
marvellous rationale cannot fairly be credited to Knight:

Georgists are aware of the "supply side" effects on all the other tax bases,
but why would the famous Laffer Curve not also apply to their single tax?
As a tax rate approaches 100% of any tax base, revenues will approach zero
in the long run. This tax on rent is not compatible with a market economy
because it would eliminate any incentive for landlords to charge rent that
would be captured by the government ... To obtain revenue, government
assessors would have to set the level of tax arbitrarily, thereby placing
virtual control of the land in the hands of the state. (p.61–62)

The Laffer Curve, which reflects the excess burden of taxation caused by
substitution effects, does indeed apply to all taxes conditioned on
productive activity. It applies, for example, to a tax on land income, just as
it does to a tax on labour income (wages), or interest, or exports, or beer
purchases. However, neither the market-estimated potential income of
land, i.e., rent, nor its capitalised value (based on discounted future rents)
is subject to the discretion of the title-holder. From his viewpoint, these
taxes are lump-sum charges; the landowner cannot reduce his tax burden

by decreasing output and income, by selling land, or by any other means. Without the Laffer Curve, however, Grant's dire prediction of market collapse, land nationalisation and Socialist tyranny has no foundation whatsoever.

A conspiracy of silence?

It is hard to imagine how anyone sufficiently familiar with both mainstream and Georgist economics to put his opinions into print can have analysed the case for the single tax so perfectly incorrectly – unless his intent is to preempt debate by portraying the Georgist proposal as dangerous nonsense, discouraging readers from ever investigating the question for themselves. We have to conclude that Dr. Grant aims to deprive the people of South Africa of an informed choice.

Though he laughs at the Georgists' suspicion "of some conspiracy of silence" (p.59) he, by his example, confirms that the shadow of Knight still obscures the fundamental issue of resource rights. "Economists," Grant tells us, "have utterly refuted much of what George had to say about the 'single tax.'" (p.60) The proposal enjoys a wave of popularity every generation or so, but economists time and again "expose its faults." (p.51) Today, boasts Grant, Georgists are "in retreat," as evidenced by the fact that they will now accept a tax rate somewhat less than 100% – say, 80% – in quiet and partial recognition of the distortions which a high rent tax would cause. (p. 62) If a rate of 80% is acceptable, he reasons, why not 50%, or 12%, or 2%? "[O]nce the mystical character of the tax is broken, a tax on land rent becomes a tax like any other." (*Ibid.*) In truth, Georgists are on the advance, as evidenced not only by an explosion of theoretical developments within academia (Feder 1993) but also by political developments in Russia, the United States and elsewhere. And despite the impressive success of the neo-classical stratagem, a not inconsiderable number of well-known and distinguished economists, Nobel Prize winners among them, eagerly support the principle of public collection of resource rents. (Tideman 1991) As alternative solutions fade like enticing mirages in the desert, the world is discovering anew that the Georgist paradigm offers a sober, peaceful, and civilised path to genuine reform.

Count-down for South Africa

And yet, for South Africa, the current debate is sadly restricted to the parameters of welfare capitalism.

The instability and the trends in the market economies of the West are hardly worth retaining in a society that has the chance of a fresh start. Why retain a system that built impoverishment into its approach? In Britain, for example – echoing the trends elsewhere in Europe and North America – the wealthiest 10% of the population increased its real income by 62% over the period 1979 to 1992 (after taking account of housing costs). The income of the poorest 10%, on the other hand, declined by 17%.

Was this the freedom about which Nelson Mandela had dreamed in his prison cell? So shameful has the record of poverty in Britain become that Oxfam, one of the leading charities that supplies aid to the poor citizens of the Third World, was moved to review the possibility of supplying aid to Britain. (Meikle 1994) But such a strategy – of private charity to supplement the failures of welfare capitalism – would not succeed. This was the explanation offered by the head of public policy of another aid agency, the Catholic Fund for Overseas Development:

> Everyone, even the World Bank, agrees that land reform is an urgent necessity in Brazil. The Catholic Church's Pastoral land Commission grapples daily with the consequences of the skewed patterns of land ownership. But British charity laws make it impossible for a British agency to support a campaign for land reform. (Gelber 1994)

If South Africa does not want to perpetuate an unjust economic system, it will have to depart from the well-tried failures of the European model.

The political rights of black citizens were recognised in the elections of April 1994, but they were not granted the constitutional right to an equal claim on the value of the land and natural resources of their country. On the basis of the present approach to taxation and tenure, Nelson Mandela will one day realise that his victory was an empty one. For with the best will in the world, it will prove impossible to satisfy the aspirations of the poor people (black and white) of his resource-rich country. And the fundamental obstacle to prosperity-for-all is the system of public finance that flows like ectoplasm from the mouths of the neo-classical economists.

References

1. In 1967 the Council of Port Elizabeth appointed a professor of economics from the local university to investigate the impact of the property tax on the city. Prof. Botha concluded that "land does not constitute a proper object of speculation". He explained:

   > Land fulfils a basic need, and society should see to it that the demand for land is satisfied at realistic prices. The problem here lies on the side of supply. In South Africa, land is available in sufficient quantities, yet the terms on which it is supplied often create an artificial scarcity, prices rise and home-ownership becomes more and more expensive. It is apparently the initial cost, the cost of acquiring the land in the first instance, that sets the pace for the price rises. (Botha, n.d.: 187)

   The professor recommended a reform of the property tax to induce a rational approach to land use. The council took no notice.

2. Grant's analysis of the Lebowa story is a curious distortion of the facts, as Stephen Meintjes observes: "In his tour through the former homeland of Lebowa, [Grant] ignores the fact that, as pointed out in the chapter on land tenure in *Chaka* (10), it was the very subversion by the apartheid-merchants of the security of tenure, which prevailed under the original tribal tenure, which prevented these rural communities from making a successful transition from the nomadic, pastoral, subsistence situation to one of intensive agriculture. In essence, the (white) government-appointed chiefs used land allocation as a means of patronage and this, together with hut and poll taxes and the migratory labour system, undermined the security of tenure based on usage, which they previously enjoyed. This process incidentally is eerily reminiscent of the way in which the Highland lairds sold their clansmen down the river". Letter to present authors, Aug. 28, 1994.

Bibliography

Botha, D.J.J. (n.d. [1970]), *Urban Taxation and Land Use*, Report of a one-man Commission appointed by the City Council of Port Elizabeth.

Brown, Harry Gunnison (1927), "Land Speculation and Land Value Taxation." *Journal of Political Economy* 35: 390–402.

Dunkley, Godfrey (1990), *That All May Live*, Roosevelt Park: A. Whyte Publishers.

Dwyer, Terence Michael (1981), A History of the Theory of Land Value Taxation. Ph.D. dissertation, Harvard University.

Feder, Kris (1993), Issues in the Theory of Land Value Taxation. Ph.D. dissertation, Temple University.

" (1994a), in Michael Hudson, G.J. Miller and Kris Feder, *A Philosophy for a Fair Society*, London: CIT.

" (1994b), in Mason Gaffney and Fred Harrison, *Land Speculation and the Business Cycle*, London: CIT.

Feldstein, Martin S. (1977), "The Surprising Incidence of a Tax on Pure Rent: A New Answer to an Old Question." *Journal of Political Economy* 85: 349–360.

Franzsen, R.C.D., and Heynes, C.H., eds. (1992), *A Land Tax for the New South Africa?* Pretoria: Centre for Human Rights, University of Pretoria.

Gaffney, Mason (1992), "Land Reform Through Tax Reform," in Franzsen and Heynes: 111–126.

Gelber, George (1994), "Relief on the home front", *The Guardian*, London, Sept. 3.

George, Henry (1879), *Progress and Poverty*. New York: R. Schalkenbach Foundation, 1971.

" (1898), *Science of Political Economy*, New York: Robert Schalkenbach Foundation.

Grant, Richard (1994), *Nationalization: How Governments Control You*, Johannesburg: The Free Market Foundation.

Knight, Frank (1953), "The Fallacies in the Single Tax", *The Freeman*: 809–811.

Meikle, James (1994), "Britain joins Third World as Oxfam moves to help nation's poor", *The Guardian*, London, Sept. 2.

Meintjes, Stephen, and Michael Jacques (1990), *The Trial of Chaka Dlamini*, Norwood: Amagi Books.

" (1994), "Locational Advantage as Tax Base", Submission to The Katz Tax Commission, Pretoria, July 28.

Tideman, Nicolaus (1991), "Open Letter to Mikhail Gorbachev." In Noyes, Richard, ed., *Now the Synthesis: Capitalism, Socialism, and the New Social Contract*, London: Shepheard-Walwyn/New York: Holmes & Meier. With William Baumol, Robert Dorfman, Mason Gaffney, Franco Modigliani, Richard Musgrave, Robert Solow, James Tobin, William Vickrey, etc.

About the Authors

KRIS FEDER, PhD

Dr. Feder taught economics at several Pennsylvania universities before receiving her doctorate from Temple University. She was appointed assistant professor at Bard College, Annandale-on-Hudson, New York, in 1991, following on to become Professor of Economics and Director of the Environmental and Urban Studies Program at Bard College where she specialised in public finance and the history of economic thought.

MASON GAFFNEY, PhD

In memorandum. Gaffney received his doctorate from the University of California (Berkeley). He had a wide and varied professional career, including professor of economics at several universities, a journalist with TIME, Inc. and the head of the British Columbia Institute for Economic Policy Analysis, which he founded. Author of an extensive list of studies on urban economics and public finance, including *The Corruption of Economics* (1994). Download the eBook here:

https://www.amazon.co.uk/Corruption-Economics-Mason-Gaffney-ebook/dp/B0B2WL6WGY/ref=sr_1_6

FRED HARRISON, MSc

A graduate of Oxford and London universities, Fred is the author of *The Power in the Land* (1983), which predicted the economic crisis of 1992. He is the Research Director of the London-based Land Research Trust. He is a prolific writer, including *Boom Bust, Ricardo's Law* and *# WeAreRent*. He is notable for his stances on land reform and belief that an over-reliance on land, property and mortgage weakens economic structures and makes companies vulnerable to economic collapse.

Listen to the recent Shepheard Walwyn podcast with Fred Harrison:

https://shepheardwalwyn.podbean.com/e/fred-harrison-corruption-of-economics-2nd-edition/

Index

Knight, F., 19, 54, 77, 80, 114,
117–122, 120–121, 243, 246,
251, 256–257
Kuhn, A., 196–197, 231, n.41

Labour, 13, 30
Laffer, A., 32, 34, 138 n.4
Laffer Curve, 256–257
Land:
– definition, 15, 21, 173
– monopoly power, 24, 180, 199
– public finance and, 15
– residential, 23
– speculation in, 18, 25, 27, 74,
94, 100, 128, 135–136
– vacant, 232 n.49
– valuation, 37
– value maps, 36
– values, 21
– taxation, 38, 41, 153, 155
See: Georgist Paradigm; Single
Tax; Neo-classical economics
*Land and Public Utility Economics,
J. of,* 98
Land and Taxation, 21, 92, 140 n.23
Land Tenure Reform Assn., 45
Landowners:
– compensation for, 45
– influence over academia,
50–51
– powers of, 23, 24, 41, 46, 62, 71,
182
Lane, F.K., 35
Lasch, C., 192
Lathrop, J., 52
Letchworth, 188

Liberal Party, 34
Lincoln, J.C., 36
Locke, J., 45, 193, 221
Lorenz Curves, 67
Los Angeles, 43
Lovelock, J., 190
Low, S., 50, 53, 60, 82, 85
Lowden, F., 98
Lutz, F. and V.S., 102

MacChesney, N., 82, 98
MacDonald, R., 112
Maastricht agreement, 206
McLure, C., 62, 142 n.39
Macro-economics, 30
Madero, F., 39
Madison, J., 222
Magna Carta, 179
Malabre, A.L., 28
Malthus, T., 31, 247
Mandela, N., 19, 237–241, 258
Manhattan Single Tax Club, 37, 76,
97
Manufacturers and Merchants
Federal Tax League, 36
Marginal cost pricing, 140 n. 29
Marginal efficiency of capital, 33
Marginal productivity, theory of, 56,
62
Marshall, A., 30, 47, 49, 57, 65–67,
71, 78, 79, 106–107
Marx, K, 8–9, 13–14, 17, 20,
53–56, 58, 61, 63, 141 n.35, 180,
192, 194, 196, 197, 207, 232
n.46
Mason, H., 143 n.48

Sage, H.W., 142
Samuelson, P., 30, 138 n.8
Seelye, J., 52, 77
Seligman, E.R.A., 30, 47, 50, 55,
    59–63, 65, 68, 71, 77, 78, 86, 101,
    106, 127, 140 n.27
Shaw, G.B., 14, 63, 112, 213
Simon, J., 42
Sinatra, F., 29
Sinclair, U., 36, 51, 90, 139 n.16
Single Tax, 19–20, 23, 34–38, 43, 54,
    71, 75–76, 92, 96, 99, 238–241,
    248–249, 253, 257
    – fiscal stimulus of, 42
    – income distribution and,
        76, 247
    – land speculation and, 18,
        245–246
    – markets and, 347, 252
    – neo-classical economics,
        impact on, 30, 60
    See: Henry George; Land;
        Neo-classical economics;
        Rent
Slavery, 21–22, 45, 118, 226
Smith, A., 12, 20, 45, 76, 79, 185–
    187, 193, 225
Smith College, 52
Snowden, P., 112
Solow, R., 170
South Africa, 26, 39, 237–242, 258
Spahr, C., 70–72, 82, 108,
    114, 124
Stagflation, 33
Stalinism, 11, 194
Stigler, G., 55, 65, 77, 120, 124

Stiglitz, J., 170, 212
Sun Yat-sen, 39, 226

"TANSTAAFL", 31
Tax capitalisation, theory
    of, 253
Tax Reform Act (1986), 55
Taxation, 97, 250
    See: Land.
Thatcher, M. 179, 189
Thomas, H.R., 188
Thunen, H. von., 202
Tobin, J., 170
Tolstoy, L., 39, 167, 175, 199, 226
Transportation, 211–212
Truman, H.S., 65
Tax-free society, 183

Ulmer, M., 191
Unemployment, 15, 30, 32, 34, 58,
    129, 174
United Nations, 59, 189
Urban sprawl, 42–43, 101
U'Ren, W.S., 35, 51
United States
    – Constitution, 220–223
    – Dept. of Agriculture, 95
    – farms, 132
USSR, 205–206, 213, 216, 247

Veblen, T., 51, 58, 86, 117, 119, 139
    n.16, 141 n.32
Vickrey, W., 59, 212

Wages, 115, 199–200
    – taxes on, 22